the road to good food in Ireland

A selective member-network providing good food. They epitomise excellence in their fields. Quality is controlled by agreed standards, member activities mutually reinforcing the group. The brand-network sustainability works through skilled marketing and promotion. Good Food Ireland shares informed understanding of consumer behaviour and market dynamics, to assist promotion at international, national, regional and individual businesses levels.

Published 2006 by:
Good Food Ireland
Ballykelly House
Drinagh
Wexford
Ireland
Tel +353 (0)53 9158693
Fax +353 (0)53 9158688

Book Trade Distribution:

Eason Wholesale Books
Furry Park Industrial Estate
Santry
Co Dublin
Ireland

Portfolio Books Ltd
Unit 5, Perivale Industrial Park
Horseden Lane South
Greenford
Middlesex
UB6 7RL
England

ISBN 0-9548797-3-2
Copyright © 2006 Good Food Ireland

This book is sold subject to the condition that it shall not, by way of trade, or otherwise, be lent, resold, hired out or otherwise circulated without the publisher's consent in any form or binding, or cover other than that in which it is published.

All rights reserved. No part of this book may be reproduced, stored in a retrieval system or transmitted by any means without permission. Whilst every effort has been made to ensure that the information contained in this publication is accurate and up to date, the publisher does not accept any responsibility for any error, omission or misrepresentation. All liability for loss, disappointment, negligence or other damage caused by reliance of information contained in this guide, or in the event of bankruptcy, or liquidation, or cessation of trading of any company, individual or firm mentioned is hereby excluded.

For all enquiries and information about Good Food Ireland properties
telephone:+353 (0)53 9158693
email: info@goodfoodireland.ie
www.goodfoodireland.ie

Editor:
Hugo Arnold

Production & Design Editor:
Margaret Jeffares

Contributing Editors:
Clare McCarthy
Jeanne Quigley

Design:
Karen Nolan Design
www.karennolandesign.ie

Feature Contributors:
Maurice Keller
Clodagh McKenna
John Wilson
Caroline Workman
Jeanne Quigley

Location Photography:
Margaret Jeffares
Failte Ireland
Kingdoms of Down
Causeway Coast & Glens
Belfast Visitor & Convention Centre
Fermanagh Lakeland Tourism
Carlow Tourism
Mark Nolan

Printed in Ireland by:
Walshe Print Ltd
59 O'Connell Street
Waterford
Ireland

For Good Food Ireland:

Managing Director:
Margaret Jeffares

Associate Food Consultant:
Hugo Arnold

Wine Consultant:
John Wilson

Operations Manager:
Susan Kerr

Marketing Manager:
Melina Magourty

A word from Margaret Jeffares

Welcome to Good Food Ireland

As director of Good Food Ireland my objective is to bring together and promote a network of quality, independent establishments, owned and run by people who have a passion for what they do. And a belief in delivering good food. This guide is all about putting you, the reader, in touch with the best that Ireland has to offer.

We offer a broad cross-section of good food, accommodation and eating establishments. If food is important to you then that goes as much for a snack as a full-blown dinner. So we include B&Bs, but only those with the best homemade breakfast; a luxury castle or hotel, if it really understands luxury; a restaurant serving fresh and local produce, when local really means just that; and a food shop, one that simply offers you all the ingredients for a great picnic. Why? Because in their chosen fields we know that getting all this right is difficult and only the best shine through.

We have also introduced a number of food producers, cookery schools and local and regional farmer's markets into our network as we believe this reflects the diverse way those interested in good food are likely to travel about the country.

We highlight the passion and excellence that is all around us, though sometimes hard to find. I hope you enjoy this guide for what it represents: food and accommodation from and for people who really care.

Margaret Jeffares
Managing Director

About this Guide

This is a unique collection of recommended places that make, sell or serve good food, as well as providing comfortable accommodation. All the establishments featured are run by people who believe passionately in what they do. Meeting customer demands is chief among their concerns. So they are constantly looking to refine their offer, to evolve and to be at the cutting edge.

In producing this compilation we do the same. We are dedicated to searching out quality, individuality, a sense of place and seasonal delights. In the following pages you will find places to stay, eat and drink that are a world away from the everyday. Some lie down back roads, some in villages off the beaten track, a few are difficult to find. But once you get there you'll experience an Ireland many thought had gone forever.

This is an Ireland where homemade jam means just that, where a bedroom is furnished correctly, where sheets are of the best linen when they say they are, where menus are primarily driven by the seasons and local produce and not some international hotch potch of ideas.

We live in an age when much is claimed and too often not delivered. Good Food Ireland is selective. There are only so many places we feel offer the individuality and standards required. They are all here. As a discerning eater we rely on your feedback to help us ensure the high standards we have both set ourselves and constantly refine. Please take the time to praise and or comment using the customer feedback form in the guide. Happy travelling.

Hugo Arnold
Editor

Contents

A word from Margaret Jeffares 3
About this Guide 4
How to use this Guide 8
Booking Information 10
Good Food Ireland Awards 2006 12

Features
Local Heros by Jeanne Quigley 40
Changing Rooms by Jeanne Quigley 48
Short & Sweet by John Wilson 84
Cottage Delight by Maurice Kelly 144
Plain & Arty by Caroline Workman 194
Underneath the Black Stuff by John Wilson 228
Artisan & Al Fresco by Clodagh McKenna 234

Regional Guide to Accommodation, Pubs, Cafés,
Restaurants and Recommended Places to Visit ..... 55 - 225
A Guide to
  Food Producers 241
  Cookery Schools 253
  Farmers' Markets 261
  Food Shops 273
  Microbreweries 277
One for the Road - Route Planners 283
Index of Establishments A - Z 299
Did You Enjoy Your Visit? 304

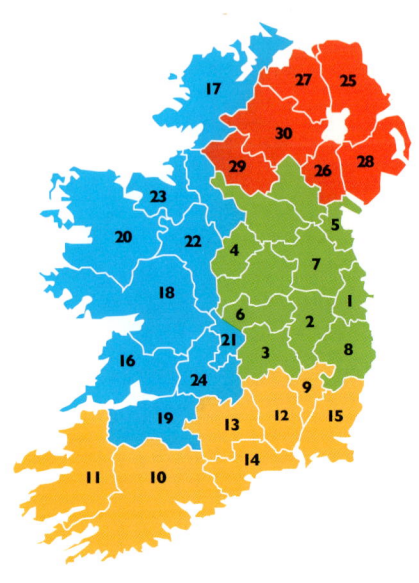

Regional Guide

	Ireland East & Dublin	**55**
1	Dublin	58
2	Kildare	75
3	Laois	76
4	Longford	76
5	Louth	77
6	Offaly (North)	79
7	Westmeath	81
8	Wicklow	81
	Ireland South	**93**
9	Carlow	96
10	Cork	98
11	Kerry	118
12	Kilkenny	130
13	Tipperary (South)	132
14	Waterford	133
15	Wexford	141
	Ireland West	**151**
16	Clare	154
17	Donegal	168
18	Galway	172
19	Limerick	181
20	Mayo	184
21	Offaly (South)	187
22	Roscommon	192
23	Sligo	193
24	Tipperary (North)	193
	Ireland North	**201**
25	Antrim	204
26	Armagh	211
27	Derry	215
28	Down	218
29	Fermanagh	224
30	Tyrone	225

How to use this Guide

Establishments are sorted first into one of four regions then alphabetically by county, placename and establishment. For a quick search by region see the top outer border edge of the pages. To find a particular establishment by its name, use the A-Z Index at the back.

Region

Place County

www.goodfoodireland.ie

◆ ✕ ● DT ♪ ⊤ ★

Establishment Name
Establishment type

Address
Tel. +353(0)65 7777777
Email. info@therestaurant.com
www.therestaurant.com

This cosy, bustling country restaurant, set in a quiet nook has a rustic cottagey décor. There are two small rooms on two floors, the former furnished in old-world Irish style, with exposed rafters, stone and subdued red rendered walls and hanging lantern-style lamps. The latter has a pine ceiling and timber floors. While the ambience is traditional

Rooms: 9 ensuite.
Double from €76. Single from €68. Family from €90.
Closed: Mid Nov - mid Feb
Other Points: Non-smoking house. Garden. Children welcome. Car park.
Directions: Situated 0.75kms outside the village of Ballyvaughan on the N67 Lisdoonvarna road.

Telephone: Numbers include the international code for dialling Ireland from abroad. To dial from within Ireland start the number with the 0 in the brackets. To dial Northern Ireland from the Republic of Ireland replace the local area code 28 with 48. From outside Ireland dial all numbers except the (0) in the brackets.

Photograph: These have all been chosen and supplied by the individual establishments.

Prices: Set meals usually consist of three courses but can include more. Where no set lunch or dinner is offered, we give the price of the cheapest main course on the menu. House wine prices are by the bottle. Prices are meant as a guideline to the cost of a meal only. All prices include VAT. In Northern Ireland prices are given in sterling £.

Symbols

- Accommodation
- Restaurant
- Café
- Pub/Bar
- Daytime opening only
- Deli
- Wine
- Bakery
- Gourmet/Farm Shop
- Leisure Centre/Spa
- CS Craft Shop
- VC Visitor Centre
- FP Food Producer

Good Food Ireland Awards

- 2002 Award Winner
- 2003 Award Winner
- 2004 Award Winner
- 2005 Award Winner
- 2006 Award Winner

Hours: Times given are opening times and annual closures.

Food serving hours: Times when food serving hours differ from above.

Rooms: For establishments offering accommodation the number of rooms is given, along with the lowest price for double and single rooms. Where this price is per person it is indicated. Prices usually include breakfast. You can check prices by calling our Central Reservations Office.
Tel. +353(0)53 9158693.

Other Points:

Children: Although we indicate whether or not children are welcome in a pub or hotel, we do not list facilities for guests with babies; we advise telephoning beforehand to sort out any particular requirements.

Disabled: As disabilities vary considerably we advise that you telephone the hotel or restaurant of your choice to discuss your needs with the manager or proprietor.

Credit cards: Very few places fail to take credit cards. Check with individual establishments.

Directions: These have been supplied by the individual establishments.

Booking Information

Our **Central Reservations Office** staff will be happy to deal with any reservations or enquiries you may have. We can suggest or tailor-make personal itineraries, book all accommodation, restaurants, pubs and cafés and show you where to find real Irish hospitality.

Accommodation Rates & Reservations

Rates are based upon two people sharing a standard double/twin room and usually include breakfast. Rates for single and family rooms have been quoted wherever possible. Some properties will also have superior rooms and suites. We have endeavoured to reflect accurate rates for 2007. Rates are a guide and subject to change without notice, please re-confirm rates when booking.

You can contact us directly
Central Reservations:

Office hours Mon-Fri. 9.00am-5.30pm
Tel. +353 (0)53 9158693
Fax. +353 (0)53 9158688
Email. reservations@goodfoodireland.ie
Web. www.goodfoodireland.ie

Cancellations

When booking please check individual deposit and cancellation policies. Each property has its own cancellation policy and we recommend that you familiarise yourself with each prior to booking.

Book Online

Be sure to visit our newly redesigned website, now with more information and easier navigation.

You can view up to the minute details on our members, read about special offers, book your car hire, see the best places to visit, choose from a number of great itineraries and make instantaneous reservations – all with the click of your mouse.

Online access to your one-stop guide to Ireland
Good Food Ireland
www.goodfoodireland.ie

Gift Vouchers
The Perfect Present

Give your friends, family or colleagues a true Irish experience in those often hard to find "real" places, run by people who have a passion for what they do, where hospitality is genuine - a refreshing change, a difference.

Vouchers can be purchased in values of €50 and €100 plus a 10% service charge for gift wrapping, postage and handling.

Purchase Online www.goodfoodireland.ie

And, why not purchase the Good Food Ireland Guide to accompany your gift voucher. For further assistance or information please telephone +353 35 9158693 or email info@goodfoodireland.ie

Ballygarry House Hotel & Spa, Tralee

Good Food Ireland
Awards 2006

The Good Food Ireland annual awards are a celebration of those members who, in the panel's opinion, excel and go the extra mile. The Nominations are open to all Good Food Ireland members who are assessed throughout the year using set guidelines. Because of the cross-section of properties, the awards embrace and epitomise our slogan "best of their type" which allows the small simple restaurant to compete with the most lavish of restaurant. The final decision rests with the panel and editor and the first and final impressions along with the "wow factor" are paramount in the final decision.

To gain entry as a member of Good Food Ireland a property must fit the Good Food Ireland criteria. Independence and breadth of choice mark out the highly regarded group of members who go through an assessment process before being recommended. Over 160 properties have made the grade, having been carefully selected for their quality, individual hospitality, good food and value for money.

In the course of assessment some members stand out as surpassing our entry standards. These members are nominated and begin the award process. All nominations are based on recommendations by our independent assessment team who are tasked with defining what and how a particular member may stand out and therefore qualify for an award.

The following nominees and award winners have impressed with the quality of their product, their attention to detail or sheer hospitality. It's all about going that extra mile in an age when uniformity is too often the order of the day.

Waterford Crystal Visitor Centre

Bed and Breakfast of the Year

Grange Lodge
Dungannon, Co. Tyrone

Gone are the days when the bed and breakfast was considered second best. Our nominees offer first class accommodation with a friendly, but unobtrusive service. The bedrooms and reception areas combine a comfortable home from home feel with stylish interiors. Breakfast is a real treat and our nominees champion the use of fresh local produce and the best of homemade food. As most are owner-managed they guarantee an interactive Irish experience.

Nominees

Viewmount House
Powersfield House

Sponsored by

Waterford Crystal
Kilbarry, Waterford
Tel. + 353 (0)51 332500
Email. visitorreception@waterford.ie
www.waterfordvisitorcentre.com

Special Award

The Bay Tree
Holywood, Co Down

It is a mark of our industry and how it has developed that every year more and more members appear that do not necessarily fit easily into any one category. Cafés that are bars that are restaurants that are art galleries that also offer bedrooms are increasingly to be found, or some combination that sets them apart. While being unusual is important for consideration in this award, the real test is about the quality of the offer, how it is delivered and expressed.

Sponsored by

Waterford Crystal
Kilbarry, Waterford
Tel. + 353 (0)51 332500
Email. visitorreception@waterford.ie
www.waterfordvisitorcentre.com

Locally Produced Food Supporters Award

O' Connell's in Ballsbridge
Ballsbridge, Dublin 4

At the core of every menu lie the ingredients used to make the dishes. This award seeks to celebrate those establishments that work hard to foster links with local growers and producers. This route is not easy; supply often being erratic and dependent on seasonal variations. Yet when it works there really is something to celebrate, a freshness and vitality that efficient distribution has done much to erode.

Sponsored by

Good Food Ireland
Ballykelly House, Drinagh, Co Wexford
Tel. +353 (0)53 9158693. Fax. +353 (0)53 9158688
Email. info@goodfoodireland.ie
www.goodfoodireland.ie

Host of the Year

Mrs Marian Walsh
The Gallery Restaurant,
Quin, Co Clare

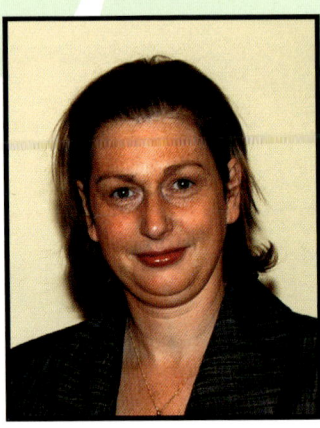

For an industry as focused on food as ours is we can often overlook the fact that at its heart lie people. This award celebrates an individual who excels at turning this fact into a key attribute. Being a good host is a complex and often fraught occupation. How to be friendly and yet efficient, how to welcome and yet offer space, how to suggest without crowding. The winner of this award can do all of this and more.

Sponsored by

Hertz
Ferrybank, Co Wexford
Tel. +353 (0)53 52512 (Reservations Ireland)
Tel. +353 (0)1 6767476 (Central Reservations)
www.hertz.ie

Restaurant of the Year

Gleesons
Clonakilty, Co Cork

While the food is crucial, service is no less important. A restaurant has to perform on many levels, more perhaps than it has in the past. It has to entertain, excite, but also comfort and calm. The sense of occasion needs to be there, but not so much that the diner feels ill at ease. The restaurant of the year must be a keen supporter of fresh, local produce in season, serving imaginative but unpretentious dishes.

Nominees
White Gables
O' Connor's Seafood Restaurant
Paul Arthurs

Sponsored by
Villeroy & Boch UK Ltd
267 Merton Road, London SW18 5JS
Tel. +44 208 871 0011. Fax. +44 208 871 1062
Email. hotel@villeroy-boch.co.uk
Represented in Ireland by Thomas McLaughlin
Tel. +353 (0)87 2800 368. Email. info@tmclaughlin

Hotel of the Year

Hayfield Manor Hotel
Cork City

All our hotels are independently run and this is evident in their friendly, personal service, individually designed interiors and quality accommodation. Our nominees successfully combine individual hospitality with a high standard of decor and many thoughtful extras. A strong commitment to good food and the use of fresh seasonal and local produce is essential to overall success.

Nominees

Kelly's Resort Hotel & Spa
Killarney Royal Hotel
Renvyle House Hotel

HOTEL & RESTAURANT

Sponsored by

Villeroy & Boch UK Ltd
267 Merton Road, London SW18 5JS
Tel. +44 208 871 0011. Fax. +44 208 871 1062
Email. hotel@villeroy-boch.co.uk
Represented in Ireland by Thomas McLaughlin
Tel. +353 (0)87 2800 368. Email. info@tmclaughlin.com

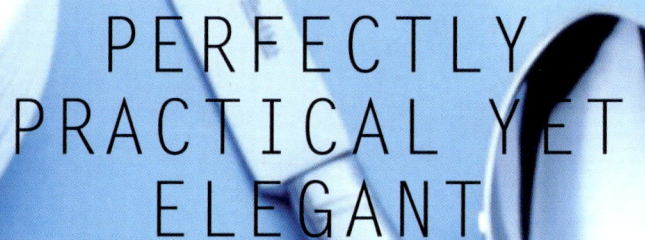

PERFECTLY PRACTICAL YET ELEGANT

Professional restaurant cutlery from Villeroy & Boch, in finest 18/10 stainless steel. With a range of designs to meet every mood, every theme and every occasion.

Villeroy & Boch (UK) Ltd. · Hotel & Restaurant Division · Tel: 020 8871 6011 (020 8875 6001, brochure line) · Fax: 020 8871 1062 · E-Mail: hotel@villeroy-boch.co.uk · www.villeroy-boch.com

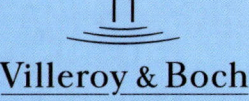

Villeroy & Boch
1748

HOTEL & RESTAURANT

Country House of the Year

Carrygerry House
Newmarket-on-Fergus, Co Clare

Rural bliss? Style, comfort and elegance and yet something of a welcoming feel with good, honest home cooking using fresh local produce were the key attributes we were looking for in this category. Country House implies a sense of getting away but the real jewels make a statement so you know you have arrived at something special. Country Houses can often imply grandeur as you imagine sweeping up the drive. We were looking for the detail of what happens after this, the detail that provides you with a really excellent visit and a knowledge that will make you want to return.

Nominees
Ghan House
Delphi Lodge

Sponsored by

Hygiene & Textile Service for Hospitality

Celtic Linen
Rosslare Road, Wexford.
Sales Manager **Mr Pat O'Dwyer**
Tel. 1890 235842. Fax. +353 (0)53 60806
Email. sales@celticlinen.ie

Guesthouse & Restaurant of the Year

Gorman's Clifftop House & Restaurant
Dingle, Co Kerry

The restaurant is certainly key in this award, yet the guesthouse element is an integral part and both must work together. We were looking for a synergy between both elements of this exciting category that reflected the commitment of the owners. What happens in the dining room has to be carried through the rest of the operation.

Nominees

Admiralty Lodge
Aherne's
Gleeson's Townhouse & Restaurant

Importer of French Food & Wines

Sponsored by
Barrell of Grapes
Carrowmeer, Newmarket-on-Fergus, Co Clare
Contact Jacques Hubert
Tel./Fax. +353 (0)61 368915
Email. info@barrell-of-grapes.com
www.barrell-of-grapes.com

Café Restaurant of the Year

The Kitchen & Foodhall
Portlaoise, Co Laois

Relaxed, accessible, easy to use and yet with fantastic food, first-class service and a friendly outlook are the kinds of characteristics we are looking for in a great café. The menu need not be long, but the ingredients and their execution have to be first class. The surroundings may be basic or indeed more than but the attention to detail is there. The winner and indeed the nominees - have turned casual into something to shout about.

Nominees
Anderson's Food Hall & Café
Emma's Café Deli
La Dolce Vita
The Yellow Door

Sponsored by
James Nicholson Wine Merchant
27a Killyleagh Street, Crossgar, Co Down, BT30 9DQ
Contact Charles O'Reilly (mob +353 872 463 778)
Tel. +44 (0)28 44830091. Tel. Lo-call from ROI 1890 667799
Email. info@jnwine.com
www.jnwine.com

Food Pub of the Year

QC's Seafood Bar & Restaurant
Cahirciveen, Co Kerry

A food pub must still be a pub, where you can have a pint. It is the atmosphere, which says it all, however. You walk in the door and what hits you is something friendly and welcoming, a sense of joining something very social. If you choose to eat food then what is presented is of the first order but there is nothing pretentious about it. Food that will complement a glass of beer as well as a glass of wine. Food to be enjoyed in a casual way.

Nominees
Hanged Man's
The Tankard Bar & Restaurant

Sponsored by

Dawn Meats Food Service
Kilmacthomas, Co Waterford
Contact **Michael Wall**
Tel. +353 (0)51 295296. Fax: +353 (0)51 295295
Email. Michael.wall@dawnmeats.com
www.dawnmeats.com

Wine List of the Year

Barça Wine & Tapas bar
Lismore, Co Waterford

We were looking for wine lists that offer the customer choice, value and interest. They did not not have to be long, nor did they have to be comprehensive. They did need to be made up of well-chosen quality wines at every price level, wines that reflected the food on offer. We looked for a selection of wines available by the glass or half-bottle. But most of all we wanted to see the passion and interest of the proprietor.

Nominees

Chapter One
Delphi Lodge
Kelly's Resort Hotel & Spa
Lacken House

Sponsored by
Febvre & Company
Highfield House, Burton Hall Road
Sandyford Industrial Estate, Dublin 18
Contact David McDonnell or Gregory Alken
Tel. +353 (0)1 216 1400. Fax. +353 (0)1 295 9036
Email. info@febvre.ie   www.febvre.ie

"Wine is constant proof that God loves us and loves to see us happy."

Benjamin Franklin.

At Febvre & Company we're strong admirers of Benjamin's line of thought. Seeing our customers happy is at the heart of everything we do. We understand the importance of reputation and we want our customers to be sure that every time they serve a Febvre wine, the care with which we select our growers shines through.

Febvre and Company Limited, Highfield House, Burton Hall Road,
Sandyford Industrial Estate, Sandyford, Dublin 18, Ireland.
Tel. +353 1 216 1400, Fax. +353 1 295 9036.
Mail. info@febvre.ie, Web. www.febvre.ie.

FEBVRE
Original thinking in wine

Guesthouse of the Year

Rusheen Lodge
Ballyvaughan, Co Clare

The winner of this award combines that rare ability to furnish their establishment as if it were as a home and yet have others to stay. As the term suggests, the establishment is still very much a house overtly not a hotel. As a guest you should feel and experience this difference. It is a difficult balance to achieve and yet when done well can provide a real point of difference. Breakfast is of equal importance and a commitment to homemade and local fresh produce is paramount.

Nominees
Aberdeen Lodge

Sponsored by
Hertz
Ferrybank, Co Wexford
Tel. +353 (0)53 52512 (Reservations Ireland)
Tel. +353 (0)1 6767476 (Central Reservations)
www.hertz.ie

Newcomer of the Year

Ballymaloe House & Cookery School
Shanagarry, Midleton, Co Cork

Each year we have a flood of new members, some have been in business a long time, others have only just started. This award celebrates the member who we feel has really brought something special, something that makes them clearly stand out from the crowd. That something is rarely one thing, more often it is a combination of factors hard to put your finger on exactly but which add up to a really memorable experience.

Nominees
Sheridan's Cheesmongers
Ballyliffin Lodge & Spa
Ballyvolane House
Newforge House
The Wolftrap Bar & Restaurant

Sponsored by
Hertz
Ferrybank, Co Wexford
Tel. +353 (0)53 52512 (Reservations Ireland)
Tel. +353 (0)1 6767476 (Central Reservations)
www.hertz.ie

Wine Person of the Year

Mr Mirco Fondrini
Farmgate Café, Cork City

We were not looking for a wine expert, instead, we wanted someone with a deep love of wine, someone who knew and could talk enthusiastically about their wine list. We wanted someone comfortable talking to a wine lover, but also with the ability to advise the less knowledgeable without talking down or patronising; someone who understood that wine and food are one of life's great pleasures, and could give the diner that extra touch.

Nominees

Tim Sacklin, Eden

Maksims Merkulovs, The Clarence & The Tearoom Restaurant

Sponsored by

GHS Classic Drinks Limited
Unit 5, OC Commercial Park, Little Island, Cork, Ireland
Contact **Hugh Murray**
Tel. +353 (0)21 451 0066. Fax. +353 (0)21 4355504
Email. sales@classicdrinks.ie www.classicdrinks.ie

Classic Drinks

A wholly owned Irish Company, working with people who are as passionate about their wines as we are.

Unit 5, OC Commercial Park, Little Island, Cork.
Tel: 021 5410066   Fax: 021 4355504
sales@classicdrinks.ie   www.classicdrinks.ie

Regional Award North

Nick's Warehouse
Belfast City

This award is open to all types of establishments within the region. The winner must show overall excellence and passion must ooze from the kitchen. Good Food Ireland Regional Winners are champions of fresh, local produce. This means that we have a network of producers around the country that serve good food at its flavoursome best. Their appreciation of regional produce is what underpins Good Food Irelands' philosophy.

Sponsored by
Tourism Ireland
5th Floor, Bishop's Square
Redmond's Hill, Dublin 2
Tel. + 353 1 476 3415
Fax. + 353 1 476 3666
www.discoverireland.com

Regional Award South

Café Paradiso
Cork City

This award is open to all types of establishments within the region. The winner must show overall excellence and passion must ooze from the kitchen. Good Food Ireland Regional Winners are champions of fresh, local produce. This means that we have a network of producers around the country that serve good food at its flavoursome best. Their appreciation of regional produce is what underpins Good Food Irelands' philosophy.

Sponsored by
Tourism Ireland
5th Floor, Bishop's Square
Redmond's Hill, Dublin 2
Tel. + 353 1 476 3415
Fax. + 353 1 476 3666
www.discoverireland.com

Regional Award East

Chapter One
Dublin City

This award is open to all types of establishments within the region. The winner must show overall excellence and passion must ooze from the kitchen. Good Food Ireland Regional Winners are champions of fresh, local produce. This means that we have a network of producers around the country that serve good food at its flavoursome best. Their appreciation of regional produce is what underpins Good Food Irelands' philosophy.

Sponsored by
Tourism Ireland
5th Floor, Bishop's Square
Redmond's Hill, Dublin 2
Tel. + 353 1 476 3415
Fax. + 353 1 476 3666
www.discoverireland.com

Regional Award West

Renvyle House Hotel
Renvyle, Co Galway

This award is open to all types of establishments within the region. The winner must show overall excellence and passion must ooze from the kitchen. Good Food Ireland Regional Winners are champions of fresh, local produce. This means that we have a network of producers around the country that serve good food at its flavoursome best. Their appreciation of regional produce is what underpins Good Food Irelands' philosophy.

Sponsored by
Tourism Ireland
5th Floor, Bishop's Square
Redmond's Hill, Dublin 2
Tel. + 353 1 476 3415
Fax. + 353 1 476 3666
www.discoverireland.com

THE FOOD ISLAND

www.foodisland.com

There are many Irelands: the scenic island finger fashioned by the Atlantic; the historic land enriched by music and literature; and there is Ireland, the Food Island. Michelin starred chef Richard Corrigan has described his home country as 'the finest food larder in the world.' Travelling around the country you'll see Ireland's gastronomic traditions coming alive in their natural habitats. Between the pasture belts and uplands where Ireland's riches in beef, lamb and dairy are carefully nurtured, you'll find growing diversity, bristling pride and newly fired enthusiasm. Take in the English Market in Cork City – a centuries old meeting place that brings the culinary treasures of Munster under one roof. Here you'll find the province's huge array of farmhouse cheeses, its pork charcuterie and its delicately smoked meat and fish. While Cork considers itself Ireland's fine food capital, Dublin too is bustling with inventive cafes, fine restaurants and great delis. On Dublin's South Anne Street you'll find Sheridan's, a cheesemonger committed to supporting native excellence in cheese and fine foods, while in bustling Temple Bar, Meeting House Square becomes an extraordinary open air pantry at the weekends.

Perhaps the best treats are those that come in the most unexpected places. In the small town of Oughterard in Co Galway you find McGeough's family butchers, whose wild boar hams and unique air dried 'prosciutto' lamb are served in the country's finest hotels. In Limerick there is The Cocoa Bean Company who have gained a reputation for being specialists in dark chocolate. And, if you're passing through Wexford or coming off the ferry at Rosslare, a visit to Ballycross Apple Farm won't disapoint. They offer some great tasting apple juices including apple and blackcurrant juice, the blackcurrants also being produced on the farm.

The weekly farmers markets run across the country are the surest barometer of the new passion for fine food and local excellence. Here, food artisans sell farmhouse cheeses, cured meats, organic produce and kitchen garden vegetables. Speciality cheeses to watch out for include Ardrahan, a well-rounded cow's milk cheese and Mossfield Organic while meat lovers should be sure to sample Staunton's Black Pudding, made to a unique recipe.

A fine dining culture has taken hold in our newly vibrant towns and villages with restaurants that source their food from local producers, fuse traditional and new wave cooking and draw rave reviews from the staunchest food critics. Watch out for the 'Feile Bia' sign when dining out. It means the restaurant is committed to sourcing quality assured produce.

From the fresh glitter of fish landed in tiny Atlantic harbours to contented cattle grazing the grasslands of Leinster and Munster; from traditional Irish stew to the exciting new passion of Irish cusine, the authentic flavour of Irish food is expressed in an endless variety of ways, and can be enjoyed in the simplest of snacks to the most dazzling of meals. There are many Irelands, but the one you'll remember most fondly is the one you come to know through personal experience. Welcome to Ireland, the Food Island. ∎

Local Heros

Do you know your blaa from your moss? Fancy whiskey in your porridge? Jeanne Quigley talks to Good Food Ireland members and sorts out Ireland's unique products and steps neatly away from the mass market.

Jeanne Quigley is a food journalist and member of the Irish Guild of Food Writers.

Ireland has a well-deserved reputation for good, fresh food. Fish straight from the pier, mountain lamb, smoked salmon, breads and cakes are all foods that the Irish - and our visitors - know and love. Over the years, Irish products have continued to improve, with many small enterprises and businesses supplying the market. In recent years, the organic market has been increasing steadily, particularly vegetables, salad leaves, fruit, meat and dairy products. The growth of Farmers' Markets around the country shows the supply and demand of fresh, local produce.

But how much importance is placed on having local foods available? Tim O'Sullivan, Head Chef at Renvyle House Hotel says ' by using local produce we get a very distinct flavour. Our guests expect to get foods from Connemara.' His menu reflects this with Connemara lamb, salmon, lobster, prawns, oysters, sausages, and black and white pudding.

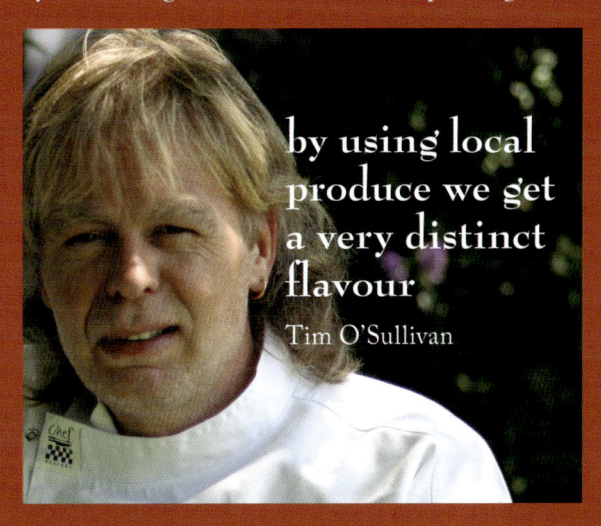

> by using local produce we get a very distinct flavour
>
> Tim O'Sullivan

> Working closely with local suppliers allows the menu to be changed constantly
>
> Denis Cotter

Denis Cotter from Café Paradiso in Cork City says that a restaurant has an obligation to become part of a community and buying locally benefits the whole area. Working closely with local suppliers allows the menu to be changed constantly.

Tom O'Connell of O'Connells in Ballsbridge echoes this thought. 'The ultimate in sourcing is when the vegetable supplier is organising his planting programme and asks us what vegetables we'll need.' He also says that customers are interested in organic produce, again a point that's consistently made.

Some of the recipes used around the country taking advantage of local produce include carrigeen moss, an edible seaweed that was valued by our ancestors because of its nutritional properties. It's usually mixed with milk, sugar and eggs to make a soufflé-like pudding. Mary Wheeler of Rathmullan House Hotel in Donegal uses an old recipe from her mother. 'Our chef collects the carrigeen moss at his front door. We serve it for breakfast with poached berries from the garden.'

'Tourists are looking for Irish produce when here on holidays,' says Norah Browne from Grange Lodge in Dungannon, Co Tyrone. 'They've left their own country so don't want their own type of food.' Norah's Bushmills porridge will, as she says, 'set them up for the day.' This is not at all surprising - large flakes of organic oats soaked overnight. Next day, double cream, brown sugar and a good dash of whiskey are added - a hearty breakfast.

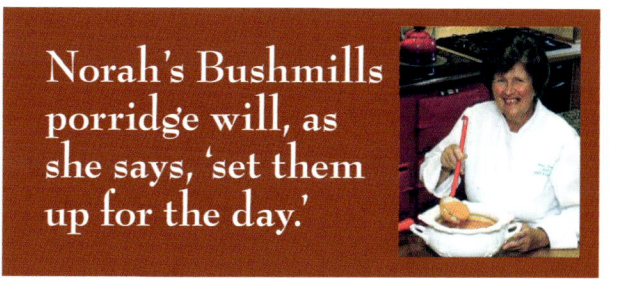

> Norah's Bushmills porridge will, as she says, 'set them up for the day.'

The Waterford Blaa causes great interest on the breakfast menu in Arlington Lodge Country House Hotel, Waterford. Maurice Keller explains. 'The Blaa dates back to the 17th century when French Huguenots arrived in Waterford. They integrated with the locals and opened bakeries in the city. The Blaa is a soft white bun eaten on a daily basis. We half the Blaa, toast lightly on each side, place a poached egg on each half, sprinkle with Kilmeaden cheddar and hey presto - the Waterford Blaa, Arlington style.'

In the Lime Tree in Kenmare, Tony Daly's popular roast flat mushroom dish has Gubbeen cheese. 'This cheese is recognised for its versatility and flavour,' he says. 'We also use Skeaghanore free-range ducks from Ballydehob. They have a lovely texture and are consistently good. We serve the breast with vanilla mashed potato and the livers are used in the duck liver parfait.'

Kate Petitt of Kate's Kitchen in Sligo says she prefers to deal with local suppliers - she can ensure the freshness of the food she sells. 'There is a huge market for anything local, not just with the local people but also with tourists. We outsource our products now, some to an ex-employee, so we know the quality is excellent.'

> The Waterford Blaa, causes great interest on the breakfast menu
>
> Maurice Keller

In the Kitchen and Foodhall in Portlaoise, Jim Tynan sees local foods from both the manufacturing and retailing viewpoints. 'We manufacture most

> Customers are interested in organic produce
>
> O'CONNELLS
> Tom O'Connell

of what we sell in the restaurant and shop. There are local free range eggs in the cakes, we cook our own hams and turkeys and my father grows the vegetables. Small producers must be encouraged.'

The importance of having local foods on menus around the country also gives a sense of pride in Irish heritage and culture. Many Irish products are known worldwide and visitors to the country are always interested in trying them out. And knowing where the food on the table is coming from is important to all - suppliers, retailers, chefs and of course, customers. ∎

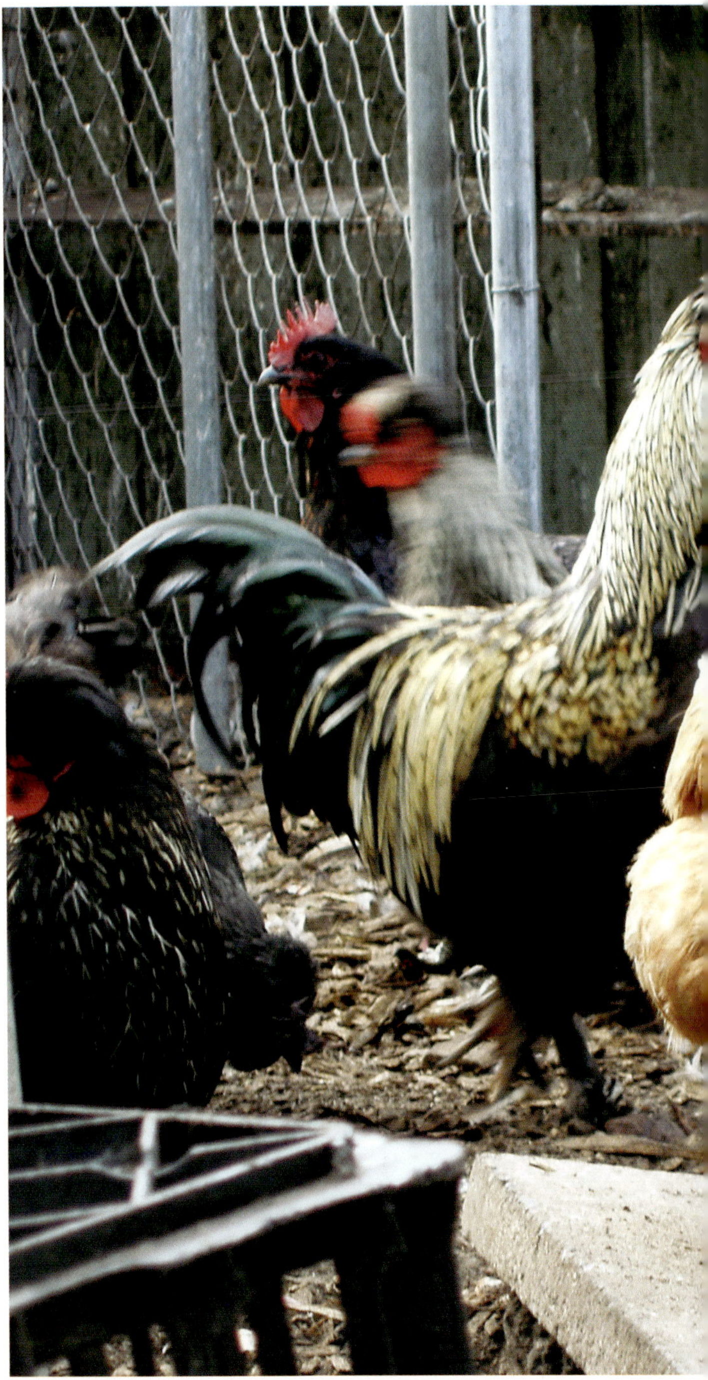

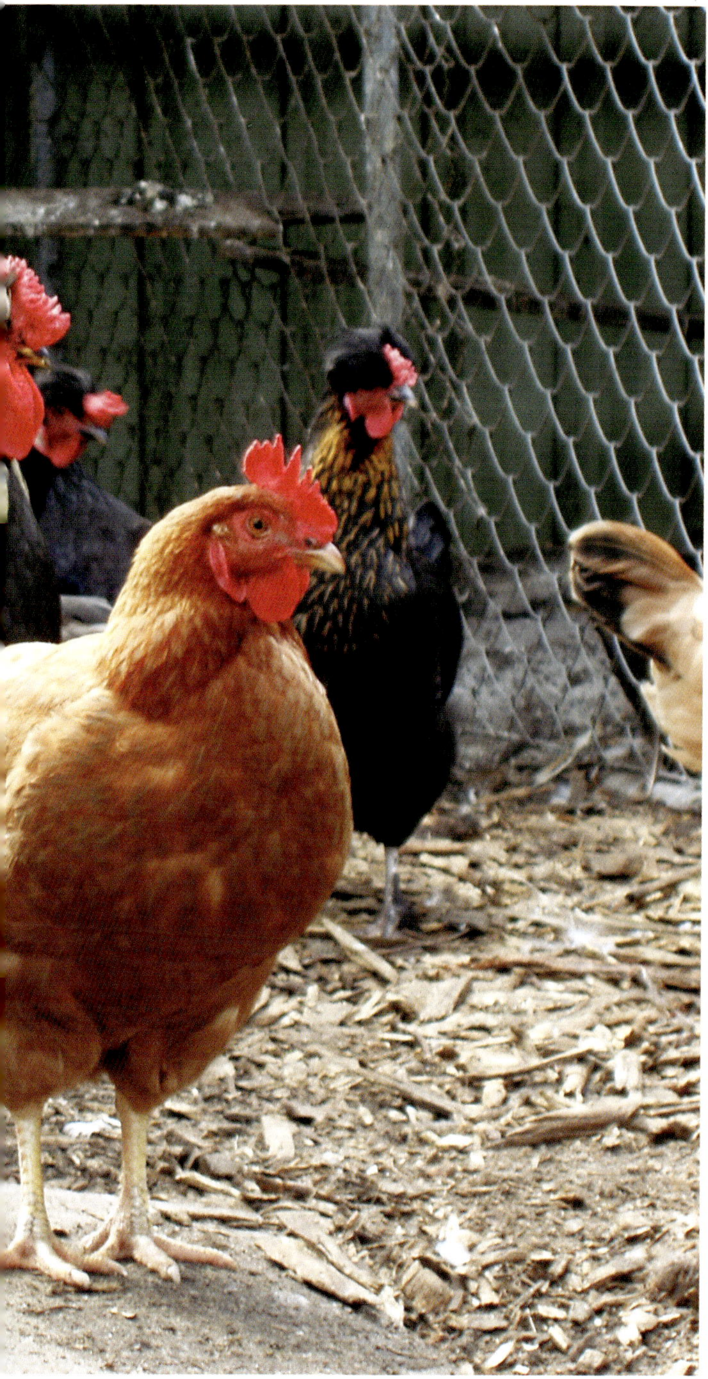

Changing rooms

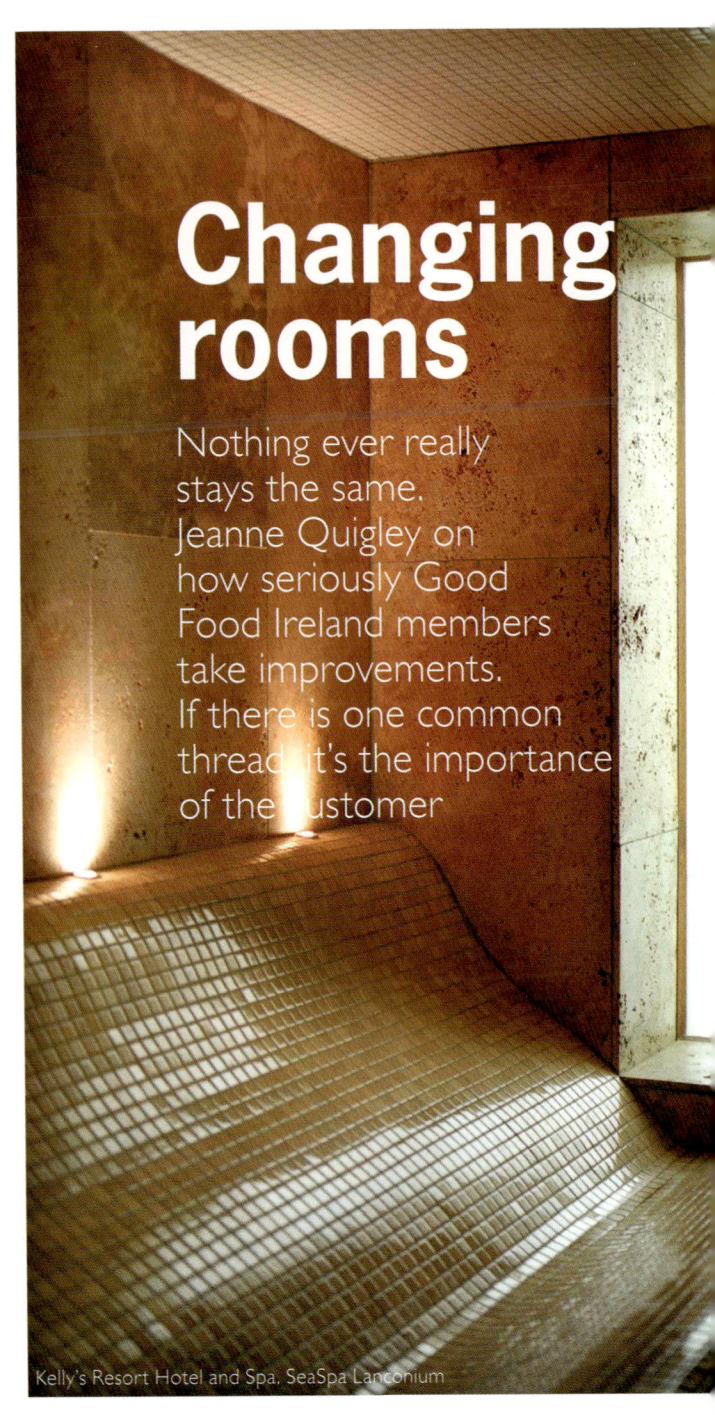

Nothing ever really stays the same. Jeanne Quigley on how seriously Good Food Ireland members take improvements. If there is one common thread it's the importance of the customer

Kelly's Resort Hotel and Spa, SeaSpa Lanconium

'It's an on-going servicing of the market,'

says Bill Kelly, owner of Kelly's Resort Hotel & Spa in Rosslare. 'Each year, for the past 20 years, we have done major or less major refurbishment.'

Kelly knows what he's talking about. Keeping the customers happy is one of the reasons that hotels and restaurants continue to upgrade. With an ever-changing market and customer demand, it's absolutely essential to keep moving forward.

As Kelly says, in today's modern world, staying put just will not do. Ten years ago, a major change to the hotel was the addition of the now extremely popular La Marine restaurant. Three years ago, the main dining-room was given a completely new look, enlarged and renamed The Beaches. And last year, the SeaSpa opened with an impressive range of luxury facilities.

Bill Kelly is the fourth generation of Kelly's to run and upgrade the Rosslare hotel, originally opened as a tea-room in 1893. His parents, Billy and Breda, gradually built Kelly's into one of the country's leading hotels. Under their management, the hotel's season was expanded from just three summer months to most of the year.

Part of this involved instigating a long-running programme of extensions and renovations that included a swimming pool, squash and tennis courts and new bedrooms.

During the Seventies and early Eighties (after Billy's death in 1977), Breda continued to expand and upgrade. Bill and his wife Isabelle took over in 1987 and have seen further major developments over the years, including the leisure centre and the modernisation of all the bedrooms.

'We have a repeat business of about 70 - 80 per cent, with customers booking each year for the same time. They can see their money being spent on upgrading, giving them a feeling of ownership,' says Bill Kelly. 'For us it means great customer loyalty'. *

Taking over O'Connor's very successful Seafood Restaurant in Bantry was a challenge in itself for Peter and Anne O'Brien. Neither had a background in the food business, but took a chance when it came on the market.

They opened in April 2003 and rather than making any immediate changes, let the business continue as it was. 'We were new to the industry and the restaurant was already successful. There were good staff already running the place who stayed with us, who identified with the business.'

Then in January 2006, the O'Briens took the plunge. 'We closed for two months and did a major refurbishment. This was part financed by selling the public bar licence. We had a layout and design and our builder was Anne's brother-in-law.'

From the customer point of view it's more comfortable but still retains a good feel and its own unique charm.

They have incorporated some of the old ideas into the new space. 'We kept the idea of the original booths but have made them much more comfortable. From being the least coveted space to dine, the new booths are now the most sought-after.' O'Brien says.

'The feedback has been very good. From the customer point of view it's more comfortable but still retains a good feel and its own unique charm. Air conditioning was necessary as the small space became uncomfortable for staff and customers when we were busy.' The old bar stools have gone but there is now an upstairs lounge with comfortable sofas where customers can have a drink before their meal.' *

The Inishowen Peninsula is close to Northern Ireland and access is made even easier with the Foyle ferry. New developments in local 4-star hotels have also brought in extra visitors to the area.

McGrory's

All this is good news for the McGrory family in Culdaff who own a very successful hotel, restaurant and pub. 'Last year, we added on seven extra bedrooms as there was such a demand in the area' says Anne Doherty, who, with her brothers Neil and John, owns McGrory's.

With the existing 10 rooms also upgraded, this major refurbishment brings the number of rooms to 17. 'The new rooms are larger and are very luxuriously furnished. We now get quite a lot of business tourists and we hope to continue with this market. We have found that since the addition of the new rooms, our restaurant and bar have been extra busy. Our backroom bar is now equipped for use as a conference centre.' Doherty says.

With 17 bedrooms, the advantage is that we can get to know our customers, many of whom return regularly. Small is a good way to be hands on.

This bar is very popular as it is one of the top live music venues in the country with many well-known acts and tribute bands. Visitors to McGrory's get an all-in package - good accommodation, excellent music and of course, a restaurant that offers local food including seafood.

'We have no further developments in the pipeline,' says Doherty. 'With 17 bedrooms, the advantage is that we can get to know our customers, many of whom return regularly. Small is a good way to be hands on.' ∎

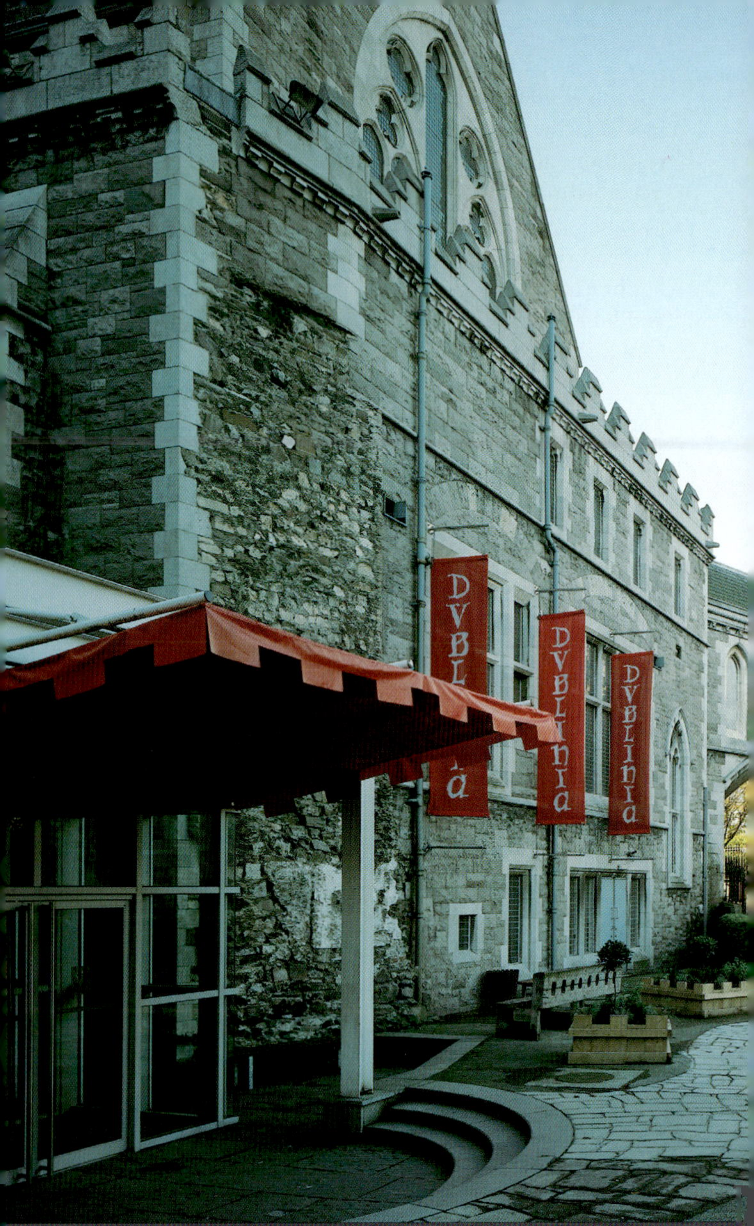
DVBLINIA
DVBLINIA
DVBLINIA

Ireland East & Dublin

Ireland East Touring Route

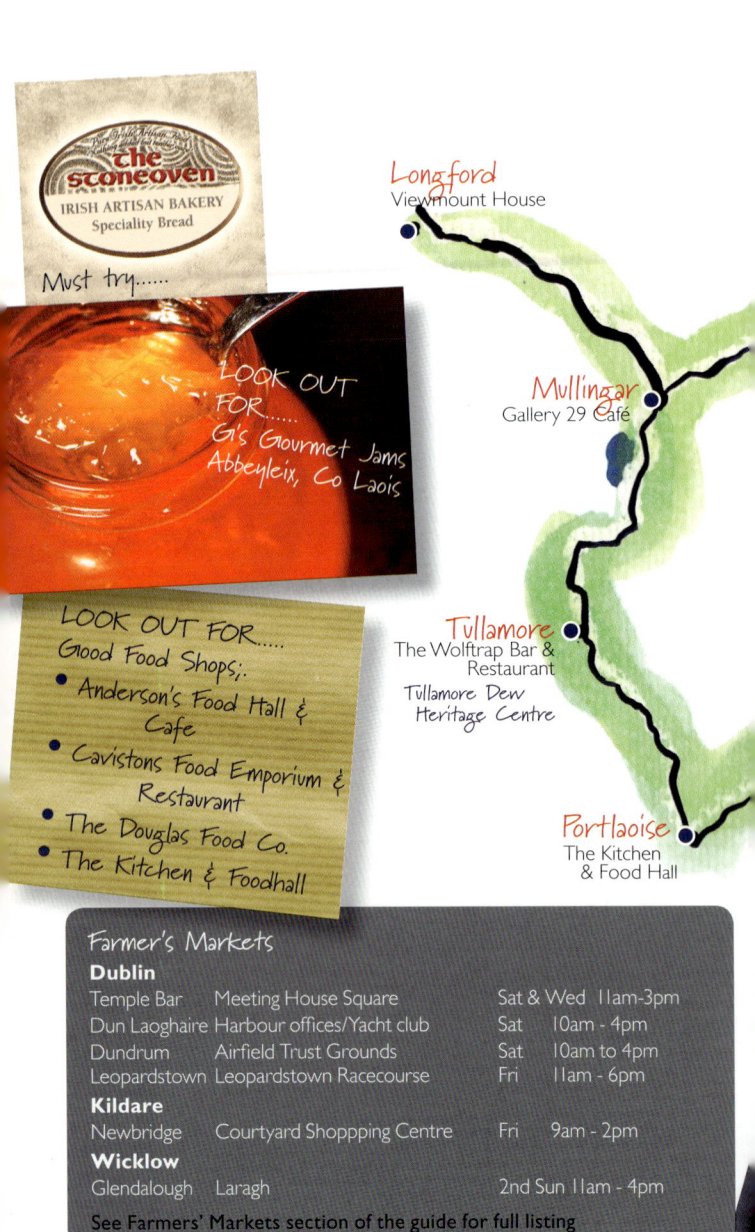

The Stoneoven
IRISH ARTISAN BAKERY
Speciality Bread

Must try......

LOOK OUT FOR......
G's Gourmet Jams
Abbeyleix, Co Laois

LOOK OUT FOR......
Good Food Shops;:
- Anderson's Food Hall & Cafe
- Cavistons Food Emporium & Restaurant
- The Douglas Food Co.
- The Kitchen & Foodhall

Longford
Viewmount House

Mullingar
Gallery 29 Café

Tullamore
The Wolftrap Bar & Restaurant
Tullamore Dew Heritage Centre

Portlaoise
The Kitchen & Food Hall

Farmer's Markets

Dublin

Temple Bar	Meeting House Square	Sat & Wed	11am-3pm
Dun Laoghaire	Harbour offices/Yacht club	Sat	10am - 4pm
Dundrum	Airfield Trust Grounds	Sat	10am to 4pm
Leopardstown	Leopardstown Racecourse	Fri	11am - 6pm

Kildare

Newbridge	Courtyard Shoppping Centre	Fri	9am - 2pm

Wicklow

Glendalough	Laragh		2nd Sun 11am - 4pm

See Farmers' Markets section of the guide for full listing

Carlingford
Ghan House

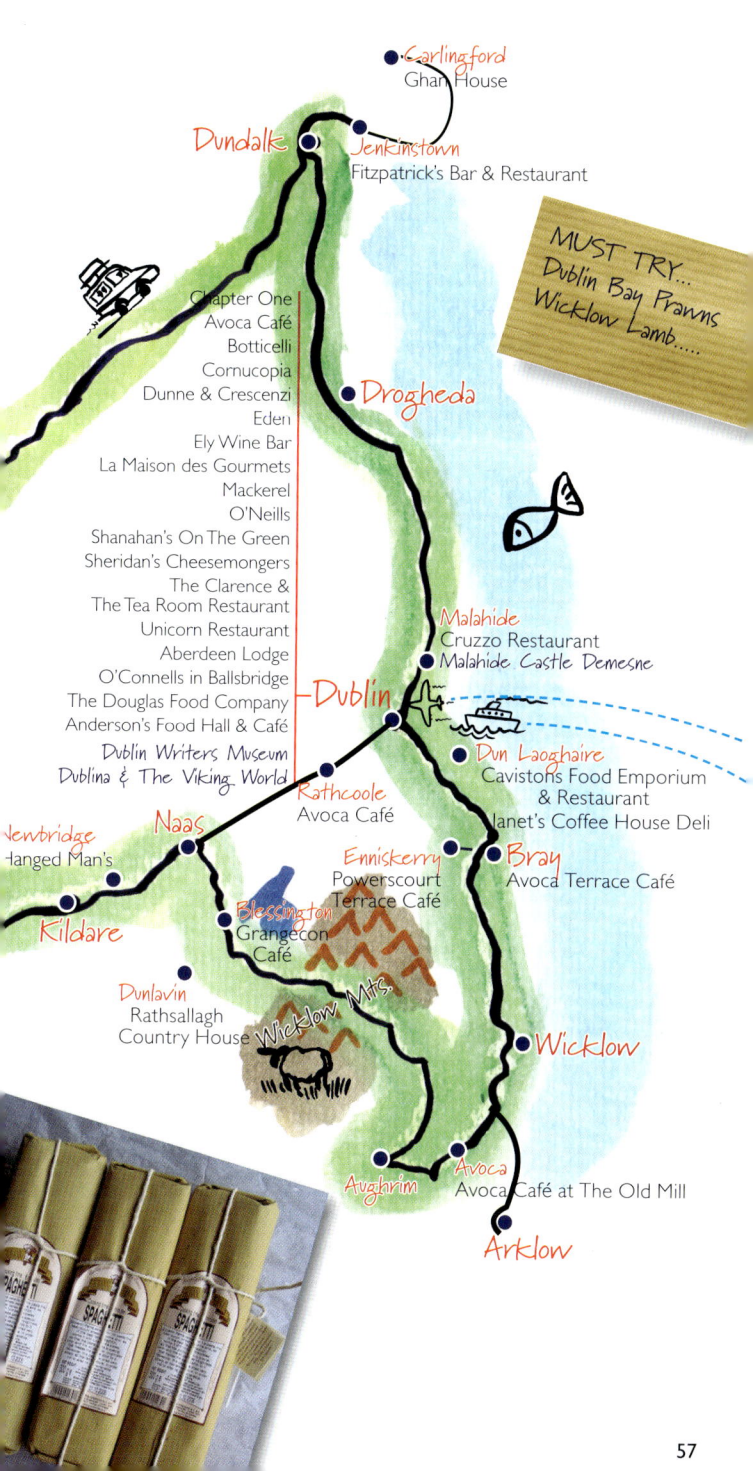

Dundalk

Jenkinstown
Fitzpatrick's Bar & Restaurant

MUST TRY...
Dublin Bay Prawns
Wicklow Lamb.....

Chapter One
Avoca Café
Botticelli
Cornucopia
Dunne & Crescenzi
Eden
Ely Wine Bar
La Maison des Gourmets
Mackerel
O'Neills
Shanahan's On The Green
Sheridan's Cheesemongers
The Clarence &
The Tea Room Restaurant
Unicorn Restaurant
Aberdeen Lodge
O'Connells in Ballsbridge
The Douglas Food Company
Anderson's Food Hall & Café
Dublin Writers Museum
Dublina & The Viking World

Drogheda

Malahide
Cruzzo Restaurant
Malahide Castle Demesne

Dublin

Dun Laoghaire
Cavistons Food Emporium
& Restaurant
Janet's Coffee House Deli

Rathcoole
Avoca Café

Newbridge
Hanged Man's

Naas

Enniskerry
Powerscourt
Terrace Café

Bray
Avoca Terrace Café

Kildare

Blessington
Grangecon
Café

Dunlavin
Rathsallagh
Country House

Wicklow Mts.

Wicklow

Aughrim

Avoca
Avoca Café at The Old Mill

Arklow

57

Ireland East & Dublin
www.goodfoodireland.ie

Dublin 1

Chapter One Restaurant
City centre restaurant

18-19 Parnell Square, Dublin 1
Tel. +353(0)1 8732266
Email. info@chapteronerestaurant.com
www.chapteronerestaurant.com

There's no denying that Chapter One is one of the capital's best restaurants, and yes, it's owned by a Corkman. With experience in London and Geneva under his belt, chef Ross Lewis returned to Ireland to open Chapter One in 1991, which he runs with business partner, Martin Corbett. The restaurant's recent remodelling has seen the addition of an oyster counter and champagne bar, with a new reception area and a fine wine cellar. Eating at Chapter One - under the Dublin Writers' Museum - is an event: service is impeccable and the food is delicious. Lunch might include brandade of cod with avocado purée and clam vinaigrette, and then spiced daube of beef with parsnip purée - or check out the goodies on the charcuterie trolley. Suppliers are credited on the menu. The impressive wine list has something to suit all pockets, and includes 14 by the glass, a good way to try something more adventurous than usual. For dinner, sample the Mediterranean fish soup and share a rack of lamb for two. The pre-theatre menu offers excellent value, and you needn't feel rushed - you can come back for dessert after the show. The Gate Theatre is around the corner, and with treats such as orange and campari jelly, coffee cream and warm chocolate mousse on offer, you won't want to miss it.

Prices: 3 course lunch menu from €32.50. Dinner main course from €30. House wine from €24.
Food served: 12.30-14.30. Tue-Fri. 18.00-22.45 Tue-Sat.
Closed: Sun, Mon, 2 weeks at beginning of August, 2 weeks at Christmas.
Cuisine: Modern European.
Other Points: Children welcome over 10 years. Private dining areas (14 and 20). Winner - Wine Person of the Year 2005. Winner - Ireland East Regional Award 2006.
Directions: Top of O'Connell Street, North side of Parnell Sq. Basement of the Dublin Writers Museum.

Ross Lewis, Chapter One

for online reservations

Ireland East & Dublin

Dublin 2

Avoca Café
Daytime café and shop

11-13 Suffolk Street, Dublin 2
Tel. +353(0)1 6726019
Email. info@avoca.ie
www.avoca.ie

The Pratt family's flagship Avoca store is a 7-level, mini-department store located in the heart of Dublin, just off Grafton Street, across from Trinity College. Awash with colour and imagination, it carries a full range of exclusive woven throws, rugs, scarves, clothing, gifts, home furnishings, children's wear, jewellery, crafts and cookery books and even boasts a secret rooftop garden. An extensive basement food hall is chock-a-block with specialist gourmet foods, giftware and kitchen gear, as well as home-baked products and freshly made salads that can be purchased for takeaway. The light-filled Avoca Café on the second floor has table service, dramatic floral arrangements and is hugely popular. Wholesome, healthy, home-cooked dishes might include sweet potato and lemongrass soup; chicken Caesar salad; shepherd's pie, chicken skewers with cous cous; and a range of impeccably fresh salads. Save room for a slice of chocolate and raspberry tart or a strawberry-orange tartlet with fresh cream.

Prices: Main course from €7.95-€13.95. House wine from €17.
Food Served: 10.00-17.30 Mon-Sat. 11.00-17.30 Sun.
Closed: 25, 26 Dec.
Cuisine: Traditional and modern Irish with international influences.
Other Points: Children welcome. Craft shop.
Directions: Turn left into Suffolk Street from the bottom of Grafton Street.

Dublin 2

Botticelli
City centre Italian restaurant

1-3 Temple Bar, Dublin 2
Tel. +353(0)1 6727289
Email. botticelli@eircom.net

This long established casual Italian restaurant, in the heart of Temple Bar, seems to draw from the lively atmosphere on the streets visible through its large windows. The menu features a wide variety of traditional Italian dishes including classic pasta dishes such as rigatoni puttanesca and lasagne al forno, while starters such as antipasto all'italiana and caprese salad are a quintessentially Italian introduction. There are plenty of meat, fish and chicken dishes, including vitello ai funghi, saltimbocca al romana, filetto al pepe verde and swordfish with capers, olives, garlic and tomato sauce. Owner Piero Cosso believes in using the best ingredients to produce the best food, and chef Luigi Palmieri's pizzas are a case in point. A thin, crispy homemade crust arrives laden with tomatoes, cheese and a wide choice of extra toppings. Homemade ice creams come in nearly a dozen flavours, including green apple and champagne and strawberry. Set lunches are good value, and there is a wide selection of mostly Italian wines. Service is courteous and professional.

Prices: Lunch (starter/main course & tea/coffee) from €8.80. Dinner main course from €10-€20. House wine from €18.95
Food served: 12.30-24.00 daily.
Closed: 25, 26 Dec.
Cuisine: Italian
Other Points: Children welcome.
Directions: Just off the square in Temple Bar.

Ireland East & Dublin

www.goodfoodireland.ie

Dublin 2

Cornucopia
City centre vegetarian restaurant and café

19 Wicklow Street, Dublin 2
Tel. +353(0)1 6777583
Email. cornucopia@eircom.net

'Cheap and Cheerful' is a term that can be thrown around and used far too loosely these days and you may still wonder about the actual quality of the food itself? The small, easy going vegetarian restaurant and café which is conveniently located just off Grafton Street in the centre of Dublin city is one such restaurant where the wonderfully wholesome and varied food may well leave you looking at vegetarian food with a whole new mindset! Fantastic soups like 'Moroccan carrot' or 'courgette, regato cheese and almond' do not disappoint and can be served with a very generous slice of homemade bread (choose from wholewheat, brown, tomato, gluten free, dairy free). All the food is clearly labelled for customers with food intolerances. For those looking for a substantial main meal there are delights like 'Butternut squash and two cheese cannelloni cooked in a sage cream' or 'Polenta bake layered with roast Mediterranean vegetables and topped basil pesto'. There is a choice of ten salads which originate from all over the globe 'Japanese rice salad' or 'Mediterranean chickpea salad with Feta cheese, rocket and roast aubergine in a sun dried tomato dressing' give you the idea. Lunch is served seven days a week but if vegetarian fare is not your first love, it may be worth considering one of their special vegetarian breakfasts which are served Mon - Sat until midday. Or if the cup of tea or coffee doesn't revive the weary shopper, they could always try one of their delicious homemade desserts or cakes like 'Coconut and passion fruit roulade' or 'Blueberry and almond tart'.

Prices: Lunch/dinner main course from €10.50. House wine from €20.
Food Served: 8.30-20.00, until 21.00 on Thursdays and 12.00-19.00 Sundays.
Closed: 25-27 Dec. 1 Jan. Easter Sun and Mon. October bank holiday Sun & Mon.
Cuisine: Vegetarian - special diets catered for.
Other Points: Children welcome.
Directions: Just off Grafton Street, take the turn at Brown Thomas.

Dublin 2

Dunne & Crescenzi
Italian restaurant, café wine bar and deli

14 & 16 South Frederick Street, Dublin 2
Tel. +353(0)1 6759892

With their ever-expanding empire of charming small Italian café-restaurants Eileen Dunne and Stefano Crescenzi have nailed a winning formula. Authentic is a word much used about D&C, and indeed this is the kind of place you could bring a visiting Italian without batting an eyelid. The South Frederick Street branch has a large selection of Italian wines (some organic), and artisan ingredients - including olive oils, pastas and preserved fruits - to purchase and take away. The atmosphere is relaxed, the service brisk but friendly, and the simple menu a reminder that the best ingredients - buffalo mozzarella, fragrant basil, ripe tomatoes - can and should stand alone. The generous antipasti (misto and vegetariano) are particularly good, and there are daily changing pasta dishes, as well as side orders of delicious breads, olives and tomato or bean salad. The competitively priced wine list gives a regional tour of Italy.

Prices: A La Carte Menu available throughout the day - dishes from €5.50. House wine from €13.
Food Served: 8.30-23.00 Mon-Sat. 12.00-18.00 Sun.
Closed: Sundays. 25 Dec for 2 weeks.
Cuisine: Italian.
Other Points: Children welcome.
Directions: Close to Grafton Street and parallel to Dawson Street.

Ireland East & Dublin

for online reservations

Dublin 2

Eden
City centre restaurant

Sycamore Street, Templebar, Dublin 2
Tel. +353(0)1 6705372
Email. eden@edenrestaurant.ie
www.edenrestaurant.ie

With its knock-out location overlooking the vibrant Meeting House Square in the heart of Dublin's cultural quarter, Temple Bar, and its light, bright modern Irish cuisine, Eden attracts a buzzy crowd of artists, musicians, business types, and out-of-towners. Its two-storey, light-filled interior, awash with amazingly lush plants, sleek white tables and chairs, and its breezy outdoor dining terrace (perfect for watching movies shown in the square) are great for lazy weekend brunches, as well as lunch and dinner, anytime. Opened in 1997, its ultra-seasonal menus, under chef Michael Durkin's direction, rely on locally sourced produce, meat, seafood, game and cheeses; breads and ice creams are homemade. Try an exotic cocktail such as an espresso martini or a cosmopolitan before tucking into a lunch starter of baked fresh figs with Parma ham, Ricotta and honey followed by lemon scented breast of cornfed chicken or for dinner seared beef carpaccio followed by roast panfried Magret duck breast with pommes Anna, green beans and kumquat relish or braised lamb shank with Moroccan spices. The wine selection is diverse and well-balanced. The pre-theatre menu represents excellent value at €25 for three courses and is available 18.00-19.00 Sunday - Thursday.

Prices: Lunch main course from €14.50. 2 courses €19.50. Dinner main course from €18. House wine from €23.
Food served: Lunch 12.00-15.00 daily. Dinner 18.00-22.30 Mon-Sat & 18.00-22.00 Sun.
Closed: Bank Holidays.
Cuisine: Modern Irish.
Other Points: Children welcome.
Directions: Next to the Irish Film Centre.

Eden

Ireland East & Dublin

www.goodfoodireland.ie

Dublin 2

ely wine bar
City centre wine bar and restaurant

22 Ely Place, Dublin 2
Tel. +353(0)1 6768986
Email. elywine@eircom.net
www.elywinebar.ie

Michelle and Erik Robson are the young, hardworking couple behind this easygoing, perennially popular wine bar, now with a newly extended basement. Upstairs, the marble fireplace, wooden floors and small bar with flattering lighting create an intimate atmosphere which induces you to linger. And what a great place this is to do just that; there are 500 wines to choose from, over 70 of them by the glass, so a spot of self-education is perfectly affordable. A delightful, uncomplicated menu melds seamlessly with the enjoyment of wine; lunch dishes such as a divine salad of home cured duck breast served with poached pear and pickled ginger partner perfectly a recommended Chilean Chardonnay. There is something for everyone on the dinner menu with choices from traditional Irish stew made with organic Burren lamb to pan fried swordfish steak. A cold charger heaped with meats and Irish cheeses is ideal for large, grazing groups. All meat is organic and from the family farm in the Burren. Berry crumbles, baked cheesecakes and plum pies are simply crying out to be matched with the dessert wines which follow.

Prices: Lunch main course from €14. Dinner main course from €14. Wine from €24.
Hours: 12.00-24.30.
Food served: 12.00-23.30 Mon-Fri. 13.00-23.30 Sat.
Closed: Sundays and one week over Christmas.
Cuisine: Contemporary Irish.
Other Points: Winner - Wine List of the Year 2004.
Directions: At the junction of Baggot Street/Merrion Row, off St Stephen's Green.

Dublin 2

La Maison des Gourmets
Café, bakery & patisserie

15 Castle Market, Dublin 2
Tel. +353(0)1 6727258

Tucked away on a pedestrians-only street in the heart of the city's smartest shopping area, this charming boulangerie and salon de The specialises in authentic French bread, viennoiserie and patisserie products, offering a true taste of France in Dublin. For breakfast indulge in the Petit Dejeuner Francais, a selection of mini viennoiseries to accompany your favourite coffee or freshly squeezed juices, to be enjoyed there or to go. Light lunch dishes, served in a chic, understated space at the top of a winding staircase might include French onion soup and tartine of Bayonne ham and artichoke or smoked salmon with chive cream accompanied by a glass of wine. After a busy day drop in for a delicious afternoon tea that includes a selection of hand made delights which are all made in full view. The shop also does a brisk trade in custom-made, ultra-rich special-occasion cakes.

Prices: Main course from €10-€12. Wine from €22.
Food served: 8.00-19.00 Mon-Sat. Lunch only served 12.00-15.00.
Closed: Sundays and bank holidays. 1 week after Christmas.
Cuisine: French.
Other Points: Children welcome. French language lessons at breakfast.
Directions: Between Georges St. Arcade and Powerscourt Shopping Centre or between Dury St. and South William St.

Mackerel, Dublin

Ireland East & Dublin

www.goodfoodireland.ie

Dublin 2

Mackerel
City centre seafood restaurant

Bewley's Café, 78/79 Grafton Street,
Dublin 2
Tel. +353 (0)1 6727719
Email. info@mackerel.ie
www.mackerel.ie

Housed in Bewley's Café in Grafton Street, the 'heartbeat of Dublin for generations', Mackerel has built up an excellent reputation in less than two years. Relax over Sunday brunch with the paper while savouring a risotto with smoked haddock and poached egg or roast artichoke heart filled with crab and red onion. Sip a Prosecco or Margarita while choosing dinner from a menu that reads like a who's who of the fish world. Begin with a starter of mussels steamed with garlic, ginger, spring onion and cider or baked crab dip with fromage frais and cheese crust. Follow this with pan fried shark with black bean salsa, gambas with chilli and lime butter, baked fresh sardines with a roast red pepper sauce, whole roast silver bream, or roast fillet of red snapper with pakchoi and satay sauce. Opt for a plateful of Sheridan's cheese or one of the tempting desserts - possibly both if stomach space allows. A light raspberry and elderflower mousse may be sufficient after this feast but if not, a hazelnut pannacotta or strawberries, Prosecco and sorbet will be splendid. A good wine list has mainly French, Italian and Spanish bottles with Portugal and Australia contributing to the whites. House wine, both red and white, comes in half bottles, ideal for lunch.

Prices: Main course from €15. Sunday Brunch dishes from €10.
Opening hours: 12.00-16.00 & 17.00-22.00. Sunday brunch 12.00-16.00.
Closed: Bank Holidays.
Cuisine: Seafood.
Directions: On left hand side of Grafton Street.

Dublin 2

O'Neill's
City centre pub

2 Suffolk Street, Dublin 2
Tel. +353 (0)1 6793656
Email. mike@oneillsbar.com
www.oneillsbar.com

O'Neill's has been a licensed premises for more than 300 years, and has been in the O'Neill family since 1927. Inside, a plaque details the amazing history of the area, including the fact that it was the site of the Viking Parliament, a temporary palace for King Henry II, and even featured entertainment and executions in Medieval times! The historic bar enjoys a great location in the city centre, across from the main tourist office. It's a popular spot with locals and tourists alike, and the crowds create a great buzz. The portions here are sizeable, the carvery runs all day, and there is also an à la carte menu and salad/sandwich bar, so there's no excuse for going hungry. Start with seared spicy chicken wings with blue cheese dip or share a combo platter. Main courses may include beef and Guinness stew, traditional Irish corned beef and cabbage or a Kerry casserole of pork, bacon, mushrooms, onions and rosemary. If you can manage any more, the home-made dessert selection will tempt you. Find an alcove and try a pint of Darcy's Dublin Stout or Revolution Red Beer or pick from the good selection of reasonably priced wines.

Prices: Lunch/dinner from €10.25. Dinner main course from €10.25. Bar snack from €3.65. House Wine from €15.25
Opening hours: 10.30-23.30 Mon-Thur. 10.30-00.30 Fri-Sat. 12.30-23.00 Sun.
Food served: 11.30-22.00 Mon-Fri. 11.30-21.00 Sat. 12.30-22.00 Sun.
Closed: Good Friday and 25, 26 Dec.
Cuisine: Modern and traditional Irish and European.
Other Points: Live traditional music every Sun and Mon night.
Directions: Opposite Dublin Tourism Centre on Suffolk Street.

Dublin 2

Shanahan's on the Green
Steakhouse and seafood restaurant

119 St Stephen's Green, Dublin 2
Tel. +353(0)1 4070939
www.shanahans.ie

Start the weekend off with a bang with Shanahan's Friday lunch. If you can set aside the afternoon, you get a surprise appetiser, which you might choose to follow by caramelised black figs and Bayonne ham, venison ragoût and passionfruit soufflé, tea and coffee and petit fours, for €45. It's a great way to sample the atmosphere of one of the capital's most renowned restaurants. Shanahan's is based in a beautifully restored Georgian townhouse on St Stephen's Green. Ideal for a special occasion, its sense of luxury is conveyed by plush carpets, gilt mirrors, crystal chandeliers and white linen. The Oval Office bar even boasts JFK's rocking chair. For dinner, you could go for pan-fried crab and potato sandwiches, followed by Alaskan halibut with caper gremolata, marinated cherry tomatoes and sakura salad, and finish with warm Belgian chocolate fondant with Baileys ice-cream and Toblerone chocolate sauce. But really, the must-try in Shanahan's is the steak. Certified Irish Angus beef is cooked in a broiler at 1600-1800F, for the perfect result. Steaks can be anything from eight to 24 ounces. The fantastic wine list offers a huge selection of New and Old World, and with the help of the knowledgeable staff, you are sure to find something you'll love.

Prices: Set lunch from €45-€50. A La Carte during December. Dinner main course from €38. Wine from €30.
Food served: 12.30-14.00 Fridays only. 18.00-22.30 daily.
Closed: Over Christmas & New Year.
Cuisine: American steakhouse & seafood.
Other Points: Winner - Wine List of the Year 2003.
Directions: On the west side of St Stephen's Green.

Dublin 2

Sheridan's Cheesemongers
Gourmet cheese and food shop

11 South Anne Street, Dublin 2
Tel. +353(0)1 6793143
Email. dublin@sheridanscheesemongers.com
www.sheridanscheesemongers.com

Sheridan's is a cosy shop. Stop by on a busy day and you are likely to be squeezing past fellow shoppers to even get in. Once there however your attention is likely to be quickly drawn to the shelves. On the left are the hard cheeses, to the right oils, vinegars and wine along with biscuits and chocolate. Up a few steps and you come to olives, lots of them and bread and on the left a fridge with softer cheeses and yoghurts. Out the back there are meats and blue cheeses. All of these are sourced with the Sheridan's well-known eye for detail from small producers. If you can, call in on a Thursday. A number of items, include Pain Poilaine bread, comes in from France the day before. Foods worth waiting for.

Opening Hours: 10.00-18.00 Mon-Fri. 9.30-18.00 Sat. (Check for Christmas opening hours).
Closed: Sundays. 25,26 Dec.
Directions: Off Grafton Street in the city centre.

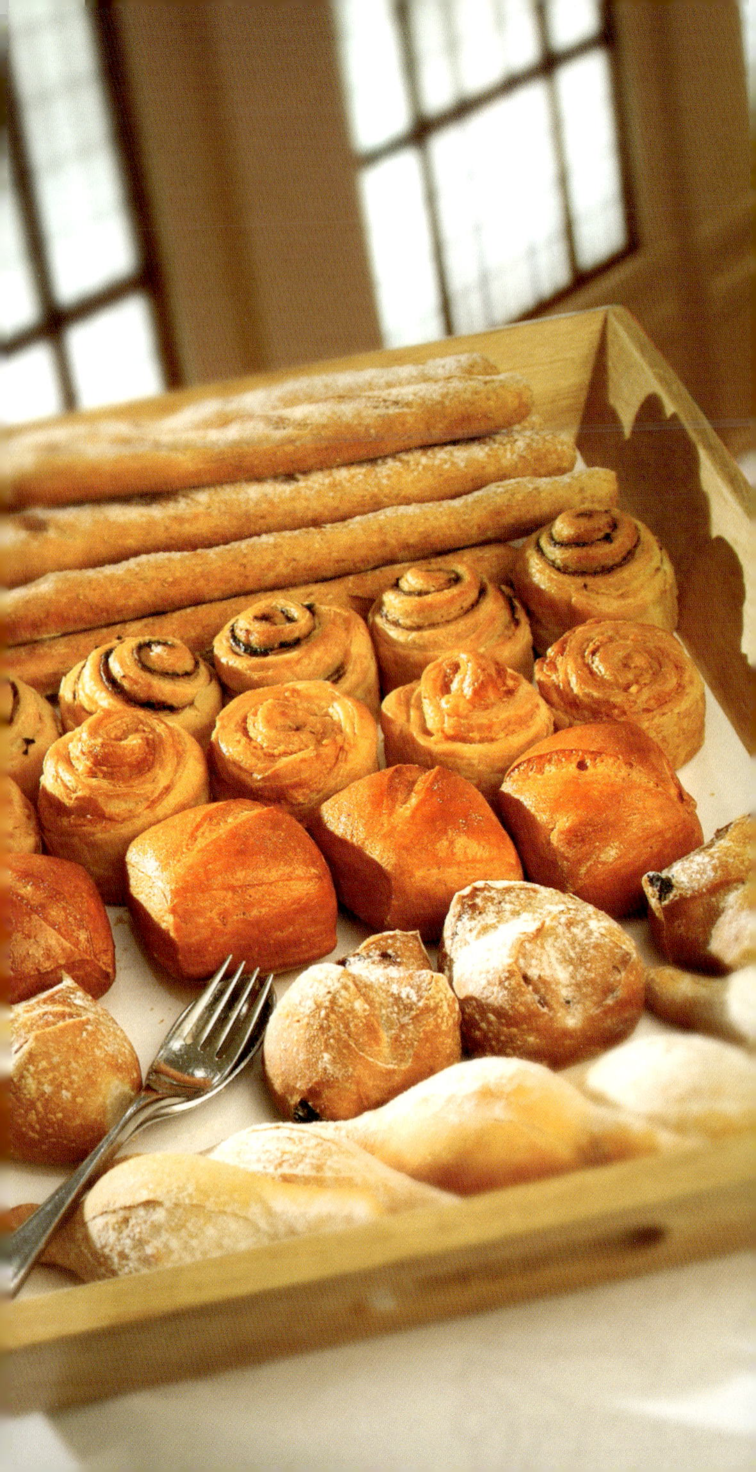

Dublin 2

The Clarence & The Tea Room Restaurant
City centre hotel & restaurant

6-8 Wellington Quay, Dublin 2
Tel. +353(0)1 4070800
Email. reservations@theclarence.ie
www.theclarence.ie

This landmark hotel in the heart of Temple Bar dates from 1852, and was famously re-opened by rock stars Bono and The Edge in 1996. The original arts and crafts features have been carefully incorporated into the contemporary design, which uses natural materials such as Portland stone and American white oak to create a mood of understated elegance. The Octagon bar with its wood panelling, and the Study, with its open fire, have become popular city centre meeting spots. The Tea Room, with its 20-foot high coved ceilings and double-height windows, is an outstandingly calm and beautiful space. Chef Fred Cordonnier produces an inventive menu of classically influenced dishes, combining luxury ingredients with the finest seasonal produce. Terrine of foie gras, orange and kumquat crumble, coriander tuile might be followed by oven roasted fillet of cod, crisp fennel, saffron and tomato dressing, black olive oil, brandade "beignets" or pan fried fillet of prime Irish Hereford beef, glazed spring onions, wild mushrooms, "marchand de vin" sauce with; followed by a dessert of mille feuille of chocolate and raspberry mousse, fresh raspberries and double cream ice cream. Chutneys, breads, ice-cream, sorbet and chocolates are made in-house and herbs come from the chef's garden. Each of the 49 rooms and suites has been individually designed

Rooms: 49 ensuite. Double from €210. Single from €210. Family from €599.
Prices: Lunch from €24 (2 courses). Dinner main course from €30. Bar snack from €6.50. House wine from €27.50.
Opening Hours: Bar - 11.00-23.00 Mon-Wed & Sun. 11.00-00.00 Thu-Sat.
Food Served: Breakfast 7.00-11.00 Mon-Fri. 7.30-11.30 Sat-Sun. Lunch 12.30-14.30 (except Sat). Dinner 19.00-22.30 Mon-Sat. 19.00-22.00 Sun.
Closed: 24-26 Dec.
Cuisine: French/Irish with a continental twist. Traditional and modern combined.
Other Points: Children welcome. Bedrooms non-smoking. Valet parking. Meeting and private dining room.
Directions: The hotel overlooks the River Liffey at Wellington Quay, southside. The Tea Room has its own entrance on Essex Street.

to provide accommodation that is simple and elegant, many have super king-size double beds. All rooms are decorated in one of the hotel's five signature colours: crimson, royal blue, amethyst, gold and chocolate and each contains Shaker-style furniture, specially crafted beds with Egyptian linens and spacious white tiled bathrooms with pedestal sinks and oak cabinets.

The Tea Room at The Clarence

Ireland East & Dublin

www.goodfoodireland.ie

Dublin 2

Unicorn Restaurant
Italian restaurant and café

12B Merrion Court
Merrion Row, Dublin 2
Tel. +353(0)1 6762182
Email. unicorn12b@eircom.net
www.unicornrestaurant.com

The Unicorn had been run by the same family for almost 60 years when the current owners took over in 1995, and they hope to match this record with the Italian restaurant. The emphasis here is on quality ingredients: vegetables are organic, eggs and ducks are free range, fish and shellfish is bought locally on a daily basis and meat is Irish and traceable. Staff at The Unicorn are friendly and efficient. A large lunch menu concentrates on Italian favourites such as meatballs and risotto, but also takes in Irish fare such as Clonakilty black budding and Dublin Bay prawns. For dinner, start with calamari or polenta, and try the traditional regional Italian treats such as, from Tuscany, slow-cooked lamb shank and from Lombardy, veal on the bone 'Milanese' with rocket and cherry tomatoes. Signature dishes at the Unicorn include chargrilled salmon 'Mari Monti', with wild mushrooms and berries on a bed of rocket, and pockets of veal stuffed with Parma ham, Mozzarella and sage. Tantalising desserts include Grand Marnier chocolate mousse or you might prefer the cheese board with onion marmalade and a glass of port.

Prices: Lunch main course from Antipasto Bar from €9.50-€16.50. Dinner main course from €12.80-€42.50. House wine from €23.50.
Food served: 12.30-16.00 and 18.15-23.00 Mon-Sat.
Closed: Sundays. Good Friday. 25 Dec to 2 Jan. All Bank Holidays.
Cuisine: Contemporary Italian.
Other Points: Piano Bar dining room open nightly Tue-Sat. Available for private dining or just dinner with live music.
Directions: East of St Stephen's Green.

Dublin 4

Aberdeen Lodge
Period guesthouse

53 Park Avenue, Ballsbridge, Dublin 4
Tel. +353(0)1 2838155
Email. aberdeen@iol.ie
www.halpinsprivatehotels.com

This grand Edwardian townhouse is set in desirable Dublin 4, close to the city centre, Lansdowne Road sports grounds and the RDS. The elegant dining room overlooks extensive landscaped gardens and cricket grounds. At Pat Halpin's luxury ivy-covered lodge, service is impeccable: you are greeted with offers of tea and newspapers. Upstairs, you'll feel pampered by the aromatherapy products, robes and slippers. Bedrooms feature four-poster beds, period furnishings and fresh flowers, as well as whirlpool spas in suites. Afternoon teas and fine wines are served on crisp white linen in the main drawing rooms and library: snacks here include warm goats' cheese crostini or an Irish farmhouse cheeseboard. For breakfast, enjoy buttermilk pancakes with maple syrup and cinnamon or kippers with herb butter, all with home-made bread, pastries, scones and preserves. Residents have use of a nearby leisure centre, with swimming pool, jacuzzi and sauna.

Rooms: 17 ensuite. Double from €140. Single from €99. Suite from €189 Some have spa bath.
Food served: Drawing Room Menu available throughout the day until 21.00.
Cuisine: European.
Other Points: Non-smoking. Complimentary wireless internet access. Garden. Children welcome. Car park.
Directions: Minutes to the city centre by Dart. By car take the Merrion Road towards Sydney Parade Dart Station and then first left into Park Avenue.

for online reservations

Ireland East & Dublin

Dublin 4

O'Connells in Ballsbridge
City centre restaurant

Bewley's Hotel, Merrion Road,
Ballsbridge, Dublin 4
Tel. +353(0)1 6473304
Email. info@oconnellsballsbridge.com
www.oconnellsballsbridge.com

Since its opening, chef and owner Tom O'Connell has focused on building a reputation for serving up impeccably-sourced Irish ingredients at affordable prices. The menu aims for broad appeal, with coeliacs well accommodated, serving everything from warm beef salad to rollmops, crispy duck pizza to fish 'n chips with pea and mint puree, chicken satay to braised shank of lamb. Flexibility is also key; many of the dishes are served as starters or main course portions, many of the wines are served in half bottles or by the glass, and their novel approach to desserts, served as 'little desserts', allow customers a taste of two for the price of one. Recent developments have included the addition of innovative weekday lunch (12.30-14.15) and teatime (17.00-19.00) BBQs in the large summer courtyard (Mon-Fri/May-Aug), and a new direction in the menu which provide more one-dish suppers for the casual diner, with an emphasis on super-fresh fish of the day, alongside lots of pasta and vegetarian dishes.

Prices: Buffet lunch main course from €10.95. Dinner: 3-courses inclusive of first course, main course, two of O'Connell's little desserts and tea/coffee and Tipperary mineral water from €28.50. House wine from €19.85.
Food Served: 12.30-22.00. 12.30-21.00 Sun.
Closed: After lunch 24 Dec to 27 Dec at 15.00.
Cuisine: Traditional and modern Irish.
Other Points: Coeliac friendly. Carpark. Winner - Wine List of the Year 2002. Winner - Locally Produced Food Supporters Award 2006.
Directions: On the junction of Simmonscourt and Merrion Road in Ballsbridge.

Dublin 4

Sheridan's Cheesemongers
Gourmet cheese and food shop

7 Pembroke Lane, Ballsbridge, Dublin 4
Tel. +353(0)1 6608231
Email. info@sheridanscheesemongers.com
www. sheridanscheesemongers.com

This is one of the most recent additons to the Dublin stable and while cheese is part of the offer there is more of a delicatessen feel to the place. Sandwiches at lunchtime, taken from the fridge or made to order are supplement with boxes of organic apples and other fruit. Like all the Sheridan outlets attention to sourcing means you gaze at one beautiful quality package after another. Will it be biscuits to go with cheese, bars of chocolate or jars of jam. Service is informative and generally knowledgable. For anyone looking to cheat your way though the first part of an evening there are excellent olives, antipasti and cured meats along with good bread. The main course too, can easily be provided for although if you are catering for anything more than six people it might well be wise to give notice.

Opening hours: 10.00-18.30 Mon-Fri. 10.00-18.00 Sat.
Closed: Sundays. 25, 26 Dec.
Directions: From City Centre turn right off Baggot St onto Waterloo Rd. take next left onto Pembroke Lane. Sheridan's is on the left.

Ireland East & Dublin

Dublin 4

The Douglas Food Company
Gourmet food shop and deli

53 Main Street, Donnybrook, Dublin 4
Tel.+353 (0)1 2694066
Email.
grainne@thedouglasfoodcompany.ie

This gourmet deli and catering company provides chic south Dublin with a classy spot for an over-the-counter lunchtime bite, as well as a one-stop shop for delectable takeaway meals. Owner Grainne Murphy takes pride in her hands-on approach and the midday rush finds her, along with her small team, serving up sandwiches, soup, coffee and delicious desserts to a busy and appreciative crowd. Then, and throughout the day, hot meals such as beef stroganoff and Mediterranean fish casserole are available, as well as colourful salads including couscous with roasted pepper, courgettes, coriander and basil dressing. Treats such as Normandy apple tart and banana and Bailey's loaf are perfect just with coffee. The shop is smart and bright, with a large window frontage in which the dishes of the day are displayed. Some unusual deli products can be found among the cheeses, wines, chocolates and coffees for sale. The top-notch catering service can accommodate special diets.

Opening hours: 10.00-18.30 Mon-Fri. 9.30-18.00 Sat.
Closed: 25 Dec to first Monday after New Year (open for catering orders on 31 Dec). Closed bank holiday Sundays and Mondays.
Cuisine: Modern Irish/Mediterranean.
Directions: Directly opposite Donnybrook rugby grounds on the Main Street.

Dublin 9

Andersons Food Hall & Café
Café, restaurant and deli

3 The Rise, Glasnevin, Dublin 9
Tel. +353(0)1 8378394
Email. info@andersons.ie
www.andersons.ie

At Andersons you can choose to eat in, or pick up something delicious for later. Noel Delany and Patricia van der Velde specialise in Irish and continental cheeses, charcuterie and breads. This beautifully restored butcher shop, which has been in the Delany family since the 1930s, retains its character with the original façade. The interior is inspired by the "bouchon", a butcher-cum-restaurant typical of the French city of Lyon. The café at the back features comfortable wood and marble furniture, and here appetisers include duo of crab and salmon terrine with mixed leaves and French rye brown bread. You can try the chicken and walnut salad, or one of the seven speciality plates. Their fish plate includes salmon, crab terrine, capers, prawns, roll mop herring and smoked mackerel. Gourmet sandwiches include Gubbeen vegetarian cheese, peppers and tomato with mixed leaves, onion, cucumber and country chutney on multigrain bread. Wines by the glass come mainly from France, Italy and Spain, and any of the 180 different bottles for sale can be drunk on the premises, for a €6 corkage. Those taking the non-alcoholic route are well catered for, with a range of speciality teas, or Lorina French lemonade in five flavours.

Prices: Lunch main course from €6.95. Dinner main course from €10.95. House wine from €16.95.
Food Served: 9.00-19.00 Mon-Wed. 9.00-20.30 Thur-Sat. 10.00-19.00 Sun.
Closed: Good Friday & Easter Sunday. Christmas (3/4 days).
Cuisine: Continental café style.
Other Points: Garden. Children welcome.
Directions: Just off Griffith Avenue. Near Drumcondra/Airport Road. Coming from the airport, turn right onto Griffith Avenue, then 2nd right.

Ireland East & Dublin

Dun Laoghaire Co Dublin

Caviston's Food Emporium & Restaurant
Seafood restaurant, deli and fish shop

59 Glasthule Road, Glasthule,
Dun Laoghaire, Co Dublin
Tel. +353(0)1 2809245/2809120
Email. info@cavistons.com
www.cavistons.com

Over its 50 years of business, this family-run seafood and gourmet mecca has built itself a steadfast reputation for high quality food and friendly well-informed service. Peter Caviston is the Southside housewife's favourite grocer, knowing as they do that they can rely on him to maintain the emporium's jovial atmosphere (no more so as on Bloomsday on June 16th) as much as its standards of excellence in everything from artfully displayed selections of the freshest seafood to European salamis, farmhouse cheeses from Ireland and elsewhere, organic vegetables, speciality breads, take-home salads and pre-cooked meals. Next door is the eponymous seafood restaurant, a bright little space popular enough to support a brusque three-sitting lunch-trade; the 3pm sitting is the one to go for if you'd like to linger a little over the imaginatively approached but simply prepared seafood. Main courses such as roast monkfish au poivre or pan seared king scallops, are served with bowls of tossed leaves and boiled baby potatoes for the table to share, emphasising the relaxed sociability of the entire enterprise.

Prices: Main course from €14.95-€28. House wine from €18.75.
Food served: Three sittings (Tue-Fri) 12.00-13.30, 13.30-15.00, 15.00 last orders. 12.00-13.45 & 13.45-15.15 Sat.
Closed: Sundays & Mondays. 2 weeks from 22 December.
Cuisine: Seafood only.
Other Points: Children welcome.
Directions: First village after Dun Laoghaire going towards Dalkey approximately 8 miles from Dublin City.

Caviston's Food Emporium & Restaurant

Ireland East & Dublin

www.goodfoodireland.ie

Dun Laoghaire Co Dublin

Janet's Coffee House Deli
Daytime town centre coffee shop & restaurant

70 Upper George's Street,
Dun Laoghaire, Co Dublin
Tel. +353(0)1 6636871
Email. janetscoffeehousedeli@eircom.net

The Janet here is Janet Hosgood, who, with her husband, chef Roberto Morsiani, offers an array of goodies like mama used to make, in a no-nonsense, all-day menu. There's a vegetarian breakfast of frittata with marinated mushrooms and cheese, fried egg, tomato and sauté potatoes. Hot paninis are named after celebrities: try the Colin Farrell - panino bread, baked ham and Vienna salami, with tomatoes, cheese and rocket salad. The patisserie features bacon and onion scones, gluten-free cookies, and home-made almond and nutella cake. Inventive daily specials might feature Aunt Mildred's cod: pieces of cod cooked in white wine and peperonata sauce, served with mixed salad, or Saltimbocca Profumati - slices of turkey breast cooked with sage, topped with Parma ham in a white wine creamy sauce, served with sautéed potatoes. You are spoiled for choice: there is a large pasta menu, including several vegetarian options, and a good-value taster menu, where rustic sausage is served in a pepper, potato and tomato sauce. Finish with one of the speciality coffees, or another glass of Italian wine. After all that, you may need a stroll in nearby People's Park.

Prices: Main course lunch from €6. House Wine from €3 per glass.
Food Served: 8.00-16.00. Mon-Fri 9.00-16.00 Sat.
Closed: Sundays.
Cuisine: Irish, Italian and European.
Other Points: Children welcome but no high chairs available.
Directions: On the left as you leave Dun Laoghaire centre heading south. Near to the People's Park.

Malahide Co Dublin

Cruzzo Restaurant
Waterside restaurant and bar

Marina Village, Malahide, Co Dublin
Tel. +353(0)1 8450599
Email. info@cruzzo.ie
www.cruzzo.ie

This fashionable waterfront restaurant, with floor to ceiling windows, has an enviable position on Malahide marina. A buzzing ground floor bar opens out on to a terrace overlooking gin palaces and assorted boats - a great place to sip a gin-and-tonic and spot a celebrity or two. Inside, the design is sleek and contemporary with light reflected from the sea bringing a fresh, clean edge. From the piano bar, an impressive staircase leads up to the spacious restaurant, where head chef Nicholas Noakes serves up a seasonal menu incorporating fresh local ingredients and combining native and European cooking styles. A typical selection from the carte could include slow roast duck, seared scallops, confit of vegetables, pickled galangal, soy, honey and shallot dressing or grilled Dover sole, salsa verdi, followed by sticky toffee pudding, roasted honeyed apple and whipped cream, for example. There is an early bird menu offering excellent which is available Mon-Fri from 18.00-19.00 and Sat from 17.30-18.30. The global wine list has a decent selection of half bottles.

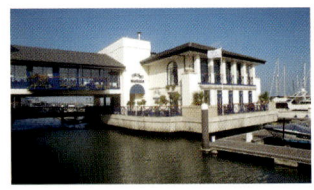

Prices: Lunch main course from €14. Dinner main course from €19.95. House wine from €20.
Opening hours: Open daily from 12.30 till late.
Food served: Lunch 12.00-14.30 & Dinner 18.00-22.00 Mon-Fri. Dinner only 17.30-22.30 Sat. Lunch 12.30-15.15 & Dinner 18.30-21.30 Sun.
Cuisine: Contemporary. Seasonal emphasis on seafood.
Other Points: Car park. Children welcome.
Directions: From M50 follow sign to Malahide, take right at lights in village, straight to end of marina.

Ireland East & Dublin

Dublinia & The Viking World
Place to Visit

St Michael's Hill, Christchurch, Dublin 8
Tel. +353(0)1 6794611
Fax. +353(0)1 6797116
Email. info@dublinia.ie
www.dublinia.ie

The Dublinia & The Viking World exhibitions are amongst Dublin's most popular visitor attractions. The exhibitions reveal fascinating glimpses of the Viking and medieval past using reconstructions, audio-visual and interactive displays. Superbly researched and imaginatively presented there is something here to interest everyone. The exhibition is housed in a beautiful neo Gothic building, formerly the Church of Ireland Synod Hall, linked to Christ Church Cathedral by an elegant covered bridge, one of the city's landmarks. Owned by The Medieval Trust, a charitable trust, income generated from the Dublinia exhibitions is used to fund the ongoing preservation of this beautiful building.

Other Points
Discounted admission tickets to Christ Church Cathedral can be purchased by visitors to Dublinia & The Viking World. A gift shop features a wide range of books, gifts and souvenirs many related to Viking and medieval themes. Guided tours available by prior arrangement. Wheelchair Accessible, Coach Parking, Toilets.

Hours
Apr -Sept: 10.00 - 17.00 Daily
Oct - Mar: 11.00 - 16.00 Mon - Fri
10.00 - 16.00 Sat, Sun & Bank Holiday
Closed 23rd, 24th, 25th & 26th Dec and 17th Mar.

Directions
Beside Christ Church Cathedral, located half way between Trinity College and the Guinness Storehouse.

Dublin Writers Museum
Place to Visit

18 Parnell Square, Dublin 1
Tel. +353(0)1 8722077
Fax. +353(0)1 8722231
Email. writers@dublintourism.ie
www.writersmuseum.com

Situated in a magnificent 18th century mansion in the north city centre, the collection features the lives and works of Dublin's literary celebrities over the past three hundred years. Swift and Sheridan, Shaw and Wilde, Yeats, Joyce and Beckett are among those presented through their books, letters, portraits and personal items. In 1991, the Dublin Writers Museum was opened to house a history and celebration of literary Dublin. The splendidly restored Georgian house is a pleasure in itself with its sumptuous plasterwork and decorative stained-glass windows. The museum holds exhibitions, lunchtime theatre and readings and has a special room devoted to children's literature. Dublin is famous as a city of writers and literature, and the Dublin Writers Museum is an essential visit for anyone who wants to discover, explore or simply enjoy Dublin's immense literary heritage.

Other Points
Multi-lingual Tours, Specialist Bookshop, Calendar of Events, Café & Conference Facilities.

Hours
Jan to Dec: Mon - Sat 10.00 - 17.00
Sun & Public Holidays: 11.00 - 17.00
Late opening Jun, Jul & Aug
Mon - Fri   10.00 - 18.00

Admission Charged

Directions
North end of O'Connell Street on Parnell Square, opposite the Garden of Remembrance.

Ireland East & Dublin

www.goodfoodireland.ie

Malahide Castle Demesne

Place to Visit

Malahide, Co Dublin
Tel. +353(0)1 8462184
Fax. +353(0)1 8462537
Email. malahidecastle@dublintourism.ie
www.malahidecastle.com

Set on 250 acres of parkland in the pretty seaside town of Malahide, the Castle was both a fortress and a private home for nearly eight hundred years, and is an interesting mix of architectural styles. The Talbot family lived here from 1185 to 1973. The history of the family is recorded in the Great Hall, with portraits of generations of the family telling their own story of Ireland's stormy history. One of the more poignant legends concerns the morning of the Battle of the Boyne in 1690, when fourteen members of the family breakfasted together in this room, never to return, as all died during the battle. Adjacent to the Castle is the Fry Model Railway, one of the largest model railways in Europe.

Other Points
Fry Model Railway, Multi-lingual Tours, Talbot Botanic Gardens, Craft Shop and Restaurant, Banqueting Facilities.

Hours
Jan to Dec: Mon - Sat 10.00 - 17.00
Apr to Sep: Sun & Public Holidays 10.00 - 18.00
Oct to Mar: Sun & Public Holidays 11.00 - 17.00

Admission Charged

Directions
North of the city centre (8 miles), go to Fairview take the turn for the Malahide Road on your left, follow the signs for Malahide and then signs for Malahide Castle.

Ireland East & Dublin

Milltown Co Kildare

Hanged Man's
Pub and restaurant

Milltown, Newbridge, Co Kildare
Tel. +353 (0)45 431515
Email. pm_keane@yahoo.ie

With over thirty years of experience under his belt, owner, Pat Keane's fine pub and restaurant is located by The Grand Canal, five miles outside Newbridge in the village of Milltown. Noted for its consistently great food, we should not overlook the friendly yet efficient staff and it's comfortable and ambient interior decorated with black cauldrons, fairy lights and candles. Two dining rooms lead off the main pub, and the view over the river through a large glass window brings a sence of tranquillty. The menu is modern Irish with some International inclusions - how about a 'New York Strip Sirloin' or for the more daring of you the 'Grilled loin of Kangaroo'? Alternatively you could opt for the 'Panfried Clonakilty black pudding and savoury potato cake served with a mustard cream sauce' to start and a 'honey roast duck served with champ' for main.

Prices: Lunch: (2 courses) from €25. Dinner main course from €18.50. House Wine from €18.
Food Served: Open 7 nights for dinner from 17.00 and Sunday lunch from 12.30.
Cuisine: Modern Irish with a twist.
Other Points: Covered balcony/deck. Garden. Car Park. Beside the Grand Canal and walking distance to Pollardstown Fen (National Nature Reserve).
Directions: 5 minutes from Newbridge. South on Main St. in Newbridge. Turn right at Post Office & Bank of Ireland. Pass Newbridge Railway Station on right. Turn right in Milltown Village, 300 yards on right.

Ireland East & Dublin

www.goodfoodireland.ie

Portlaoise Co Laois

The Kitchen & Foodhall
Daytime restaurant, café and food shop

Hynd's Square, Portlaoise, Co. Laois
Tel. +353(0)57 8662061

Jim Tynan's wonderful food emporium and excellent day time restaurant is a real gem in the near-centre of Ireland and worth a special visit if you are in the vicinity or en-route from Cork to Dublin. It has been in existence for twenty-three years and its success must be attributed to the consistent, fantastic, wholesome food; a welcoming, warm and relaxed atmosphere and of course to the fantastic Irish speciality products for sale in the food hall. Not to mention those that are especially chosen and imported by Jim from abroad and those which are made by him on the premises. His loyal clientele come from far and wide to purchase his jams, chutneys, terrines, breads, desserts and speciality Christmas products - especially his world famous Christmas puddings! There are two entrances, two large front windows and a small outdoor eating area. Within, it's three unpretentious slate-floored rooms on two floors feature cosy open fireplaces and the restaurant seats 175. Hereford prime beef with organic vegetables or a

Prices: Lunch main course from €10.50. House Wine from €10.99.
Food served: 9.00-17.30 Mon-Sat.
Closed: Sundays, 25 Dec-3 Jan incl. Good Friday & bank holidays.
Cuisine: Traditional Irish/Mediterranean.
Other Points: Children welcome. Winner - Café Restaurant of the Year 2006
Directions: Entrance on Church Street beside the courthouse or through Hynd's Square off Main Street.

selection of salads from the buffet table are a speciality and one that delivers every time. This wonderful food can be complemented with a great bottle of wine, which can be bought from the shop for the restaurant without paying a corkage charge - What more can be said? You can also check out the Art at "The Tynan Gallery" upstairs at the Kitchen with a new artist every month from February to October.

Longford Town

Viewmount House
Country house bed and breakfast

Dublin Road, Longford
Tel. +353(0)43 41919
Email. info@viewmounthouse.com
www.viewmounthouse.com

This is a most appealing 1750s Georgian house, set amid four acres of lovely wooded gardens. Formerly owned by Lord Longford, the house has graceful architectural details including a white "flying staircase" which leads to six ample bedrooms furnished with large antique beds, tasteful woven rugs and garden views. Bathrooms are good-sized and well appointed. James and Beryl Kearney's warmth and attention to detail is evident throughout the house. Breakfast, served in a unique vaulted dining room with pine woodblock flooring, Georgian blue walls and crisp white linens, includes freshly squeezed orange juice or fruit salad, homemade muesli with natural yogurt, and a choice of a "full Irish" breakfast, scrambled eggs and smoked salmon, cheese/mushroom omelettes, or pancakes topped with

Rooms: 6 ensuite. Double/twin from €100. Single from €60.
Closed: Never
Other Points: Non-smoking house. Garden. Car park. Children welcome.
Directions: Coming from Dublin leave the N4 at first roundabout towards Longford town. After (30) speed limit sign you see Viewmount House sign. Turn very sharp left and the house is on your right - five hundred metres.

pecans and maple syrup, served with crispy bacon. This is an ideal base to explore the midlands, the River Shannon Corlea Trackway, Belvedere House, Strokestown House, Tullynally Castle and eight championship golf courses are within a 30-mile radius.

Carlingford Co Louth

Ghan House
Coastal country house, restaurant & cookery school

Carlingford, Co Louth
Tel. +353(0)42 937 3682
Email. ghanhouse@eircom.net
www.ghanhouse.net

Paul Carroll's attractive Georgian country house and cookery school stands in walled grounds in a lovely village close to Carlingford Lough. The small lake to the front catches the reflection of the long, white, two-storey building and breathtaking views of Slieve Foy encircle the house. Inside, a large hallway with old timber floors and an open fireplace create an atmosphere of warmth and comfort which permeates the house. The twelve ensuite bedrooms, all with mountain views, are furnished with family antiques and filled with fresh flowers and old-fashioned attention to detail. The restaurant offers intimate dining in classic surroundings, with home-baked bread and dishes such as ceviche of tuna loin with spicy lime dressing, or roasted local red legged partridge setting the elegant tone. Vegetables and herbs come from the garden and fresh local produce is used where possible including Cooley lamb, Carlingford mussels and oysters.

Rooms: 12 ensuite. Double from €180. Single from €75.
Prices: Dinner main course from €27.50. House Wine from €18.50.
Food Served: Fri, Sat, Sun (booking recommended) and at any other time by prior arrangement.
Closed: 24-26, 31 Dec. 1-6 Jan.
Cuisine: Modern Irish.
Other Points: Garden. Dogs welcome in stable. Children welcome. Cookery school. Private dining.
Directions: 1 hour from Dublin & Belfast Airports, 15 minutes from N1, signposted to Medieval Carlingford. Ghan House is a tree length away from Carlingford.

The cookery school attracts high calibre guest chefs such as Ursula Ferrigno and Paula McIntyre, and the impressive programme of events includes fishing trips on Carlingford Lough, whiskey tasting and eight-course gourmet nights.

Ireland East & Dublin

www.goodfoodireland.ie

Jenkinstown Co Louth

Fitzpatrick's Bar & Restaurant
Country pub and restaurant

Jenkinstown, Rockmarshall,
Dundalk, Co Louth
Tel. +353(0)42 9376193.
Email.fitzpatricksbarandrestaurant
@eircom.net
www.fitzpatricks-restaurant.com

Situated beside the Cooley Mountains, Carlingford Lough and several fine beaches, only fifteen minutes from Dundalk and less than an hour from Dublin, Fitzpatricks Bar & Restaurant provides a consistent welcome and unique environment oozing with character for the weary traveller! Owned and run by Danny and Dympna Fitzpatrick whose commitment and attention to detail have ensured a winning formula either for some fine food or just a relaxing drink. You will be enthralled at the décor whether you choose the Lounge Bar with it's remarkable collection of memorabilia from times gone by or you could opt for their well presented but also distinctly decorated beer garden with it's charming nostalgic character which once again sets Fitzpatricks ahead of the rest. Old favourites like traditional fish n' chips with salad, chips and mushy peas, with the fish straight from the boat at Clougherhead, may tempt you or you may prefer roast crispy duck breast with grilled fresh

Prices: Lunch main course from €10.50. Set Sunday lunch €25. Bar snack from €19. Dinner main course from €25.50. House wine from €18.50
Hours: Bar 12.30-23.30 Mon-Wed. 12.30-24.30 Thurs-Sat. 12.30-23.00 Sun.
Food served: 12.30-22.00 Tue-Sun.
Closed: Mondays except for Bank Holidays and high season. Good Friday and 25 Dec.
Cuisine: Modern Irish.
Other Points: Garden. Children welcome. Car park. Winner - Dining Pub of the Year 2004.
Directions: Go north through Dundalk, take the Carlingford Road, Fitzpatrick's is approx. 5 miles down the Carlingford Road on the left hand side.

figs and cherry jus for something a little bit different. A comprehensive children's menu, which includes healthy alternatives to the usual 'nuggets or sausages' question means that everyone is catered for and should leave with a big smile on their face wondering when next they will return?

Symbols

- Accommodation
- Restaurant
- Café
- Pub/Bar
- Daytime opening only
- Deli
- Wine
- Bakery
- Gourmet/Farm Shop
- Leisure Centre/Spa
- CS Craft Shop
- VC Visitor Centre
- FP Food Producer

Good Food Ireland Awards

- 2002 Award Winner
- 2003 Award Winner
- 2004 Award Winner
- 2005 Award Winner
- 2006 Award Winner

Ireland East & Dublin

Tullamore Co Offaly

The Wolftrap Bar & Restaurant
Town centre bar & restaurant

William Street, Tullamore, Co Offaly
Tel: +353 (0)57 9323374
Email. info@thewolftrap.ie
www.thewolftrap.ie

Since taking over The Wolftrap two years ago, Gina and Shane Murphy, with Gina's husband Padraig McLoughlin, have adopted a hands-on approach that's good news for customer service. Named after a mountain in the nearby Slieve Blooms, the bar has polished oak floors and leather seating, and does a lively trade. Food spans both modern and traditional: the bar menu could feature saffron-flavoured fish, then meatballs with tagliatelle and garlic bread. Chef Ronan Fox keeps things lively with a lunch menu that changes daily, and in the restaurant section, a dinner menu that changes every five weeks. The stylish restaurant, which has its own separate bar, is tastefully decorated with neutral colours and dark wood, with a wall of wine bottles as a focal point. Here, a sample menu might include ketaffi-wrapped prawns with a lemon aioli and an onion and pepper marmalade, followed by corn-fed chicken with game sausage, fondant potato and a silver skin onion and thyme jus. All desserts, such as crumbles, cheesecakes and brownies, are hand-made in the kitchen. Wines are divided by country and there's a good selection of half-bottles. There's also a beer garden that smokers will appreciate. You may get to meet Padraig and Ronan at Tuesday's traditional music session: they are both musicians!

Prices: Lunch main course from €9.50. Dinner main course from €17.00. Bar snack from €3.50. House wine from €18.
Hours: 12.00-23.30 Sun-Thurs. 12.00-0.30 Fri. 12.00-02.00 Sat.
Food served: 12.00-20.30 daily in bar, except Sat: 12.00-20.00. Restaurant: 18.30-22.30 Tues-Sat.
Closed: Restaurant closed Sundays and Mondays. Bar and restaurant closed 25 Dec and Good Friday.
Cuisine: Restaurant: modern Irish fine dining. Bar: traditional and modern.
Other Points: Children welcome. Car park.
Directions: Tullamore town centre, at the junction of William Street and Harbour Street.

Ireland East & Dublin

www.goodfoodireland.ie

Tullamore Dew Heritage Centre

Place to Visit

Bury Quay, Tullamore, Co Offaly
Tel. +353(0)57 9325015
Fax.+353(0)57 9325016
Email. tullamoredhc@eircom.net
www.tullamore-dew.org

The Tullamore Dew Heritage Centre, housed in the 1897 Bonded Warehouse, relates the story of Tullamore Dew Whiskey/ Irish Mist Liqueur and the development of Tullamore town. Visitors can wander through the various recreated working stations of the distillery such as malting, bottling or cooperage areas and learn how the whiskey was made. Throughout the tour, visitors can interact with the artefacts, admire bees collecting honey for the production of Irish Mist, try out outfits worn on canal barges in the 1850's and learn about the history of Tullamore Town. Audiovisual presentation, guided and self guided tours, complimentary tasting of Tullamore Dew Whiskey or Irish Mist Liqueur.

Other Points
Coffee Shop, Restaurant, Fully licensed bar, Tourist Office and Gift Shop.

Hours
May to Sept: Mon to Sat 9.00 - 19.00
Sun 12.00 - 17.00
Oct to Apr: Mon - Sat: 10.00 - 17.00
Sun 12.00 - 17.00

Admission Charged

Directions
Located on the banks of the Grand Canal. Just 6 minutes off the N6 at Kilbeggan, on reaching Tullamore, take an immediate right after the bridge and drive along the quay. From the N52, drive through the town and take a left before the Grand Canal

Ireland East & Dublin

Mulllingar Co Westmeath

Gallery 29 Café
Daytime café and restaurant

16 Oliver Plunkett Street, Mullingar, Co Westmeath
Tel. +353(0)44 9349449
Email. corbetstown@eircom.net

Ann and Emily Gray's popular café makes the most of its handsome black-painted 19th-century façade and refurbished interior featuring seating for 50 people. This delightful eatery has a lively open kitchen, and tempting displays of the Grays' home-baked goodies: breads, scones, muffins, baked puddings, tarts and gateaux. Hearty breakfast favourites include pancakes with lemon and sugar; or baked potato cake with tomato and crispy bacon. The lunch menu offers delicious soups; a large choice of sandwiches on freshly baked focaccia bread or demi baguettes; and hot dishes such as pan fried salmon and smoked haddock fish cake with lemon and herb mayo served with roast baby new potatoes and greens or chicken and red pepper curry with basmati rice. Of course, there's always room for coffee and a homemade pastry or one of their delicious desserts

Prices: Lunch main course from €8.95-€10.90.
Food Served: 9.00-18.00 Tue-Sat.
Closed: Sun & Mon. 25 Dec to 10 Jan.
Cuisine: Modern Irish with European/Asian twist.
Other Points: Children welcome. Fully air-conditioned.
Directions: Take any of the three exits from the Mullingar bypass to the town centre. Gallery 29 Café is about fifty yards from the Market Square on the main street.

such chocolate walnut and orange tart served with whipped cream. Ann and Emily's philosophy of sourcing local and organic produce and creating "good honest food cooked with passion" shows in all their offerings.

Avoca Co Wicklow

Avoca Café at The Old Mill
Daytime café and shop

The Old Mill, Avoca, Co Wicklow
Tel. +353(0)402 35105
Email. info@avoca.ie
www.avoca.ie

Owned and operated by the Pratt family, Avoca Handweavers is well-known for its beautifully woven throws, rugs, scarves, clothing, accessories and handcrafts. Much of the fabric seen in this, and all the other Avoca stores, is woven here at a restored mill dating from 1723. It is the oldest working mill in Ireland, and visitors are welcome to see the entire weaving process first-hand by taking a free tour of the mill. The store also carries soft furnishings, toys, gifts and food from the Avoca Pantry range. A self-service café, like all the other Avoca cafes, is renowned for its wide selection of high-quality, homemade food: tomato and roasted pepper soup; shepherd's pie; chicken and broccoli encroute; home-cooked ham; oak-smoked trout;

Prices: Main course from €10.95. House wine from €19.
Food Served: 9.30-17.00.
Closed: 25, 26 December.
Cuisine: Traditional and modern Irish.
Other Points: Garden. Children welcome. Car park. Historic working mill.
Directions: Turn off the N11 at Rathnew and follow the signs to Avoca.

sweet chilli salmon; and chicken breast with sesame. Mouth-watering desserts include home-baked scones with butter and preserves, and strawberry meringue roulade. The picturesque village is the fictional home of the BBC's popular "Ballykissangel.

Ireland East & Dublin

www.goodfoodireland.ie

Blessington Co Wicklow

Grangecon Café
Daytime cafe, restaurant and foodshop

Kilbride Road, Blessington,
Co Wicklow
Tel.+353(0)45 857892
Email. grangeconcafe@eircom.net

Jenny and Richard Street opened this lovely little daytime café 6 years ago. Hidden away in a sleepy village among verdant countryside, close to the N81, it's a gem of place with a firm commitment to all things organic, homemade and local. Specialist produce is on show all around. The owners admit to keeping things simple to keep down costs, but customers - including those who come to stock up on Grangecon's excellent ready-meals - are the richer. A breakfast menu is available daily and aside from delicious homemade soup, there are sandwiches, meltingly good quiches, sausage rolls made from organic pork, salads - baked St Tola cheese with roasted red pepper, mixed leaves and hazel nuts - and shepherd's pie. On the sweet side, there are freshly baked apple pies and brownies, with Illy coffee, Crinnaughton apple juice and ginger beer or homemade lemonade to round things off. Bring your own wine.

Prices: Lunch main course from €9.95.
Food served: 9.00-16.00 Mon. 9.00-17.30 Tues-Sat.
Closed: Sundays. 25 Dec - 1 Jan.
Cuisine: Simple
Other Points: Children welcome. Dogs welcome.
Directions: Left at the Downshire Gallery in Blessington, the café is 3 doors along on the left.

Dunlavin Co Wicklow

Rathsallagh Country House
Country house, golf club and restaurant

Dunlavin, Co Wicklow
Tel. +353 (0)45 403112
Email. info@rathsallagh.com
www.rathsallagh.com

Rathsallgh House has been in the O'Flynn family for almost 30 years. The 18th-century home enjoys a spectacular 530-acre parkland setting, but combines a warm welcome with these grand surroundings. Its 18-hole championship golf course was designed by Irish professional Christy O'Connor Jnr. Chef John Kostuik has been with Rathsallagh for 21 years, and uses locally produced beef and fish, as well as Rathsallagh's own organic vegetables and herbs. Dinner might consist of Duncannon scallops with girolle mushrooms and sweet pea puree, followed by passionfruit and apricot sorbet, then roulade of guinea fowl supreme with wild mushroom stuffing served with gratin potato and balsamic vinegar jus. For dessert, there's chocolate fondant with mocha crème Anglaise and Mascarpone ice-cream. The wine list is so extensive you may want to do some preparation on their website. Spoil yourself by ordering one of their special baths and while you enjoy your dinner, staff will pour you an aromatic bath, complete with fairy lights and relaxing music. Supplement your evening with a bottle of champagne and a movie DVD. Next morning, enjoy a fabulous selection from the sideboard - dishes such as Rathsallagh Ham on the bone, salamis, Irish farmhouse cheese, a full Irish and a selection of homemade breads and jams or choose some healthy options which may include homemade muesli and seasonal fruit compote or the fish of the day.

Rooms: 29 ensuite. Double from €270. Single from €195
Prices: Lunch main course from €7.50. Five-course set dinner €65. Bar snack from €4.50. House wine from €25.
Food served: Lunch and afternoon tea available to residents only 12.30-16.00. Dinner: 19.00-21.00.
Cuisine: French/Irish
Other Points: Children welcome over 12 years. Garden. Car park. All bedrooms non-smoking. Dogs welcome by prior arrangement. Jacuzzi & steam room. Tennis court. Snooker room. 18 hole championship golf course.
Directions: 50km south-west of Dublin, 1.5km south of Dunlavin on the road to Baltinglass.

82

for online reservations

Ireland East & Dublin

Enniskerry Co Wicklow

Powerscourt Terrace Café
Daytime café and shop

Powerscourt House and Gardens,
Enniskerry, Co Wicklow
Tel. +353(0)1 2046066
Email: info@avoca.ie
www.avoca.ie

Powerscourt House and Gardens is situated 12 miles south of Dublin and is one of the worldís great Italianate gardens, stretching over 47 acres. The Powerscourt Terrace Café, owned by the Pratt family of Avoca Handweavers, is located in the 18th century Palladian house overlooking the estate's gardens and fountains with breathtaking views to Sugarloaf Moutain. The bright, airy eatery is self-service and extends to a large outdoor eating area that buzzes in good weather. The menu changes daily and might include beef and Guinness stew, Lakeshore pork, Spanish meatballs and chicken and broccoli crumble, as well as a selection of quiches, and wine in quarter, half and full bottles. An extensive range of homemade desserts bring raspberry tart, apple pie, strawberry roulade, chocolate fudge cake and

Prices: Main course from €10.95 House wine from €15.
Food served: 10.00-17.00. Sunday until 17.30.
Closed: 25, 26 December.
Cuisine: Traditional and modern Irish.
Other Points: Children welcome. Outdoor terrace. Car park. Private dining.
Directions: 2 miles from Enniskerry Village.

delicious scones - perfect for tea after a walk round the gardens or a browse through the wonderful Avoca shop for gifts, clothes and deli produce.

Kilmacanogue Co Wicklow

Avoca Terrace Café
Daytime cafe, shop and garden centre

Kilmacanogue, Bray, Co Wicklow
Tel. +353(0)1 2867466
Email.info@avoca.ie
www.avoca.ie

Situated in 11 acres of gardens in the old Jameson (of whiskey fame) estate, just 30 minutes from Dublin at the gateway to scenic Wicklow county, this Avoca shop, like all the others in the enterprise, combines great shopping with delicious, country-style eating. As in all the stores, this one sells its own range of clothing for men, women and children; throws, scarves and hand-knit designer sweaters; toys; accessories; pottery and books. It also has a garden centre. The foodhall's specialty food offerings include deluxe flavoured olive oils and vinegars, fancy chocolates, and Mongetto pasta sauces. The attractive self-service terrace cafÈ with outdoor seating has a strong wholefoods, salads and international orientation. Typical tasty dishes include freshly baked breads, carrot and coriander soup, home-cooked ham with a selection of salads, roasted Mediterranean vegetables,

Prices: Main course from €11.45. House wine from €15.
Food served: 9.30-17.30 Mon-Fri. 10.00-17.30 Sat-Sun.
Closed: 25, 26 December.
Cuisine: Traditional and modern Irish
Other Points: Garden and outdoor terrace. Children welcome. Car park. Craft shop. Highly Commended - Café of the Year 2003. Winner - Café of the Year 2004.
Directions: On the N11 signposted before Kilmacanogue village.

Mexican chilli beef, and assorted quiches and pizzas. Save room for the strawberry and fresh cream roulade, cheesecake, and chocolate cakes.

Short and sweet

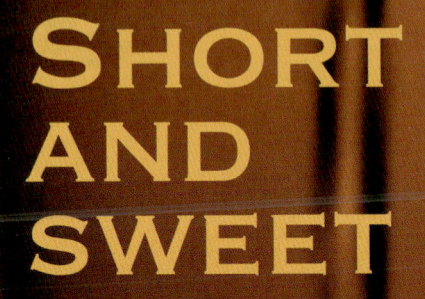

The perfect wine list is not nearly as difficult as some would have you believe. It should be short and to the point says John Wilson

We are sitting in the drawing room of the country house hotel of my dreams. It is a wonderful summer's evening, the sun slowly going down over the horizon. Having spent the day hill-walking with my partner, I have built up a healthy appetite, and am anticipating dinner with some relish. We have ordered our food; we are sipping a glass of nicely chilled Champagne, one of a dozen or so wines available by the glass. I open up the wine list.

The list is short but very well-chosen, allowing us full scope to indulge our preferences and passions. She adores lighter white wines, not too high in alcohol, and definitely un-oaked. Her normal tipple is an aromatic, fruit-filled New Zealand Sauvignon, or if we are on a budget, a crisp fresh dry white from the Côtes de Gascogne. But the list offers her plenty of choice; there is a very tempting-looking Soave from Italy, a Rias Baixas from Spain, two very good Sauvignons, one from Casablanca, the hot new white wine region of Chile, another from Robertson in South Africa; then there are a few Rieslings too - a light crisp trocken from Germany, and a wonderful Clare Valley Riesling from Australia; any of these would go very nicely with the plate of seafood she has ordered. I myself would probably have gone for the Sancerre, or maybe the Muscadet, the prefect partner for Fruits de Mer; but instead she opts for the Chablis. It is from one of the top estates, a small grower whose wines are exemplary. It will go perfectly with those prawns, mussels and oysters. Even better, it is available in half bottle.

My own starter is very different; I am having foie gras, and need something rich, possibly sweet, but certainly powerful to drink with it; there is plenty of choice. If I felt like pushing the boat out, there is a maturing Puligny-Montrachet; a rich Viognier from the northern Rhône, or the big toasty Australian Chardonnay will certainly stand up to the robust flavours. In the end, I opt for a glass of Sauternes, a sweet wine that would be the traditional accompaniment in France; helpfully the restaurant offer it by the glass to go with my goose liver.

On then to the main courses; again we are having different dishes. She has gone for the full monty - grilled prime sirloin steak, with chips and a Béarnaise sauce. I have chosen grilled black sole with herb butter. Winewise, we need something that will stand up to her steak, but not overwhelm my fish.

The list includes a few well-chosen clarets - not a page of them, and not at stratospheric prices either - a few five-ten year old Bordeaux, good wines from lesser vintages, rather than lesser wines from good vintages. There are two or three red Burgundies too, each a different style, and at a different price. The big busty Barossa Shiraz will overwhelm my main course; likewise the Californian Zinfandel. There is a very young fruity Rioja, a great all-rounder that would probably suit both our choices, and the Merlot from Chile is also a distinct possibility.

Fairly quickly I narrow my choices down to two or three; there is a Chinon, a light red from the Loire Valley, one of my favourite kinds of wine, provided it is from a good vintage; then there are a couple of Pinot Noirs - one reasonable-priced one from Burgundy, and one from New Zealand. I have never tried either, so I ask the wine-waiter. So far, she has been very pleasant and seems knowledgeable. Her advice is short and succinct. The Burgundy might be a bit heavy and tannic for the fish, but either of the other two would do the trick; we go for the New Zealand Pinot Noir, and hit the jackpot. It is light, fruity and easy-drinking, and sits sweetly with my fish. With her steak, it is equally successful – the fruit and light acidity acts like a piquant fruity sauce, the prefect foil for the rich meaty flavours.

On then to the final courses. She goes straight for the something deeply chocolaty. I don't have a sweet tooth, but the cheese board looks interesting, the cheeses local and properly matured. I ask for the wine list once more, and with a large single slice of farmhouse cheddar, I make heavy inroads into a half-bottle of Bordeaux. The dessert list is short, only four wines, but each is available by the glass. The wine waiter suggests an Orange Muscat from California, a pairing that works brilliantly. Feeling rested, full and full of bonhomie, we retire to the drawing room. I look at the digestif list and decide to have a Calvados with my coffee. She being more traditional, has a cognac. The perfect end to my perfect meal. ∎

Mostly, I eat out in modest establishments. Here are five things I look out for on a wine list.

1 SIZE
A short list - I am there to enjoy the company of my guests, not read a giant tome.

2 SELECTION
Small should not limit my choices.
In a good wine list, each wine is different, from a good producer, and makes me want to try it.

3 PRICE
Fairly priced - I know running a restaurant is expensive, but I don't see why wine-lovers should be penalised.

4 ADVICE
I enjoy talking to a **knowledgeable wine waiter** - I don't need a fully trained sommelier - just someone with a bit of enthusiasm, who has tried out the wines, and can explain how they taste. Either that, or some properly written tasting notes.

5 SIZE AGAIN
If I am eating alone or with one other person, I love to choose from a selection of wines by **the glass or half-bottle.**

Five tips if you don't know anything about wine.

ASK FOR HELP
Most Good Food Ireland member restaurants will have someone who knows something about wine. Don't be afraid to ask – they will be delighted to help you.

ALL PURPOSE WINES
If there are more than one of you, go for wines that suit a wide variety of dishes. For white wines, un-oaked Chardonnay, most new world Sauvignon, Pinot Grigio, Alsace Riesling, will happily partner most fish, seafood, and even white meat dishes. For all-round reds, look at Australian Shiraz, Chilean Merlot, most Pinot Noir, Rioja, Beaujolais, or Côtes du Rhône.

PAY A LITTLE MORE
The rewards are great if you are prepared to trade up a little, and pay a few euros more than house wine.

TRY TO AVOID
the big, well-known producers and regions. Quite often the value lies elsewhere.

LOOK FOR
or ask about wines by the glass and half-bottles – they are an option at every part of the meal.

féile bia
Certified Farm to Fork

When eating out choose Féile Bia and know where your food is coming from.

When you see the Féile Bia plaque or logo displayed in a restaurant, hotel, pub or workplace, you can be sure of how the food is produced and where it comes from.

Féile Bia is your reassurance that the fresh meat and eggs are sourced from suppliers approved under recognised Quality Assurance Schemes and can be traced back to the farm where they came from.

Visit www.bordbia.ie to see the full list of Féile Bia members by county.

www.bordbia.ie

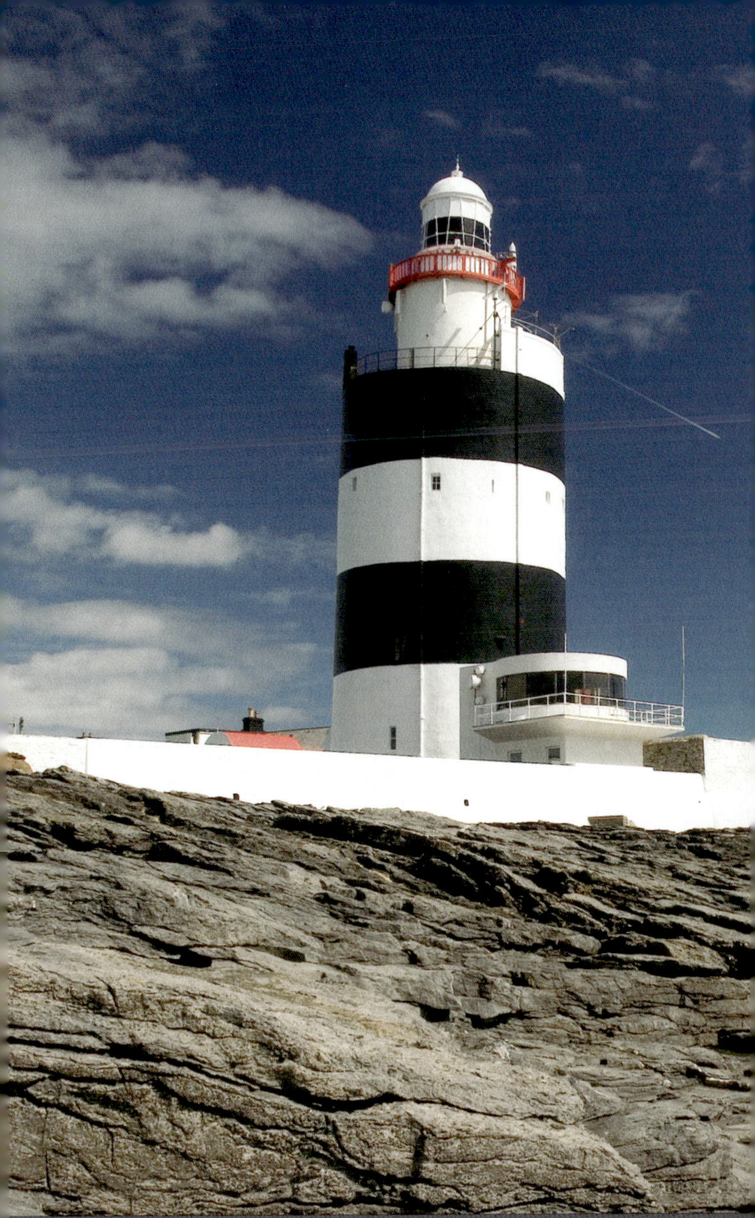

Ireland South

Ireland South Touring Route

Ballybunion — Íragh Tí Connor

The Tankard Bar & Restaurant
Restaurant David Norris
Ballygarry House Hotel & Spa

Tralee

Ballydavid

Dingle Penninsula

Slieve Mish Mts.

The Laurels Pub & Restaurant
Mentons at the Plaza
Killarney Royal Hotel
Murphy's Ice Cream
Muckross House, Gardens & Traditional Farms

Dingle
Gorman's Clifftop House and Restaurant
Murphy's Ice Cream

Killorglin

Killarney

Macgillycuddy Reeks

Knightstown

Cahirciveen
QC's Seafood Bar & Restaurant

Ring of Kerry

Moll's Gap Avoca Café

Kenmare
Lorge Chocolatier

Beara Penninsula

Bantry
O'Connor's Seafood Restaurant

Durrus
Carbery Cottage Guest Lodge

Goleen
The Heron's Cove
Mizen Head Signal Station

Skibbereen
Skibbereen Heritage Centre

MUST VISIT......
The English Market, Cork City

MUST TRY......
- Tripe & Drisheen
- Crubeens "Pigs Feet"
- Corned mutton
- Hot buttered eggs

LOOK OUT FOR.....
Bellvelly Smoked Salmon

MUST TRY......
Murphy's Ice cream
takeaway latte

Knockmealdown Mts.

Boggeragh Mts.

• Mallow

Fermoy
Munchies Gourmet
Coffee House
Ballyvolane House

Lismore
Barça
Wine & Tapas Bar
Farmgate Restaurant & Country Store
Ballymaloe House & Cookery School

Café Paradiso
Farmgate Café
Fenn's Quay Restaurant
Franciscan Well Brew Pub
Hayfield Manor Hotel
Isaacs Restaurant
Lotamore House
Nash 19 Restaurant
Nakon Thai Restaurant
Fota House & Gardens

Cork

Midleton

Youghal
Aherne's Townhouse &
Seafood Restaurant

Cobh
Knockeven House
Cobh – The Queenstown Story

Kinsale
Blue Haven Hotel
Old Bank House

Clonakilty
Gleesons Restaurant
An Sugan

Farmer's Markets
Cork

Clonakilty	McCurtain Hill	Thur & Sat 10am - 2pm
Cork City	English Market, Grand Parade	Open every day
Fermoy		Sat
Midleton	Hospital Road	Sat 10am - 2pm
Skibbereen	Old Market Square	Sat 9am - 1.30pm

Kerry

Dingle	Opposite the harbour	Fri 10am - 4pm
Kenmare	An Cro, Bridge Street.	Wed-Sun 10am - 6pm
Killarney	Parish Hall, Anne's Rd.	Fri 11.30 - 1.30

See Farmers' Markets section of the guide for full listing

Ireland South

Leighlinbridge Co Carlow

Lord Bagenal Inn
Waterside hotel and restaurant

Leighlinbridge, Co Carlow
Tel. + 353(0)59 9721668
Email. info@lordbagenal.com
www.lordbagenal.com

James, Mary and the Kehoe family run a confident yet relaxed and friendly establishment eight miles from Carlow town, in the picturesque, heritage village of Leighlinbridge. Located on the River Barrow and with it's own private marina it is perfectly situated for a short break to explore Ireland's sunny South East. The restaurant has a reputation for good food that is complemented by a wonderfully selected and personalised wine list. There is something for everyone with the house wines alone ranging from €18 - €23. Meat, game and seafood are all sourced locally where possible, and you could expect to find "Pigs crubeen braised in port & stuffed with truffle, sweetbreads and glazed with honey and rosemary" or you could choose from the daily bar menu which has a well priced selection of dishes, and serves until 10pm. Refurbishment through Summer 2006 brings a new fine dining restaurant located on the waterfront as well as additional bedrooms, with suites overlooking the river, so undoubtedly their loyal clientele over the last twenty six years or so will be able to continue visiting but also bring along their friends!

Rooms: 39 ensuite. Double from €130. Single and family room-rates on request.
Prices: Lunch main course from €8.75. Sunday hot carvery lunch from €10.50. Dinner main course from €22. House wine from €18.
Food Served: 12.00-22.00 Mon-Thurs. 12.00-22.30 Fri & Sat. 12.00-21.00 Sun.
Closed: 25 Dec.
Cuisine: Modern Irish.
Other Points: Children's play area. Private marina. Car park. Winner - Pub Wine List of the Year 2003.
Directions: Just off the main N9 Dublin/Waterford road in Leighlinbridge.

Symbols

- Accommodation
- Restaurant
- Café
- Pub/Bar
- Daytime opening only
- Deli
- Wine
- Bakery
- Gourmet/Farm Shop
- Leisure Centre/Spa
- CS Craft Shop
- VC Visitor Centre
- FP Food Producer

Good Food Ireland Awards

- ★ 2002 Award Winner
- ★ 2003 Award Winner
- ★ 2004 Award Winner
- ★ 2005 Award Winner
- ★ 2006 Award Winner

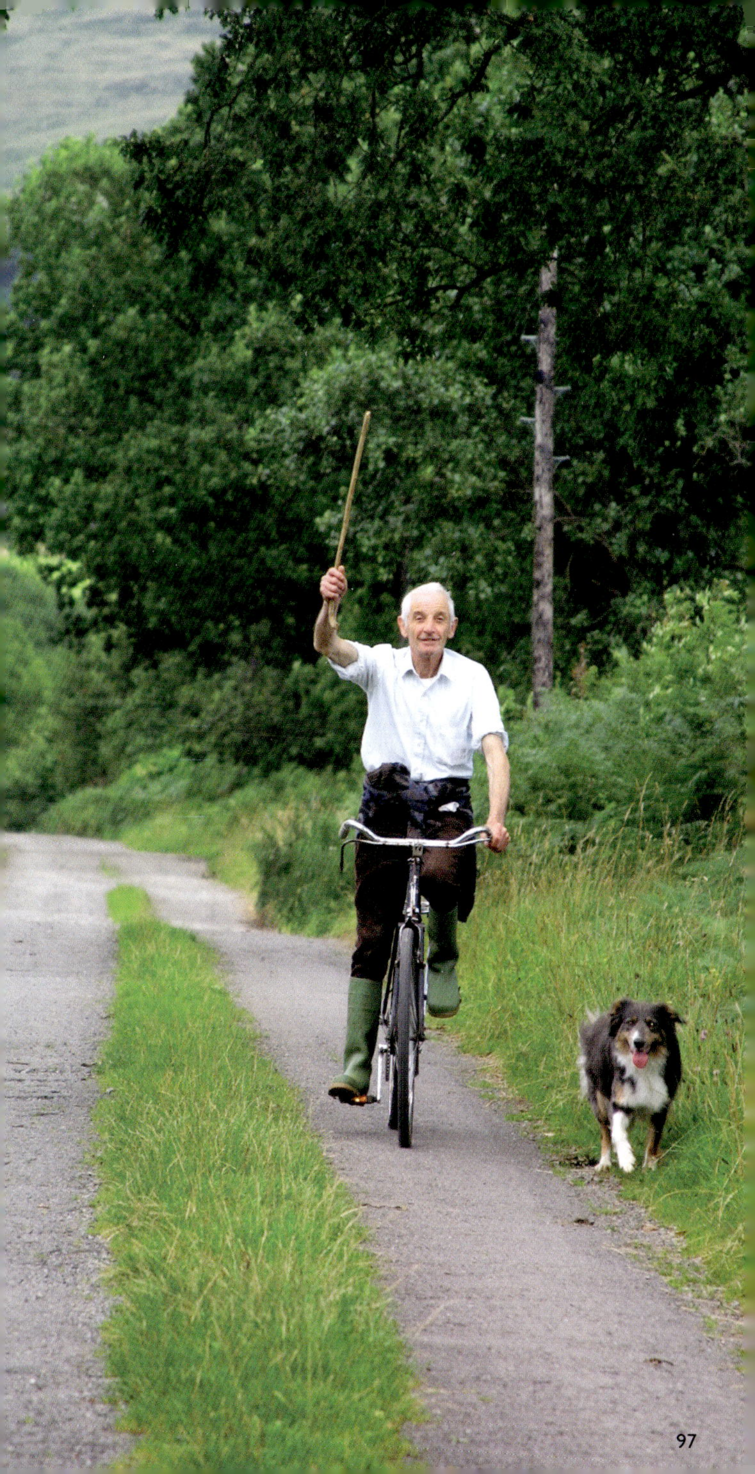

Ireland South

Bantry Co Cork

O'Connor's Seafood Restaurant
Seafood restaurant and bar

The Square, Bantry, Co Cork
Tel. +353(0)27 50221
Email.oconnorseafood@eircom.net
www.oconnorseafood.com

You can't miss O'Connor's in the heart of Bantry - Peter O'Brien and his wife Anne (great grand-daughter of the original owner) have completely renovated the restaurant in the past year, and the shop front features three striking sailboats. Inside has a sleek, modern finish that retains its comfortable booths. As owner/operators, the O'Briens have really made their mark on Bantry dining, with their attention to detail showing on everything from the food, wine and service down to the décor and even the choice of music. As you would expect from the port location, the menu caters well for seafood lovers. But if you start with the house speciality mussels, or choose to share oysters from their seawater tank, you can then try Skeaghanore duck breast on creamed potato with ginger and orange sauce and finish with warm toffee and apple cake. Lunch includes hot open sandwiches and O'Connor's seafood chowder. All breads and stocks are made daily on the premises. The global wine list is affordable and offers interesting choices by the glass. Nearby is the Sheep's Head walking route to its south, Garnish Island to its north, and, in the picturesque setting of Bantry House, the West Cork Chamber Music Festival and the traditional music festival, Masters of Tradition.

Prices: Lunch main course from €10. Dinner main course from €19. House Wine from €19.
Food Served: 12.15-15.00 daily, 18.00-22.00 Mon-Sat. 18.00-21.00 Sun from May to November.
Closed: Sundays & Monday evenings November to April.
Cuisine: Traditional/Modern Irish/Seafood Specialities
Other Points: Children welcome before 20.00.
Directions: On the square in Bantry across from the fountain, beside Bantry Bay Hotel.

Clonakilty Co Cork

An Sugán
Town centre pub and restaurant

41 Wolfe Tone Street, Clonakilty,
Co Cork
Tel. +353(0)23 33498
Email.ansugan4@eircom.net
www.ansugan.com

Well-known An Sugán, run by the O'Crowley family for the past 20 years, stands on a corner in the centre of Clonakilty. Seafood is a speciality in this colourful pub, where you can sit by the open fire in the rustic bar, or enjoy a traditional feast in the kitchen-style dining room. The walls are adorned with interesting paintings and photographs, as well as shelves of delph. Fish and shellfish come from nearby Union Hall or Castletownbere, meat comes from Macroom, and the kitchen bakes all its own breads. An Sugán does comfort food at its best, with a lunch menu including home-made seafood chowder, seafood pie, salmon and potato cakes, and fresh crab salad. There's plenty for meat-eaters too: for dinner, start with the obligatory Clonakilty black pudding with chutney, then try the roast half duckling with orange and Armagnac sauce. A new dining room and beer garden are on the cards for 2007.

Prices: Lunch main course from €10.90. Dinner main course from €12.90 Bar Snack from €6.90. House Wine from €18.
Opening Hours: 12.30-23.30 Mon-Sat, 12.30-23.00 Sun.
Food Served: 12.30-21.30 daily.
Closed: Good Friday, 25,26 Dec.
Cuisine: Seafood
Other Points: Children Welcome, Garden.
Directions: On entering the town from Cork, go straight through roundabout for the centre of town and An Sugan is on your left.

Clonakilty Co Cork

Gleesons
Town centre restaurant

3 Connolly street, Clonakilty, Co Cork
Tel. +353(0)23 21834
Email. gleesonsrestaurant@eircom.net
www.gleesons.ie

Robert and Alex Gleeson have brought their experience from London's Dorchester to Clonakilty. Their town-centre gem goes for understated elegance. The look is stylish but simple, which means the food gets a well-deserved chance to shine. At Gleeson's, everything is made in-house - chutneys, bread, cheese biscuits, pesto and ice cream all come from this industrious kitchen and they also grow their own herbs. Soups and sauces are made without flour, so most of the menu is suitable for coeliacs. Menus change every two months but at time of going to press, lunch included everything from Woodcock Smokery cold smoked haddock with potato and baby spinach salad and chive beurre blanc to Thai green chicken curry with turmeric and ginger flavoured basmati rice. Fish is a strong point, caught in nearby Skibbereen and Castletownbere, and for dinner it might be served with warm nicoise vegetables and bearnaise sauce. Only Irish meats are used, and fruit and vegetables come from numerous local small garden producers. And, of course, the Gleesons don't have to look far for that famous black pudding! Alex's comprehensive wine list is expertly annotated, and there is a good half-bottle selection.

Prices: Lunch main course from €12.50. Dinner main course from €16.95. House Wine from €19.50
Food Served: Lunch 12.00-14.30 Thur-Fri, 12.30-15.00 Sun. Dinner 18.00-21.30 Tue-Sat
Closed: Sunday and Monday evenings. 3 weeks in Jan/Feb.
Cuisine: Modern Irish/French
Other Points: Children over 7 welcome. Parking nearby. Early bird menu available 18.00-19.00 each evening, incl. Sat and all evening on Wed. Winner - Restaurant of the Year 2006
Directions: Located on Connolly Street, adjacent to Scannell's Pub, almost directly opposite the junction with Kent Street, location for Old Mill Library and Town Hall.

Café Paradiso

Knockeven House

100

Ireland South

Cobh Co Cork

Knockeven House
Country house bed and breakfast

Knockeven, Rushbrooke
Cobh, Co Cork
Tel. +353(0)21 4811778
Email. info@knockevenhouse.com
www.knockevenhouse.com

This handsome Victorian house has been run as a Bed & Breakfast by welcoming hosts Pamela and John Mulhaire since 2003, deservedly winning an award in this guide within just one year. With its glimpses out onto the bay below, and surrounded by mature gardens, one of the house's great attractions is the abundance of natural light in its various reception rooms and bedrooms, all of which have been beautifully furnished to create an elegantly welcoming ambience. There is excellent attention to detail throughout, evidenced in the tasteful use of colour and choice of fabrics from bedlinen to furnishing coverings. The drawing room is a particularly attractive space, thanks to the comforts of an open fire and several stylish antique period pieces, and the adjoining drawing room is a smart place to take breakfast, which ranges from a full Irish to scrambled eggs with Frank Hederman smoked salmon to homemade brown bread, scones and preserves.

Rooms: 4 ensuite. Double from €130. Single from €80. Family room - price on request.
Other Points: Garden. Car park. Winner - Bed & Breakfast of the Year 2004.
Directions: N25 in direction of Rosslare, Wexford/Waterford and take Cobh exit 624. Pass Fota Wildlife Park, over the bridge turn right at Great Island garage, sharp left and first right avenue to Knockeven House.

Cork City

Café Paradiso
City centre vegetarian restaurant

16 Lancaster Quay, Cork
Tel. +353(0)21 4277939
Email. info@cafeparadiso.ie
www.cafeparadiso.ie

The care that goes into the dishes at this Cork gem is apparent from even a glance at the detailed menu: Denis Cotter and Bridget Healy have satisfied Corkonians since 1993 with their unique and tempting vegetarian treats. At lunch, you might try salad of purple potatoes and broad beans with baby salad leaves, mint, basil, Knockalara sheep's cheese and a citrus dressing. In the evening, sit back and enjoy choosing from mouth-watering starters that include oyster mushrooms and samphire in a gingered miso broth with spring onion gnocchi. The main course might bring aubergine parcels of spinach, pinenuts and Coolea cheese with tomato-caper sauce, crushed potato cake and summer beans. Save room for vanilla-poached apricots with lemon polenta cake and yoghurt. The wine list places its emphasis on Italy and New Zealand. Wines by the glass have several organic options. Emerge on the high moral ground after all those fruit and veg portions, and try the recipes at home with the Café Paradiso cookbook. Even the most voracious meat-eater will be converted.

Prices: Lunch main course from €12. Dinner main course from €22. House wine from €20.
Food Served: 12.00-15.00 and 18.30-22.30 Tue-Sat.
Closed: Sundays and Mondays and one week over Christmas.
Cuisine: Modern seasonal vegetarian.
Other Points: Children welcome. Winner - Restaurant of the Year 2004. Winner - Ireland South Regional Award 2006
Directions: On Western Road, opposite Jury's Hotel.

101

Cork City

Farmgate Café
Daytime café

Old English Market,
Princes Street, Cork
Tel. +353(0)21 4278134

Located in the gallery above the wonderfully acclaimed, 200 year old food emporium called the 'English Market', Farmgate Café is perfectly poised to enjoy local ingredients that are on offer throughout this landmark, 'foodie' location! As well as sampling the hustle and bustle of market life - under cover it should be mentioned! Produce really doesn't get more local, seasonal or fresher than this! Buying directly from the producers - a lot of which are selling from stalls within this busy and atmospheric space means that the Farmgate menu always reflects what the seasons and weather conditions have to offer. Salad is supplied from Devoy's Organic Farm in Rosscarbery, West Cork or from Martin's Farm at Waterfall, Cork. Jack the fishmonger at the market may supply rock oysters and owner Kay Harte or her daughter Rebecca may recommend a glass of Prosecco Casa Bianca to the weary shopper - not a bad way to break up the day! Old favourites like 'Shepherd's Pie' or 'Irish Lamb Stew' could hit the spot on a cold winters day... Or for a real stab at traditional Cork fare why not try 'Tripe & onions, with or without Drisheen' or 'Market Corned Beef' or 'Corned Mutton' served with a choice of seasonal vegetables or salad. If you have space, do try some wonderful local cheeses eg. Gubbeen, Carraigaline Smoked, or Ardrahan, which are served with Arbutus artisan bread or Farmgate's own soda bread. For those with a sweet tooth and an easy-going schedule, try some homemade 'Bread and Butter Pudding' or 'Fruit Crumble'. However, if you want to carry on exploring the town or sampling more of Cork's retail therapy maybe 'Seasonal Fruit with natural yoghurt or cream' might be a better choice - just for the extra energy... All in all, it is a fantastic place to visit, to sample the wholesome food and to enjoy real 'value for money'!

Prices: Main course from €8.50. House wine from €17 (€5 per glass).
Food served: 8.30-17.30 Mon-Sat.
Closed: 1 Jan, Good Friday, 25-26 Dec.
Cuisine: Traditional Irish and Modern European.
Other Points: Children welcome. Winner - Café of the Year 2003. Winner - Wine Person of the Year 2006.
Directions: In the Old English Market, off Patrick Street in Cork City.

Lotamore House, Cork

for online reservations **Ireland South**

Cork City

Fenns Quay Restaurant
City centre restaurant and café

No 5 Sheares Street, Cork
Tel. +353(0)21 4279527
Email. polaryl@eircom.net
www.fennsquay.ie

This bright, modern restaurant is full of interesting art, and if it's fine you can enjoy a seat outdoors. Owner/managers Pat and Eilish O'Leary place the emphasis on local ingredients. Fish comes from Union Hall in West Cork, as well as Cork city's "English Market". Chef Kate Lawlor creates the fresh fish recipe daily, according to what's delivered each morning. The attention to detail is readily apparent: even the simplest of dishes gets the Fenn's Quay twist. Lunch might include warm chicken salad with roasted peppers and tomato compôte, or Parmesan tartlet with beetroot and Feta filling and roast sweet potato. Dinner features Ardsallagh goats' cheese with spiced pear and succulent lamb chump kebab with hummus and ratatouille, or chargrilled sirloin steak with roast flat-cap mushroom and red onion confit. Gluten-free double chocolate mousse (a layer of white and

Prices: Lunch main course from €10.95. Dinner main course from €16.95. House wine €17.95.
Food served: 10.00-22.00 Mon-Sat.
Closed: Sundays and Bank Holidays, 25 Dec.
Cuisine: Progressive Irish.
Other Points: Children welcome.
Directions: 2 minutes from Courthouse/city centre.

dark) is a good way to round off, or try the house speciality: V'ice cream (sweet Pedro Ximénez sherry with vanilla ice-cream). An all-Irish cheese plate comes from local producers, including Gubbeen and Cashel Blue. An informative and reasonable wine list is divided by country. There's also a good-value early bird menu.

Cork City

Franciscan Well Brew Pub
Brewery pub

North Mall, Cork
Tel. +353(0)21 4393434
Email. shane_long@hotmail.com
www.franciscanwellbrewery.com

Founded in 1998 on Cork's North Mall, across the street from the river, the Franciscan Well Brewery is built on the site of an old Franciscan Monastery dating back to 1219. It was believed that water from the well had miraculous and curative properties, though you'll have to try the brewery's own lager, ale, stout and wheat beer yourself to see if they could claim similar benefits. All the beers brewed here are free from chemical additives and preservatives. Enjoy them from the taps of the large serving vessels behind the bar. Try the creamy Shandon stout, the fruity Blarney Blonde ale or the robust Rebel Red ale with a distinct caramel flavour.

Opening hours: 15.00-23.30 Mon-Wed. 15.00-24.00 Thur. 15.00-00.30 Fri-Sat. 16.00-23.00 Sun.
Directions: Head straight down North Main Street, cross over the North Gate Bridge and then turn left.

Several European beers are also available. There's a barbecue every Thursday and Friday from May to September, and regular traditional live music, as well as beer festivals twice yearly: at Easter and the October bank holiday weekend, inspired by the German Oktoberfest. What would the monks have made of it all? Find out more on a special brewery tour.

Ireland South

Cork City

Hayfield Manor Hotel
City centre hotel, restaurant & spa

Perrott Avenue, College Road, Cork
Tel. +353(0)21 4845900
Email. enquiries@hayfieldmanor.ie
www.hayfieldmanor.ie

This red-brick hotel offers peaceful seclusion in the heart of the city. Joe and Margaret Scally with daughter Anne-Marie, run this luxury hotel which they have tastefully renovated and extended. Guests can enjoy Hayfield Manor's famous afternoon tea in the drawing room or take an after-dinner drink by the fire in the library. The oversized bedrooms are individually decorated with Margaret's impeccable style, and feature crisp, white linen, luxury toiletries, bathrobes, slippers and fresh flowers. In the new elegant setting of Orchids Restaurant, chef Alan Hickey uses the finest organic ingredients from the local area, and offers contemporary Irish cuisine in an elegant setting. Here you can enjoy fillet of turbot with baby potatoes, green beans, tomato and baby carrot ragout, followed by mango tarte fine with vanilla and mango salsa, and passionfruit sorbet. The international wine list includes helpful regional introductions. Perrotts restaurant serves more informal food, such as gnocchi with sage and smoked bacon, followed by grilled fillet of seabass with saffron and lemon risotto. The Vine private dining space is used for wine and whiskey tastings, meetings, receptions and private lunches and dinners. The hotel's new treatment rooms offer Elemis spa therapy. Altogether, it's a top-class establishment.

Rooms: 88 ensuite. Double from €280. Single from €250.
Prices: Lunch main course from €17. Perrotts Restaurant: Dinner main course from €17. Orchids Restaurant: Three course set dinner €55. House wine from €32.
Food Served: 12.30-14.15 & 18.00-22.30 daily.
Cuisine: 2 restaurants. Orchids - contemporary Irish cuisine, Perrotts - casual style, international.
Other Points: Suite of treatment rooms. Indoor heated pool. Outdoor Jacuzzi. Steam room and gym. Drawing room and library. Gardens. Bird aviary. Private dining rooms. Car park. Children welcome. Winner - Hotel of the Year 2006.
Directions: Leaving from outside the City Library at Grand Parade, continue straight through one set of traffic lights and at the next traffic lights, turn left on to Washington St. Continue straight for about a half mile. You will pass Jury's Hotel and come up to a set of traffic lights. The main gates to University College Cork will be in front of you. Turn left on to Donovans Road and continue straight up the hill. At the top of this road, turn right on to College Road and take the next immediate left, up Perrott Ave. The entrance to Hayfield Manor is directly in front of you.

for online reservations **Ireland South**

Cork City

Isaacs Restaurant
City centre restaurant and café

48 MacCurtain Street, Cork
Tel. +353(0)21 4503805
Email. isaacs@iol.ie

One of Cork's busiest and vibrant restaurants. Michael Ryan's bistro style, informal restaurant doesn't fail to deliver on value for money, quality of food or service. The inviting atmosphere which is somehow spacious and cosy at the same time could transport your imagination back to Victorian times with its' bricked walls and high ceilings dating back to the 18th Century! However, the menu is not quite of the same era! It marries together International favorites from around the globe for example a plate of tapas alongside some of the most popular Irish dishes. You could go for 'potato cakes served with Clonakilty Black Pudding, glazed apples and whole grain mustard sauce' or for the non meat-eaters a 'fried Ardsallagh goats cheese salad with roast beetroot, chickpeas and basil oil'.

Prices: Lunch main course from €8.90-€12.90. Dinner main course from €14.80-€25.90. House wine from €17.50.
Food served: 10.00-14.30 and 18.00-22.00 Mon-Sat. 18.00-21.00 Sun.
Closed: One week at Christmas.
Cuisine: Modern Irish/Mediterranean.
Directions: Opposite the Gresham Metropole Hotel, on MacCurtain Street.

Food is presented in a clever yet unpretentious way and at a competitive price - as is its' easy to follow, no-nonsense wine list.

Cork City

Lotamore House
Georgian guesthouse

Tivoli, Cork
Tel. +353(0)21 4822344
Email. lotamore@iol.ie
www.lotamorehouse.com

Geri McElhinney's Lotamore House is an elegant Georgian building, boasting views of Cork Harbour and its own beautiful gardens. Inside you are welcomed by roaring fires and warm colours, and period features such as the large, stained-glass window visible from the entrance hall. The house, recently refurbished, is furnished throughout with fine antiques. There is an afternoon and early evening snack menu, or you may choose to visit one of Cork city's many restaurants, within just a few minutes' drive. On your return, you can help yourself to the well-stocked honesty bar. No two rooms are alike, but they share a tasteful touch, and feature oversized beds, deep armchairs and the finest fabrics. Luxury toiletries and fluffy white towels will complete a restful stay. Follow the aromas of freshly cooked food to the dining room for breakfast, which could be the full Irish,

Rooms: 20 ensuite. Double from €130. Single from €85. Family from €155.
Other Points: Bedrooms non-smoking. Garden. Children welcome. Car park. Winner - Guesthouse of the Year 2004.
Directions: 5 minutes drive from the city centre off dual carriageway heading east out of the city.

or perhaps free-range eggs and a bakery basket, served with great attention to detail. Some of the many activities nearby include boating, scenic walks, horse-riding and golf.

Ireland South

Cork City

Nash 19 Restaurant
City centre restaurant and café

19 Princes Street, Cork
Tel. +353(0)21 4270880
Email. info@nash19.com
www.nash19.com

Situated in the heart of Cork's business district, just a stone's throw from the renowned English Market, this lively café has been serving excellent modern Irish food for over 15 years. Aromas of freshly baked scones, traditional pastries and hot coffee fill the air from the early morning hours, when scores of breakfasters stop in en route to work. Owner Claire Nash is committed to using the best regional produce, and a myriad of local suppliers deliver on a daily basis. All fish, meat and poultry are supplied by the English Market. Seasonal menus change regularly. Choose from such wholesome lunch specialties such as tomato and basil soup; calamari and cod pasta tagliatelle; Mexican chicken and warm salad with salsa, guacamole and tortilla crisps; and Irish blue cheese, broccoli and cherry tomato

Prices: Main course from €11.90. House wine from €19.50
Food Served: 7.30-16.30. 7.30-16.00 Sat.
Closed: Sundays, Bank Holidays and 25 Dec to 2 Jan.
Cuisine: Modern Irish with European influences.
Other Points: Children welcome.
Directions: Located on Princes Street Lower between Patrick Street and South Mall, close to the Old English Market.

tart. And delicious homemade desserts such as rhubarb and blackberry crumble. The service is efficient and friendly, and there's a small selection of wines, bubbly and beer.

Douglas Co Cork

Nakon Thai Restaurant
Thai restaurant

Tramway House, Douglas Village, Co Cork
Tel. +353(0)21 4369900
www.nakonthai.com

David and Sineerat McGreal offer the tastiest Thai lessons in town. At Nakon Thai, you are greeted with a warm "sawadee" (meaning welcome), and all your dishes are freshly cooked, using no artificial flavourings (or MSG). Their Combo platter allows you to try several starters, from the Thung Tong (a mixture of minced pork, tiger prawns, crab-meat and Thai herbs wrapped in pastry and served with plum sauce) to the Angel Wings (chicken wings with minced pork, vermicelli and coriander). The main course could consist of stir-fried sliced roast duck in red curry with basil, chillies and herbs, or fried squid with onion and celery in chilli sauce. Seafood is from Cork's famous English Market and meat from a local supplier. Soups range from mild to spicy, and the broad

Prices: Main course from €14.50. House wine from €15.95
Food served: 17.30-23.00 Mon-Sat. 17.00-22.00 Sun.
Closed: 24-27 December and Good Friday.
Cuisine: Thai.
Other Points: Children welcome. Air-conditioning. Convenient Parking.
Directions: In Douglas Village, opposite the Rugby Club.

dessert selection includes rich chocolate pudding and the "summer fruit teardrop" - vanilla flavoured mousse on a shortbread base topped with redcurrant, peach and blackberry. The wine list is extensive and well-annotated, or you could try the premium Singha beer.

Hayfield Manor, Cork

Ireland South

www.goodfoodireland.ie

Durrus Co Cork

Carbery Cottage Guest Lodge
Coastal bed and breakfast

Durrus, Co Cork
Tel.+353(0)27 61368
Email. carberycottage@eircom.net
www.carbery-cottage-guest-lodge.net

Situated on the Sheep's Head peninsula, overlooking Dunmanus Bay and the Mizen peninsula, Carbery Cottage is a relaxed and modern guest lodge. Mike Hegarty and Julia Bird offer the personal touch: they want guests to enjoy their home, set on two acres of lawned, south-facing gardens, which accommodates a maximum of six guests. Choose from the homely Dunmanus room, the large Fastnet suite for views over the bay, or the ground-floor Seefin suite with French doors to the terrace and pond. If you are looking for a lie-in, this is the B&B for you: full Irish breakfasts are served in the dining room until midday. Evening meals are also available, using organic, locally sourced produce where possible, and with seafood a speciality as Mike himself is a fisherman. Dinner might include crab and avocado stuffed mushroom, then steak and Guinness pie with local new potatoes, and finally lemon and lime cheesecake with Carbery raspberries. There are several options for short walks, cycling, fishing and golf, as well as well-known gardens to visit nearby.

Rooms: 3(2 ensuite). Double from €80. Single €40. Family from €100.
Prices: Standard supper menu from €15. Set dinner from €40. (Residents only)
Cuisine: Local organic produce, specialising in fresh seafood.
Other Points: Garden. Dogs welcome. Smoking areas. Credit cards not accepted.
Directions: When you reach Durrus village the road forks, take the right hand fork which is sign posted Ahakista, Kilcrohane and the Sheepshead Peninsula. Follow this road for exactly 2.4 miles. You will pass a lay-by on the right and then see a turn on the right (sign posted The Sheeps Head Cycle route). Turn right up this road for about 0.2 of a mile the road turns to the left then 50 yds later there is a turn to the right going up the hill between two farms. We are about 300 yds on the left.

Fermoy Co Cork

Munchies Gourmet Coffee House
Daytime coffee shop and restaurant

Lower Patrick Street, Fermoy, Co Cork
Tel. +353(0)25 33653
Email. munchiesfermoy@eircom.net

Since it's opening in 2002, Jason and Fiona Hogan's bright, clean coffee house has established a reputation for its exceptionally warm and friendly atmosphere. The hardworking pair have clearly passed on this sunny outlook to their well-presented staff, who deal with customers with smiling efficiency. The interior is simple and clean, with pine tables, a dresser bearing pastas and sauces and a chalkboard displaying the daily menu. All food is fresh, with fruit, veg and herbs from the Hogan's' organic plot, and meats supplied from their local family butcher and made on the premises daily - for breakfast, there's French toast, pancakes with maple syrup and a huge choice of speciality teas alongside the excellent Segafredo coffee. Lunch might bring homemade soup - nicely presented on a white china with a swirl of cream and freshly baked soda bread, fresh panini, baps and wraps and of course traditional Irish Stew and homemade lasagnes all served with roast vegetables, bacon mash and salad. There's a daily selection of gluten free soups, lunches and deserts and a small selection of wines by the glass.

Prices: Main course lunch from €8.90.
Food served: 9.00-17.00 Mon-Sat.
Closed: Sundays, Christmas week, Public Holidays.
Cuisine: Traditional Irish
Other Points: Outside seating area. Children welcome. Car park.
Directions: On Tallow Road, next to the Mart car park.

Fermoy Co Cork

Ballyvolane House
Historic country house

Castlelyons, Nr Fermoy, Co Cork
Tel. +353(0)25 36349
Email. info@ballyvolanehouse.ie
www.ballyvolanehouse.ie

Justin and Jenny Green's family heritage home has an early Italianate style, providing elegance and comfort. With seven acres of beautifully landscaped gardens, there are some wonderful walks through the woodlands and lakes. As you would expect, food is country house style, menus varying with seasonal, weather and fishing conditions. Ingredients are sourced from local artisan food producers, organic where possible. The walled garden provides an abundance of fruit for jams and chutneys and the range of vegetables grown includes seakale, asparagus and fennel. There are complimentary fruit cordials and homemade chocolate biscuits in the bedrooms. Starters include delights such as pear and Gabriel cheese pine nut salad or garden beetroot soup with chive cream. Follow with a main course of baked Ballycotton hake with salsa verde or roast Caherbeg organic loin of bacon. Wonderful old-fashioned puddings include sticky toffee or rhubarb bread-and-butter. The global wine list includes a Lebanese, a Greek organic and a UK award-winning sparkling wine.

Rooms: 6 ensuite. Double from €170-€200. Single from €130.
Prices: Lunch from €35 (two courses). Dinner from €50 (four courses). Bar snack from €6.50. House wine from €23. Picnic lunch €15 (available daily by prior arrangement only). Afternoon tea daily at €6.50.
Food served: 7.30-12.00. Dinner at 20.00 daily.
Closed: 24 Dec - 4 Jan.
Cuisine: Country house
Other Points: Bedrooms non-smoking. Gardens. Children welcome. Car park. Dogs welcome. Salmon and trout fishing. Bicycles. Badminton. Croquet.
Directions: From Cork - turn right off N8 at the River Bride just before Rathcormac onto the R628. Take second turn right towards Midleton at a crossroads approximately two miles later. Take the next left, a half-mile up the hill - the house is on the right about a half-mile from the last turn.

Ballymaloe House, Cork

Ireland South

Goleen Co Cork

The Heron's Cove
Waterside restaurant and bed & breakfast

The Harbour, Goleen, Co Cork
Tel. +353(0)28 35225
Email. suehill@eircom.net
www.heroncove.ie
www.heronscove.com

Situated just outside the village of Goleen (meaning small inlet), Sue Hill's charming bed and breakfast makes a great base for a West Cork trip, with Schull Planetarium, Bantry House, Barleycove and the Mizen Head Visitor Centre all within easy reach. Goleen was built during the 19th century at a crossroads where a cattle fair was held. There is a hidden harbour down to the left, which gives the village its name. The Heron's Cove was originally built on the site of an old farmhouse. Three of the bedrooms have private balconies with lovely views of the harbour. The à la carte menu includes locally smoked sprats with capers, onion and melon, followed by Bantry Bay scallops, pan-fried with a smoked bacon cream sauce and the Heron's Cove signature dessert - a baked chocolate and vanilla cheesecake. Choose a bottle from the reasonably priced rack of wines and it is opened at your table. Next morning, breakfast is entirely up to you - although you will get plenty of suggestions, such as oats, omelette or pancakes, nothing is too much trouble for Sue's guests.

Rooms: 5 ensuite. Double from €80. Single from €50. Family from €100 (3 adults or 2 adults & 2 children).
Prices: Dinner main course from €20. House wine from €19.75 (litre).
Food served: Daily from 19.00 - by reservation only Oct-Apr.
Closed: 24 Dec-1 Feb.
Cuisine: Irish.
Other Points: Garden. Car Park. Full drinks licence.
Directions: Turn off the N71 and follow the R592 to Goleen. Turn left down to the harbour.

Murphy's Ice Cream, Kerry

Ireland South

www.goodfoodireland.ie

Kinsale Co Cork

Blue Haven Hotel
Coastal hotel and restaurant

3/4 Pearse Street, Kinsale, Co Cork
Tel.+353(0)21 4772209
Email.info@bluehavenkinsale.com
www.bluehavenkinsale.com

Kinsale considers itself the culinary capital of Ireland. The historic town has a great buzz, and is packed with galleries and craft shops as well as eateries. Enjoy a one-hour walking tour or take a harbour cruise and imagine you're part of the yachting set. A stay in this stylish "boutique" hotel will also make you feel special. It stands on the site of the original Kinsale fish market. Service here is excellent, under the watchful eye of owner Ciaran Fitzgerald. The elegant restaurant, blu, features modern Irish cuisine with international influences. All jam, marmalade, preserves, pickles and relish are homemade,the beef is Irish and local produce is used where possible. Starters include Vichyssoise, either cold with freshly shucked oyster or hot with herbed crutons. Follow with grilled John Dory with cous cous, roasted tomatoes and black olive tapenade, and, if you still have room, share the chef's selection tasting plate for dessert. The wine list includes fair trade options by the bottle or glass, features a choice of wines of the week,

Rooms: 17 ensuite. Double from €160. Single from €120.
Prices: Lunch main course from €13.50. Dinner main course from €22.50. Bar snack from €6.50. House Wine from €20.
Opening Hours(Bar): 10.30-23.30 Mon-Sat 12.30-23.00 Sundays.
Food Served: 12.00-22.00 daily.
Cuisine: Modern Irish with an international twist.
Other Points: Garden. Children welcome. Bedrooms non-smoking.
Directions: Follow signs for Cork Airport, continue to Five Mile Bridge and take R600. Drive through Riverstick, Belgooly and arrive in Kinsale.

and is helpfully categorised by country of origin. Bedrooms are luxuriously decorated, and the breakfast menu includes smoothies, buttermilk pancakes in four flavours, eggs Benedict or smoked haddock.

Blue Haven Hotel

Ireland South

Kinsale Co Cork

Old Bank House
Georgian residence

Pearse Street, Kinsale, Co Cork
Tel. +353(0)21 4774075
Email. info@oldbankhousekinsale.com
www.oldbankhousekinsale.com

The Old Bank House has recently been refurbished, with sumptuous new soft furnishings and pocket-sprung beds added. However, owner/manager Ciaran Fitzgerald has managed to retain the old-world charm of this luxurious Georgian residence, and all of the antique furniture has remained. Located in the centre of Kinsale it is close to its sister property the Blue Haven Hotel and to the many shops and galleries in this popular harbour town. The beautiful bedrooms and suites are individually and tastefully decorated to the highest standards, and most have lovley views of the town. Enjoy the overstuffed sofa and fresh flowers of the comfortable sitting room, with its high ceiling and stone fireplace. Cooked breakfast features a vegetarian as well as traditional fry-up which includes local bacon and sausage and Clonakilty Black Pudding, omelettes, French toast, oatmeal porridge and scrambled egg with smoked salmon from Kinsale victualler John Coholan. There's also a seasonal fresh fruit platter, yoghurt and local cheeses, accompanied by a selection of home-made bread, marmalade and preserves. Outside are the many shops and galleries. of Kinsale.

Rooms: 17 ensuite. Double from €170. Single from €170. Family from €215.
Other points: Winner - Guesthouse of the Year 2005.
Directions: In the Centre of Kinsale between Supervalue and the Post Office.

Midleton Co Cork

Farmgate Restaurant & Country Store
Restaurant and country store

Coolbawn, Midleton, Co Cork
Tel. +353(0)21 4632771

Marog O'Brien's food store and restaurant - in the picturesque town of Midleton - has been a popular spot for food lovers for over 20 years. At the front is the shop, where farm-fresh produce, organic fruit and vegetables, cheeses and home-baked treats are sold. At the back is the homely restaurant, where the lunchtime menu takes in sandwiches, salads and cheese plates, as well as hot dishes such as traditional Irish stew or catch of the day. On Thursday, Friday and Saturday nights, dishes become a little more elaborate - but always firmly anchored around local produce - with starters bringing warm salad of lamb's kidney with mushrooms and pink peppercorns. Main courses might include Farmgate free-erange duck with sage and onion stuffing, with a sumptuous double chocolate mousse gateau for dessert. A well-considered wine list has a strong showing from France. This is a sister restaurant to the Farmgate Café in Cork (see entry).

Prices: Lunch main course from €10.95 Dinner main course from €16. House wine from €20.
Hours: 9.00-21.30.
Food served: Lunch 12.00-16.00 Mon-Sat. Dinner 19.00-21.30 Thurs-Sat.
Closed: Sundays, Bank Holidays, 10 days over Christmas and Good Friday.
Cuisine: Traditional Irish and Modern European.
Other Points: Children welcome. Garden.
Directions: Follow the signs for the Irish Distillery off the Waterford to Cork Road. Farmgate is located in the town centre.

Ireland South

www.goodfoodireland.ie

Shanagarry Co Cork

Ballymaloe House
Period country house, restaurant & cookery school

Shanagarry, Midleton, Co Cork
Tel. +353(0)21 4652531
Email. res@ballymaloe.ie
www.ballymaloe.ie

With a history dating back to 1450 when a Norman Castle was built on lands at Ballymaloe, this is one of Ireland's best-known guesthouses. The buildings in use today are built into and around the castle. In 1967, rooms were built for guests and these continue to provide comfort and olde-world charm. New rooms have been built over the years, offering guests all the luxuries associated with this charming guesthouse. Eating in Ballymaloe is always a treat, whether it's breakfast, lunch or dinner. With the highest quality ingredients in the capable hands of head chef Jason Fahy, cooking is inspired. Lunch may be warm salad of Gubbeen cheese and bacon or escalope of beef. After an aperitif in the drawing room, a five-course dinner may begin with Ballycotton fish soup or locally smoked fish tart, followed by roast Kassler or guinea fowl. With Irish Farmhouse cheeses and homemade biscuits and a dessert from the trolley, you may just manage coffee and petit fours. Ballymaloe is unusual in that it still lays down stocks of fine vintage wines. The list has some 200 carefully selected wines.

Rooms: 33 ensuite. High season rates - double from €260. Single from €160. Family from €410.
Prices: Lunch (4 course) from €35. Dinner (5 course) from €70. House wine from €25.
Food served: Lunch 13.00 daily. Dinner 19.00-21.00 daily.
Closed: Christmas and 2 weeks in Jan.
Cuisine: Traditional Irish.
Other Points: Cookery School. Afternoon tea and light lunches residents only. Bedrooms non-smoking. Children welcome. Garden. Car park. Heated outdoor pool (summer). Tennis. Five-hole golf course. Croquet. Children's outdoor play area. Annual Wine Weekend Courses in March and April. Craft shop. Winner - Newcomer of the Year 2006
Directions: From Cork airport, turn left towards the city. At the Kinsale roundabout follow road markings and signs for N25 East. At the roundabout at the end of the tunnel take the third exit heading for Rosslare. Bypass Midleton at the roundabout, take the third exit and watch for signs for Cloyne and Ballycotton. Ballymaloe is 2 miles beyond Cloyne on the Ballycotton road.

Ballymaloe Cookery School
Cookery School

Shanagarry, Midleton, Co Cork
Tel. +353(0)21 4646785/4646727
Email. enquiries@cookingisfun.ie
www.cookingisfun.ie

You could be forgiven for thinking the Ballymaloe Cookery School is somebody's house. The building is a delight, the garden a sea of green and everywhere happy smiling faces. Students range in age from the young to the not so young, from those taking time out to those embarking on careers. You don't just learn how to cook at Ballymaloe. It starts with the ingredients; eggs from the farm, fish from nearby Ballycotton, herbs and vegetables from the strictly organic garden, fruit from the trees that boarder the outside seating areas.

The kitchens themselves are homely and welcoming with large generous demonstration areas and lots of natural light. And seemingly everywhere is the dominating, infectious enthusiasm of Darina Allen, the guiding force behind what has become a world-wide name for quality and integrity.

for online reservations **Ireland South**

Youghal Co Cork

Aherne's
Townhouse and seafood restaurant

163 North Main Street, Youghal,
Co Cork.
Tel. +353(0)24 92424
Email. ahernes@eircom.net
www.ahernes.com

Aherne's is a Youghal institution, having been in the Fitzgibbon family for three generations. The small, luxurious townhouse and seafood restaurant features the freshest local produce, so the menu changes daily. But ingredients always include the day's catch from the harbour, locally reared beef and lamb, and a variety of home-baked breads. A typical menu might feature bruschetta of Ardsallagh goats' cheese or home-made chicken liver paté to start. Chef David Fitzgibbon creates imaginative dishes with attention to detail, such as roasted monkfish tail with spinach risotto and chargrilled vegetables. A fixed-price value menu is available seven days a week. The extensive and informative wine list includes plenty of half-bottle options. Two richly furnished traditional bars also offer meals cooked to order, including prawns, smoked 'Yawl Bay' salmon, oysters, Irish beef and seafood chowder. The bright, comfortable and spacious bedrooms and suites contain large beds with crisp white linen, and are furnished with antiques. Upstairs bedrooms feature little balconies overlooking a courtyard.

Rooms: 13 ensuite. Double from €160. Single from €115. Family room - rates on request.
Prices: Dinner main course from €25. Bar snack from €7.50. House wine from €18.50. Two-course value menu from €35. Full dinner menu from €45.
Food served: Bar food 12.00-22.00. Dinner 18.30-21.30 daily.
Closed: 6 days over Christmas.
Cuisine: Seafood a specialty.
Other Points: Children welcome. Car park. Non-smoking house. Winner - Guesthouse and Restaurant of the Year 2005.
Directions: Located in the town centre.

Ireland South
www.goodfoodireland.ie

Cobh, The Queenstown Story
Place to Visit

Cobh Heritage Centre, Cobh, Co Cork
Tel. +353(0)21 4813591
Fax. +353(0)21 4813595
Email. info@cobhheritage.com
www.cobhheritage.com

The story of Cobh's unique origins, its history and legacy are dramatically recalled at The Queenstown Story - a multimedia exhibition at Cobh's restored Victorian Railway Station. Explore the conditions on board the early emigrant vessels, including the dreaded 'Coffin Ship'. Learn about an 'Irish Wake' - the special farewell for emigrating sons and daughters - many of whom never returned to Ireland. Experience life on board a convict ship leaving Cove for Australia in 1801. Discover Queenstown's special connections with the ill-fated Titanic, which sank on her maiden voyage in 1912. Relive the horror of World War 1 and the sinking of the Lusitania off Cork Harbour with the loss of 1,198 lives. Learn about Annie Moore and her two brothers who left Cobh for a new life in America and how she was the first emigrant ever to be processed in Ellis Island.

Other Points
Genealogy Record Finder Service, Self Guided Exhibition, French Speaking Guide available, Restaurant, Full Wheelchair Access, and Hourly train service from Cork Station to Cobh Heritage Centre.

Hours
May 1 to Oct 31 daily 9.30-18.00
Nov 1 to Apr 30 daily 9.30-17.00
Last admissions 1 hour before closing
Closed from Dec 22 to Jan 2

Directions
Cobh is situated 15km east of Cork City, just off the N25 take the Cobh Road and turn right at the bridge as you cross on to Cobh Island.

Fota House & Gardens
Place to Visit

Fota Island, Carrigtwohill, Co Cork
Tel. +353(0) 21 4815543
Fax. +353(0) 21 4815541
Email. info@fotahouse.com
www.fotahouse.com

Fota House is Ireland's finest example of Regency period architecture with superb magnificent neoclassical interiors. Formerly owned by the Smith Barry family, Fota House began life as a humble hunting lodge. Expanded and redesigned by Sir Richard Morrison the lodge was transformed to a superb Regency residence. Within the house are some of the finest neo-classical interiors to be found in Ireland. Fota House was designed to form the centrepiece of a great ornamental estate. The gardens contain a large number of exotic plant species from around the world, which flourish due to the benign climate of the South West Coast.

Admission Charged
Free entry to Fota Gardens and Arboretum.

Hours
Jan 01st - 31st Mar	11.00 - 16.00
Apr 01st - 30th Sept	10.00 - 17.00
Oct 01st - 31st Dec	11.00 - 16.00

(IMPORTANT NOTE: Fota House can on occasions be closed due to the holding of private functions. People or groups intending to visit the house should ring ahead to check opening times on the day of their proposed visit.)

Other Points
Tours of the house are self-guided. The property is wheelchair accessible. There is also a small shop and of course a Tea Room serving light lunches, snacks, teas and coffees (home baked). Car Park on site (€2.00 fee applies)

Directions
Fota House is Located about 12 Kilometres east of Cork City, just off the main Cork - Waterford Road (N25). Take exit for Cobh and continue for about 1.6 kilometres. The entrance to Fota is shared with Fota Wildlife Park. Access also available by train (Cork Cobh line).

Mizen Head Signal Station

Place to Visit

Mizen Head, Goleen, West Cork
Tel. +353 (0)28 35115/35225
Fax. +353 (0)28 35422
Email. info@mizenhead.ie
www.mizenhead.ie
www.mizenhead.com

Mizen Head Signal Station, the must-see award-winning Visitors Centre at Ireland's most Southwesterly Point. If you miss the Mizen you haven't done Ireland. Experience the Irish Lights Signal Station, the 99 Steps, Spectacular views of the south and west coasts, Navigational Aids Simulator, the Fastnet Lighthouse Model, the famous Bridge with seals below. Mizen Head is spellbinding in any weather.

Other Points
Guided tour of the Signal Station, Audiovisual DVD 'Mizen Head Carn ui Neid', Gift/Souvenir Shop specialising in Maritime and West Cork themes, Café, Car Park.

Hours
Jun to Sep daily 10.00 - 18.00
Mid Mar to May & Oct
daily 10.30 - 17.00
Nov to mid Mar
Weekends 11.00 - 16.00

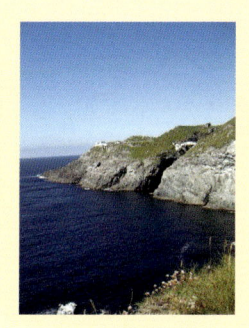

Directions
From Killarney follow N71 to Bantry, outside Bantry turn right to follow signs to Crookhaven on R591, go through Goleen, then follow signs for Mizen Head Drive. From Cork follow N71 to Ballydehob then follow signs to Mizen Head R592 through Schull to Goleen.

Skibbereen Heritage Centre

Place to Visit

Old Gasworks Building
Upper Bridge Street
Skibbereen, West Cork
Tel. +353 (0)28 40900
Fax. +353 (0)28 40957
Email. info@skibbheritage.com
www.skibbheritage.com

Enjoy a visit to the Skibbereen Heritage Centre, located in the award winning, beautifully restored Old Gasworks building. **The Great Famine Exhibition** - learn about this period of Irish history using the latest in multimedia technology. Skibbereen was one of the worst affected areas in Ireland, as testified by the mass graves at Abbeystrewery, where almost 10,000 are buried. **The Lough Hyne Visitor Centre** reveals the unique nature of this marine lake, Ireland's first Marine Nature Reserve. Find out about the history, folklore and formation of this renowned natural phenomenon. **Genealogy information** is also available including the 1901/1911 censuses for Skibbereen and district.

Other Points
Archaeology information, gift shop, salt-water aquarium, multi language audiovisuals and twice weekly guided historical walks of Skibb town. Wheelchair friendly and car park adjacent.

Hours
Mid Mar - mid May
10.00 - 18.00 Tue - Sat
Mid May - mid Sept 10.00 - 18.00 Daily
Mid Sept - 31st Oct
10.00 - 18.00 Tue - Sat
Feb & Nov 10.00 - 18.00 Mon - Fri

Directions
Skibbereen Heritage Centre is centrally located in Skibbereen, one of West Cork's picturesque towns. From Cork City: Take the N71 road through Bandon and Clonakilty, approximately 50 miles. From Killarney: Take the N71 road via Kenmare and Bantry. Follow the road signs to Skibbereen, approximately 50 miles.

Ireland South

www.goodfoodireland.ie

Ballybunion Co Kerry

Íragh Tí Connor
Guesthouse, restaurant and bar

Main Street, Ballybunion, Co Kerry
Tel. +353(0)68 27112
Email. iraghticonnor@eircom.net
www.golfballybunion.com

The name of this lovely 19th-century country house, which translates as 'the inheritance of O'Connor' says volumes about the care which owners John and Joan O'Connor have lavished upon it. Set in its own walled gardens, but close to Ballybunion's world-famous golf links and the bustle of the town itself, the house has 17 spacious bedrooms furnished with antiques to complement the convenience of satellite television, large bathrooms and direct-dial phones. Downstairs, the public rooms are also inviting, with open fireplaces and period furniture. The restaurant, with its crisp white and rose-coloured linens and baby grand piano, is the perfect backdrop for the elegant menu, which includes crab and shrimp crème brûlée with toasted brioche and seasonal leaves for starter and for main course pan fried fillet steak with a blue cheese and mushroom ragout, balsamic onions, potato gratin and a girolle and black truffle sauce or grilled turbot with a smoked salmon and dill veloute, buttered green vegetables and braised sweet potato. Delicious desserts might include a warm chocolate and orange fondant with a white chocolate sauce and rum and raisin ice cream or homemade banoffi pie. Breads and preserves are homemade, and the wine list is a treat for connoisseurs and novices alike.

Rooms: 17 ensuite. Double from €195. Single from €150.
Prices: Dinner main course from €19.95. House wine from €18.
Food served: 17.30-21.30. 13.00-21.30 on Sunday.
Closed: Closed Dec and Jan.
Cuisine: Modern Irish.
Other Points: Children welcome. Garden. Car park. Commended - Guesthouse with Restaurant 2003.
Directions: On the N69 north coastal route from Limerick to Tralee, at the top of Main Street.

Killarney Royal Hotel

Cahirciveen Co Kerry

QC's Seafood Bar & Restaurant
Restaurant and bar

3 Main Street, Cahirciveen,
Ring of Kerry, Co Kerry
Tel. +353(0)66 9472244
Email. info@qcbar.com
www.qcbar.com

Kate and Andrew Cooke own this renowned seafood restaurant, housed in an 18th-century building in the centre of Cahiciveen. All their fish is wild and locally caught, supplied by the family fish business, Quinlans Kerry Fish. Call in at lunch for home-made soup or chowder with home-made bread. Try the Basque-inspired chorizo tagliolini with spicy tomato sauce, or the QCs best-seller, deep-fried lemon sole in beer batter with home-made tartar sauce. At dinner, appetisers include salad of fresh fig and buffalo Mozzarella or sizzling fresh crabmeat and crabclaws with garlic, chilli, onion and tomatoes in olive oil. Chef Eddy Gannon trained under Ross Lewis, and his main course could be pan-seared baby squids or a mixed seafood crèpe with cod, monkfish and prawns. Daily specials might include ray wing fillets pan-fried with black butter, followed by wild halibut with a leek purée and champagne sauce. Wines are, of course, largely chosen for how well they partner fish; several are imported directly from Spanish bodegas. QCs run a 'tack and snack' package, where you can whet your appetite on a luxury 37-foot yacht from Caherciveen Marina, taking in Valentia, Beginish islands and Fort William lighthouse. The Cookes plan to extend QC's into the courtyard and garden for the 2007 season.

Prices: Bar snack from €4.95. Lunch main course from €7.50. Dinner main course from €17.50. House wine from €17.50.
Food Served: Lunch 12.30-14.30 Tue-Sat. Dinner 18.00-21.30 Tue-Sun. Apr-Oct. Open 7 days July & August. Dinner 18.00-21.30 Fri-Sun. Nov-Mar.
Closed: Closed 7th Jan to mid Feb.
Cuisine: Modern Irish with Spanish influences.
Other Points: Garden. Car park. Patio/walled courtyard. Winner - Food Pub of the Year 2006.
Directions: In the centre of town. On the right hand side as if coming into town from Waterville.

Symbols

- Accommodation
- Restaurant
- Café
- Pub/Bar
- Daytime opening only
- Deli
- Wine
- Bakery
- Gourmet/Farm Shop
- Leisure Centre/Spa
- CS Craft Shop
- VC Visitor Centre
- FP Food Producer

Good Food Ireland Awards

- ★ 2002 Award Winner
- ★ 2003 Award Winner
- ★ 2004 Award Winner
- ★ 2005 Award Winner
- ★ 2006 Award Winner

Ireland South

www.goodfoodireland.ie

Dingle Peninsula Co Kerry

Gorman's Clifftop House & Restaurant
Seaview guesthouse and restaurant

Glaise Bheag, Ballydavid,
Dingle Peninsula, Co Kerry
Tel. +353(0)66 9155162
Email. info@gormans-clifftophouse.com
www.gormans-clifftophouse.com

Vincent and Síle Gorman have created quite a haven. Here, in the heart of the Gaeltacht, you can watch the sunset over the Atlantic from the garden, or sit by the open fire as the waves crash on the rocks below. They encourage guests to mingle and plan their trips in the lounge during the evening. The Gormans source local produce wherever possible. Bread and cakes are made in-house, eggs are free-range, teas and coffees are fair trade. Breakfast is bursting with variety: you could start with prune and apricot salad, hot from the kitchen comes the traditional Irish breakfast, and vegetarians will be pleased to see the cashew nut and sunflower seed plate, with tomatoes and olives. Dinner might consist of crab potato salad with wild Atlantic smoked salmon, followed by grilled scallops with toasted hazelnuts and coriander butter. To finish, try the blueberry and nectarine cake with Mascarpone cream. The wine selection spans from Austria to Australia. All double rooms, boasting magnificent views of either ocean or mountains, have king-size beds and DVD players, and feature handmade waxed pine furniture, Louis Mulcahy pottery lamps and wall hangings by a local tapestry artist, Lisbeth Mulcahy.

Rooms: 9 ensuite. Double from €100. Single from €75. Family from €150.
Prices: Dinner (set menu) €36.50. House wine from €18.50.
Food served: 18.30-20.30 Mon-Sat. By reservation only Nov-Mar.
Closed: Restaurant closed Sundays.
Cuisine: Seafood & modern Irish.
Other Points: Garden. Children welcome. Car park. Bicycle hire. Situated on Dingle way walking route. Broadband available. Winner - Little Gem Award 2001. Winner - Guesthouse with Restaurant Award 2006.
Directions: Straight across roundabout west of Dingle signposted "An Fheothanach" 8 miles, veer to left but do not turn left.

Dingle Co Kerry

Murphy's Ice Cream
Dessert house & coffee bar

Strand Street, Dingle, Co Kerry
Tel. +353(0)66 9152644
Email. sean@murphysicecream.ie
www.murphysicecream.ie
www.icecreamireland.com

You might be forgiven for thinking Murphy's in Dingle is a pub. It almost looks like one and the name certainly sounds right. Inside however it is not creamy pints of Guinness you will find but creamy tubs of ice-cream made by brothers Sean and Kieran Murphy. Kerry cream to be precise which is what many claim lies at the heart of Murphy's deliciousness. Others think it is the flavours; top-quality Valrhona chocolate, top flight vanilla, home made caramel. Suffice to say you can sit back in the comfort of this relaxed café and enjoy a scoop or several. You can also enjoy coffee, or one of the freshly made cakes. This is dessert heaven, there is very little reason to want to go home. Unless that is you buy something to take home which is always an option.

Opening Hours: Daily. 11.00-22.00 summer. 11.00-18.00 winter.
Closed: Dec to Feb.
Directions: In the centre of town, close to the marina and Post Office.

Ireland South

Kenmare Co Kerry

Lorge Chocolatier
Chocolate & gourmet shop

Bonane, Kenmare, Co Kerry
Tel. +353(0)87 9917172
Email. chocolatecrust@eircom.net

What used to be a post office in Kenmare has now become Lorge Chocolatier. You can sample, see chocolates being made, enrol on a course and make them yourself or, best of all, buy some to take home. Previously pastry chef at the nearby Sheen Falls, Benoit Lorge has a passion for chocolate and what started out as a way to raise money for charity has since been turned into a business. He supplies shops and top hotels with his creations but is happiest when selling from his own shop direct to the public. He runs popular courses including one specially geared to children. Awards keep coming his way, including two golds from the Great Taste Awards. This is a must-stop for anyone interested in the fascinating complexities of this ancient food.

Opening Hours: 10.00-18.00
Closed: Jan.
Directions: Between Kenmare and Glengariff on the N71 before the church in the village of Bonane.

Kenmare Co Kerry

The Lime Tree Restaurant
Town centre restaurant

Shelburne Street, Kenmare, Co Kerry
Tel. +353(0)64 41225
Email. benchmark@iol.ie
www.limetreerestaurant.com

Escape to another world in the Lime Tree, an old stone schoolhouse tucked away in a fairytale garden. A former winner of our Restaurant of the Year award, the Lime Tree prides itself on its friendly and efficient staff. The judges were looking for somewhere that was relaxed, yet fostered a sense of occasion, serving imaginative dishes using fresh local produce - and here they found their prizewinner. The building dates back to 1832, and as you step inside, the open fireplace and exposed stone set the mood. Tony and Alexandra Daly have been running this treasure since 1994, offering great value for money in an informal setting. Head chef Conal Breheny will spoil you with home-made free range duck liver parfait, followed by griddled loin of local lamb with roasted Mediterranean vegetables, cauliflower and goats' cheese fondue and white truffle oil.

Prices: Dinner main course from €18.95. House wine from €20.
Food Served: 18.30-21.30 daily.
Closed: From end of Oct to end of Mar.
Cuisine: Modern Irish & seafood.
Other Points: Car park. Winner - Restaurant of the Year 2005.
Directions: At the top of town, next to The Park Hotel.

You might choose to finish with honey and almond semi-freddo with pecan praline and caramel tuile. The wine list makes your choice easy by classifying according to flavour. The Lime Tree Art Gallery next door features work by artists who have drawn inspiration from the beautiful surrounding area.

121

The Lime Tree, Kenmare, Co Kerry

Ireland South

Killarney Co Kerry

Killarney Royal Hotel
Town centre hotel and restaurant

College Street, Killarney, Co Kerry
Tel. +353 (0)64 31853
Email. info@killarneyroyal.ie
www.killarneyroyal.ie

The Killarney Royal, dating back to 1900, has been in the same family for generations, and it shows. Rooms are furnished with antiques, and the large marble bathrooms complete the sense of luxury. The hotel, owned by Margaret and Joe Scally, is convenient for town and country - it's near Killarney's shopping streets and within easy reach of Muckross House, Killarney National Park, and several golf courses. The breakfast buffet has a selection of cereals, juices, fruit, cheese and meat, and you can follow hot porridge with the Full Irish, or indulge a sweet tooth with pancakes and Danish pastries. Lunch brings Kerry coast seafood and shellfish, and sirloin of beef with Irish whiskey and peppercorn cream sauce, with fresh pear and red wine mousse gateau and wild berry compôte. For dinner, enjoy home-made tomato and basil soup, followed by fillet of beef Wellington en croûte, and a glazed, vanilla-flavoured crème brûlée. In the bar, appetisers include baked organic goats' cheese tartlet and there is an extensive menu of main courses, such as pan-fried Dover sole or crisp honey-roast duck. The informative wine list makes suggestions for partnering with your food, and a connoisseur's selection offers great value.

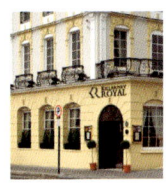

Rooms: 29 ensuite. Double from €130-€250. Single from €120-€205. Family from €250.
Prices: Lunch main course from €9.50. Dinner main course from €14.95. Bar Snack from €4.50. (bar snacks served all day). House wine from €18.50.
Food served: 12.30-21.00 daily. Early bird menu 18.30-19.30.
Closed: 24-27 Dec.
Cuisine: Modern Irish.
Other Points: Children welcome. Dogs welcome.
Directions: Just off the N22 on College Street.

Killarney Co Kerry

Mentons at the Plaza
Town centre bistro

Killarney Plaza Hotel, Killarney, Co Kerry
Tel. +353(0)64 21150
Email. info@mentons.com
www.mentons.com

This split-level bistro is a feast for the eyes as well as the palate. It boasts a grand setting, in the Killarney Plaza hotel, and features include the vaulted ceiling, polished wooden floors and arched windows. Visit for lunch to try the salmon, mussel and leek pasta in a dill cream sauce with fennel and grana padano, or the lemon, oregano and black pepper paillette of chicken with a warm bean and olive salad and tomato dressing. For dinner, chef patron Gary Fitzgerald's inventive menu could include puff pastry tartlet filled with roast parsnips and topped with goats' cheese and aubergine caviar. Meat-eaters may choose to follow with chargrilled fillet steak with fondant potato, pancetta, salsa verde and thyme jus, and their friends may opt for warm hummus strudel with nicoise salad, gaspacho and basil pesto. But for dessert, they need look no further than the passionfruit and ginger nut cheesecake, with blackberry coulis and lemon sorbet. The tempting early bird menu features pave of butterfish with a warm baby potato and green bean salad, followed by warm banana bread with butterscotch sauce and raisin ice cream. There's a choice of wines by the glass, including dessert wines.

Prices: Lunch main course from €7.95. Dinner main course from €14.95. House wine from €18.
Food served: 12.30-21.00 daily.
Cuisine: Modern and European.
Directions: Located in The Killarney Plaza Hotel in the town centre.

123

Ireland South

Killarney Co Kerry

The Laurels Pub & Restaurant
Restaurant, pub and wine bar

Main Street, Killarney, Co Kerry
Tel. +353(0)64 31149
Email. info@thelaurelspub.com
www.thelaurelspub.com

The Laurels, dating back 100 years in the same family, keeps the traditional touch with beamed ceilings, tiled floors and log fires. Con and Kate O'Leary source their ingredients locally, either from suppliers or the farmers' market. Lunch concentrates on favourites such as deep-fried brie, baked potato, warm smoked chicken salad or fish 'n' chips. At dinner, main courses might include Irish stew with Kerry lamb, traditional potato cakes with smoked bacon and chicken in a field mushroom cream sauce, and Irish beef fillet steaks with sautéed onions and mushrooms and wilted spinach. But The Laurels also has international touches, serving sizzling fajitas and stone-baked pizza with a huge array of toppings. All desserts and breads are home-made and change daily: try the raspberry bakewell tart if it's on offer. The compact global wine list is reasonably priced, and there are traditional music and Irish dancing nights in high season.

Prices: Lunch main course from €8.95. Bar snack from €6. Dinner main course from €13.95. House wine from €17.
Hours: Bar: 10.30-23.30, until 00.30 Fri-Sat. 12.30-23.00 Sunday.
Food served: Lunch: 12.00-15.00. Bar Snack: 15.30-17.30 (summer). Dinner: 18.00-21.45 Mon-Sat.
Closed: Restaurant closed Nov to Apr. Call ahead for seasonal changes.
Cuisine: Traditional Irish and International.
Other Points: Children welcome.
Directions: Centre of Killarney Town.

Molls Gap Co Kerry

Avoca Café
Daytime café and shop

Molls Gap, On the Ring of Kerry, Co Kerry
Tel. +353(0)64 34720
Email. info@avoca.ie
www.avoca.ie

This outpost of the County Wicklow handcrafts company is situated high up at Moll's Gap on the Ring of Kerry, overlooking Carrauntoohill (Ireland's highest mountain), the Gap of Dunloe and the famous lakes of Killarney. The Gap is named after Moll Kissane, who reputedly ran a shebeen (a hostelry of dubious reputation) in this area in the 1800s. As in all the Pratt family's Avoca stores, this one features the company's own clothing range for men, women and children, using soft wools and other natural fibres, as well as tasteful accessories and handcrafts. The attractive, self-service café serves up wholesome, home-cooked foods including roasted carrot, courgette and almond soup; shepherd's pie; selection of quiches and freshly made salads; and chicken and mushroom pie. Choose from such tempting desserts as double chocolate cheesecake, mascarpone cheesecake, lemon curd cake, strawberry meringue roulade, berry crumble, and blue cheese tart. Wine includes a selection of quarter bottles.

Prices: Main course from: €9.50.
Food Served: 9.30-17.00.
Closed: 8 Nov - 10 Mar.
Cuisine: Traditional and modern Irish.
Other Points: Children welcome. Craft shop.
Directions: Located in Molls Gap on the Ring of Kerry.

for online reservations | **Ireland South**

Killarney Co Kerry

Murphy's Ice Cream
Dessert house & coffee bar

37 Main Street, Killarney, Co Kerry
Tel. +353(0)66 9152644
Email. sean@murphysicecream.ie
www.murphysicecream.ie
www.icecreamireland.com

Right in the heart of Killarney on Main Street Murphy's beautifully blends the art of shop and café. You can buy to go, or buy to stay. It might be a coffee. It could be one of the freshly baked cakes but for most it is the ice-cream which attracts. There is a passion inherent in Murphy's ice-cream. And its not just the great flavours. You may pick from pure chocolate, rum and raisin or great, rather than just, vanilla but it is also Kerry milk and cream. Why not sit and enjoy a scoop or three. Wash them down with a coffee or maybe wait a while. The ice-cream tends to linger. The flavours are long in this part of the world. Should you wish to takes some home that is unlikely to be a problem. That is if you can wait that long.

Opening Hours: Daily. 11.00-22.00 summer. 11.00-18.00 winter.
Closed: Jan.
Directions: In the centre of town.

Tralee Co Kerry

Ballygarry House Hotel & Spa
Country manor hotel, restaurant & spa

Killarney Road, Tralee, Co Kerry
Tel. +353(0)66 7123322
Email. info@ballygarryhouse.com
www.ballygarryhouse.com

For those of you familiar with, and loyal to Padraig McGillycuddy's Ballygarry House Hotel over the years, you must be over the moon with the addition of its' new Spa. The Spa is called 'Nadur', the Irish word for 'nature', which immediately conjures up images of beautiful landscapes, organic ingredients and gentle, relaxing sounds - a 'Spa' drawing inspiration like this is the perfect place to relax, unwind and indulge yourself for the time you are there. Their 64 elegant and luxurious bedrooms, which are tastefully decorated complete with crisp, white bed linen and fluffy towels, carry on the general mood of peaceful ambience, which can so often be hard to find in the hustle and bustle of everyday life. Situated off the main road from Tralee to Killarney, the Hotel and Spa are perfectly located within six acres of tranquil grounds populated with landscaped gardens and mature woodland. Brooks Restaurant's modern Irish cuisine with 'contemporary twists' is always fantastic, with an emphasis on seasonal, local produce. Try the 'Freshly Shucked Oysters', which are served with a 'twist of lime' or the 'Honey Roasted Silverhill Duck'. If dining al fresco is to your liking you could try their latest addition 'The Courtyard' and enjoy the beautifully landscaped gardens while you enjoy a good Irish breakfast, a long, leisurely lunch or even a casual bite in the early evening. The quality is second to none wherever you are in Ballygarry!

Rooms: 64 ensuite. Double from €150. Single from €100. Family from €185.
Prices: Lunch Main course from €9.95. Set Sunday lunch €25. Dinner main course from €20. Bar snack main course from €12.50. House wine from €20.
Food served: Bar -12.30-21.30 daily. Restaurant 18.30-21.30 daily.
Closed: 23-28 Dec.incl.
Cuisine: Traditional with a contemporary twist.
Other Points: Garden. Children welcome. Car park. Library. Licence for Civil Weddings. Winner - Hotel of the Year 2005. Spa Facilities.
Directions: Situated off the main Tralee to Killarney road, 5 minutes from Tralee town centre and 10 minutes from Kerry International Airport.

125

Ireland South

www.goodfoodireland.ie

Tralee Co Kerry

Restaurant David Norris
Town centre restaurant

Ivy House, Ivy Terrace, Tralee, Co Kerry
Tel. +353(0)66 7185654
Email. restaurantdavidnorris@eircom.net

It's easy to sense the personal touch here. Chef/proprietor David Norris sources meat and fish from Kerry and Cork, ingredients are organic where possible, all breads, chutneys and jams are made in-house, and David grows all the herbs himself. Starters include goats' cheese mousse with poached pears, crisp wontons and walnuts. You might follow with handmade potato and Parmesan ravioli served with chargrilled leeks and wild mushrooms, or maybe glazed spring lamb shank with date mash and orange and raisin jus, and end with coconut and lime parfait, pineapple wafers and spiced pineapple coulis. The global wine list shows great care in both selection and description. Across from Siamsa Tíre and the Brandon Hotel, it's ideal for a pre-theatre stop-off for the great-value early bird menu at €25.95 (5.30-7pm, Tues-Fri). If you're anywhere near Kerry, this is the place to go.

Prices: Dinner main course from €18.50. House wine from €19.95
Food Served: 17.00-22.00 Tue-Fri. 18.30-22.00 Sat.
Closed: Sun and Mon. One week in Jan, one week in Feb.
Cuisine: Modern Irish.
Directions: Facing Siamsa Tíre in Tralee Town.

Tralee Co Kerry

The Tankard Bar & Restaurant
Coastal bar and restaurant

Kilfenora, Fenit, Tralee, Co Kerry
Tel. +353(0)66 7136164/7136349
Email. tankard@eircom.net

A long established and well-respected family run pub and restaurant, perfectly situated on Tralee Bay, with fantastic food and wine menus, sounds hard to beat and this one definitely comes up trumps! The Tankard, which claims to be the oldest pub in the area, has been in the family for a few hundred years and is owned by Jerry and Mary O'Sullivan. With a choice between a bar menu for those in a casual mood, which has a range of salads, sandwiches, pastas, burgers, steaks and fish dishes, as well as a children's menu, or if you would like something a bit more upscale, the a la carte restaurant menu equally caters for the seafood or meat lover or indeed the vegetarian! Favouring local and organic produce where possible, the seafood lover could go for oysters from the oyster bed just in front of the pub, followed by the house "speciality" - The Seafood Symphony (for 2) which consists of half lobster, scallops, prawns, mussels, grilled oysters, crab claws, salmon and plaice. For those who would rather not go in that direction, there is a boule of mozzarella served with black and white Clonakilty pudding, apple compote and crisp leaves or perhaps for mains the rosemary encrusted lamb rack, ovenbaked and served with a honey and rosemary sauce. They have a comprehensive wine list with a very good half bottle selection for the more modest consumer!

Prices: Lunch main course from €11.75. Dinner main course from €13.75. Bar snack from €3.50. House wine from €17.
Food served: 12.00-22.00 daily.
Cuisine: Modern Irish.
Other Points: Children welcome. Car park. Garden. Open Christmas Day.
Directions: 7km on the bayside of Tralee, a bright yellow building.

Ireland South

for online reservations

Muckross House, Gardens & Traditional Farms   *Place to Visit*

The National Park, Killarney, Co. Kerry
Tel. +353(0)64 31440
Fax. +353(0)64 33926
Email. muckrosshouse@duchas.ie
www.muckross-house.ie

Situated close to the shores of Muckross Lake, amidst the beautiful scenery of Killarney National Park, the house is the focal point within the Park and is the ideal base from which to explore it's terrain. The elegantly furnished rooms portray the lifestyles of the landed gentry, while downstairs in the basement, experience the working conditions of the servants employed in the house. From April to July Muckross Gardens are spectacularly adorned with the red and pink flowers of mature Rhodendrons. Take a stroll down memory lane at Muckross Traditional Farms, which recreate and portray the traditional farming methods and way of life, of a typical local, rural community of the 1930's.

Admission charged to House and Traditional Farms. Gardens Free.

Other Points
Multi-lingual Guided Tours, Walled Garden Centre, Mucros Craft Shop and Workshops including Mucros Weaving and Mucros Pottery and Garden Restaurant.

Hours
Open daily all year round (except the Christmas period).
Muckross House:
Daily Jul to Aug 9.00 - 19.00
Daily Sep to Jun 9.00 - 18.00
Traditional Farms:
Weekends & bank holidays
Mar 20 to Apr 29
Daily May to Oct

Killimer-Tarbert Car Ferry   *Place to Visit*

Shannon Ferry Group Limited
Killimer, Kilrush, Co Clare
Tel. +353 (0)65 905 3124
Fax. +353 (0)65 905 3125
Email. enquiries@shannonferries.com
www.shannonferries.com

Killimer-Tarbert Car Ferry, "Bridging the Best of Ireland's West", links the main tourist routes of the West of Ireland from Killimer, Co. Clare to Tarbert, Co. Kerry as part of the N67. With scheduled sailings every day, this pleasant twenty minute journey across the Shannon Estuary will save 85 miles /137 km from ferry terminal to ferry terminal providing a staging point for the many attractions of Clare, Kerry and adjoining counties. Take some time to enjoy our visitor centre, which stocks an extensive range of books, souvenirs, music, tea, coffee, sweets and ice-creams.

Timetable
Service every day of the year except Christmas Day (weather permitting)

1st April to 30th September

	Departure	Mon-Sat	Sun
1st Ferry	Killimer every hour on the hour	7.00 - 21.00	9.00 - 21.00
	Tarbert every hour on the 1/2 hour	7.30 - 21.30	9.30 - 21.30

Mid May - end Septmber (Additional Sailings)

2nd Ferry	Killimer every hour on the 1/2 hour.	10.30 - 17.30	
	Tarbert every hour on the hour.	11.00 - 18.00	

1st October to 31st March

	Departure	Mon-Sat	Sun
1st Ferry	Killimer every hour on the hour	7.00 - 19.00	9.00 - 19.00
	Tarbert every hour on the 1/2 hour	7.30 - 19.30	9.30 - 19.30

Ireland South Touring Route

Look out for......
- Gallweys Chocolates
- Boozeberries Classic Irish Liqueur

Thurles
Inch House

Kilkenny
Lacken House & Restaurant
Marble City Bar
Kilkenny Hibernian Hotel

The Horse & Jockey Inn

Cashel

Cahir
Galtee Mts.

Clonmel
Comeragh Mts.

Grannagh
The Thatch

Ballymacarbry
Glasha Farmhouse

Waterford
Arlington Lodge Country Hse Hotel
The Belfry Hotel
Fitzpatrick's Manor Lodge Restaurant
Gatchell's Restaurant
Waterford Crystal

Dungarvan
Powersfield House

MUST TRY......
Wexford Mussels
Bannow Bay Oysters
Kilmore Quay Prawns
Carne Crab
Dunmore East Fish

MUST TRY......
The Waterford "Blaa."
A distinctive, soft, round white bread bun. Originally introduced by French Hoguenots that settled in Waterford during the 17th century.

128

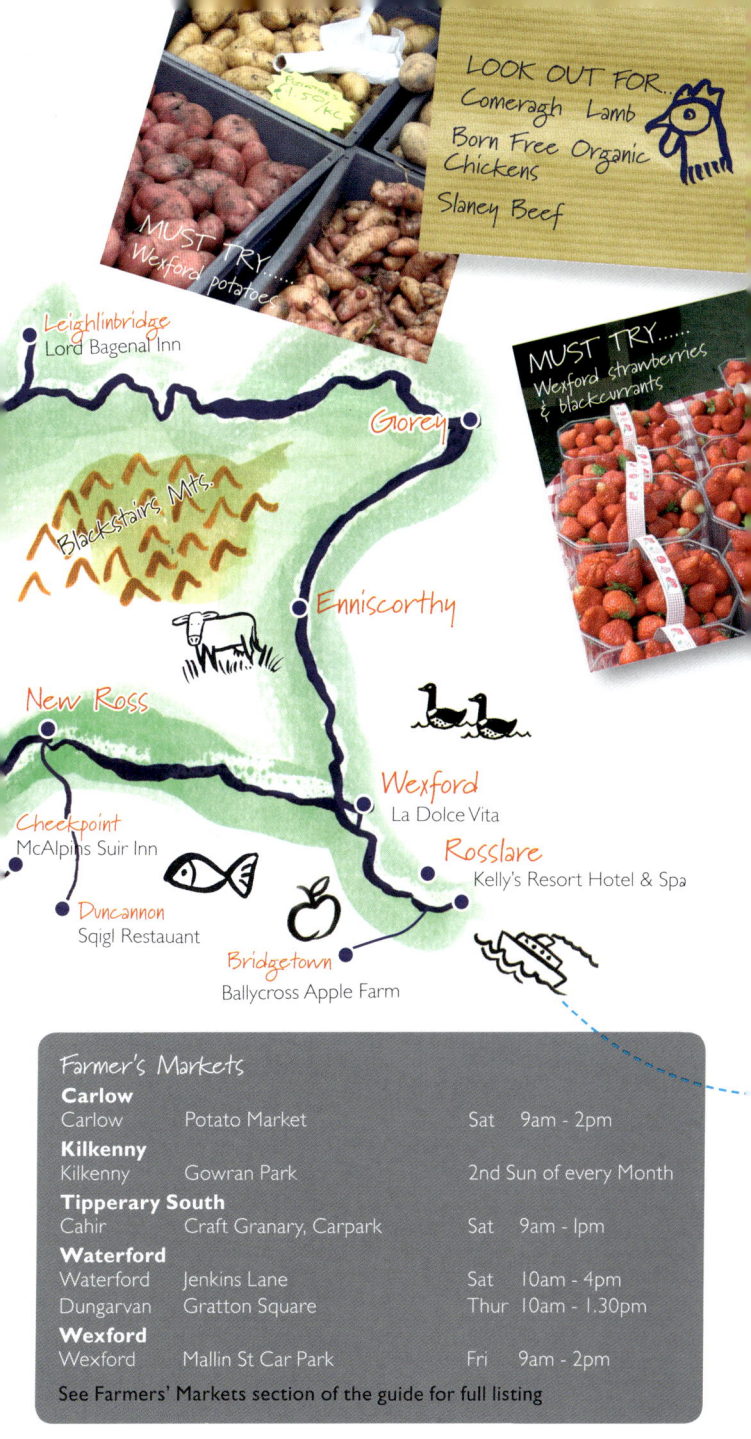

LOOK OUT FOR...
Comeragh Lamb
Born Free Organic Chickens
Slaney Beef

MUST TRY..... Wexford potatoes

MUST TRY..... Wexford strawberries & blackcurrants

Leighlinbridge — Lord Bagenal Inn

Gorey

Blackstairs Mts.

Enniscorthy

New Ross

Wexford — La Dolce Vita

Cheekpoint — McAlpins Suir Inn

Rosslare — Kelly's Resort Hotel & Spa

Duncannon — Sqigl Restauant

Bridgetown — Ballycross Apple Farm

Farmer's Markets

Carlow
| Carlow | Potato Market | Sat | 9am - 2pm |

Kilkenny
| Kilkenny | Gowran Park | | 2nd Sun of every Month |

Tipperary South
| Cahir | Craft Granary, Carpark | Sat | 9am - 1pm |

Waterford
| Waterford | Jenkins Lane | Sat | 10am - 4pm |
| Dungarvan | Gratton Square | Thur | 10am - 1.30pm |

Wexford
| Wexford | Mallin St Car Park | Fri | 9am - 2pm |

See Farmers' Markets section of the guide for full listing

Ireland South

www.goodfoodireland.ie

Kilkenny City

Kilkenny Hibernian Hotel
City centre hotel & restaurant

1 Ormonde Street, Kilkenny,
Tel. +353(0)56 7771888
Email. info@kilkennyhibernianhotel.com
www.kilkennyhibernianhotel.com

This converted Victorian bank in the shadow of Kilkenny castle is a buzzing focal point in this sociable city. It combines vibrant bars and cosy snugs with an atmospheric restaurant, 46 comfortable bedrooms and many original features. The Hibernian Bar with its leather sofas and wooden floors serves a 'Modern Irish' menu throughout the day, while the more upbeat Morrisons is a lively place for a nightcap. The Jacob's Cottage restaurant is an elegant, subtly-lit dining room, serving a range of contemporary dishes using fresh Irish produce, some of which is sourced from the local farmers' organic market. Starters could include Duncannon seafood chowder, followed by marinated haunch of wild venison or Fillet of Irish Angus Beef with a choice of sauces and to finish a selection of Irish farmhouse cheese with crackers, homemade chutney and fruit or for the chocoholics, hazelnut shortbread pots filled with chocolate truffle, rich fudge centre, bouquet of fresh berries and toffee ice cream. The wine list has a good selection from France and the New World. The smartly decorated bedrooms, including penthouses with jacuzzi baths, are all en-suite, with carved mahogany headboards and top-drawer soaps and shampoos.

Rooms: 46 ensuite. Double from €110. Single from €80.
Prices: Lunch main course from €9.95. Set Sunday lunch €22.50. Dinner main course from €17.95. Bar snack from €7.25. House wine from €19.95
Food served: Bar:12.00-20.00 Sun-Thurs. 12.00-17.00 Fri-Sat. Restaurant: 12.30-14.30 & 18.30-22.00 Mon-Sat. 12.30-15.00 & 18.30-21.00 Sun.
Closed: Christmas Eve night & Christmas Day.
Cuisine: Modern Irish.
Other Points: Children welcome. Secure public car park adjacent to hotel.
Directions: From N10 travel to Waterford road roundabout on ring road, take exit to city centre. Hotel is located on corner of Patrick St. and Ormonde St.

Kilkenny City

Marble City Bar
Contemporary city centre pub

66 High Street, Kilkenny
Tel. +353(0)56 7761143
Email. reservations@langtons.ie

Eamon Langton's successful bar in the heart of Kilkenny is hard to miss with its eye-catching, stained-glass window of undulating red and white stripes. This is the most stylish joint in which to enjoy your morning rashers. Come at 10am, though, for the MCB full Irish breakfast, and you may end up staying all day. International hotshot designer, David Collins, has created a striking, low-lit space with brown leather seating opposite a long bar, widening at the rear to accommodate tables. The lack of daylight gives the sense of a cosy microclimate where one could chat, eat and drink all day long. Rub shoulders with a mix of sharply dressed locals and tourists, and enjoy a pint, a hot chocolate or a café latte. Lunch brings bistro-style dishes such as salmon en-croute stuffed with spinach & cream cheese on a chive & Parmesan mash, while there are daily pasta and stir-fry specials. Dinner might include canon of lamb with basil pesto barley risotto and grilled aubergine and to finish Baileys filled profiteroles with chocolate sauce. Service is sleek and attentive.

Prices: Lunch main course from €9. Dinner main course from €11. Bar snack from €4. House wine from €20.
Food served: 10.00-20.30 daily.
Closed: Good Friday and 25 Dec.
Cuisine: Modern Irish.
Directions: On the main shopping street, after the Town Hall, 150 metres on the same side.

Ireland South

Kilkenny City

Lacken House & Restaurant
Victorian house and restaurant

Dublin Road, Kilkenny
Tel. +353(0)56 7761085
Email. info@lackenhouse.ie
www.lackenhouse.ie

If you have it in your head to tour the sunny South East, and particularly take in the vibrant and picturesque 'Creative Heart of Ireland' Kilkenny, then Lacken House is just the place for you. This beautiful Victorian house with ten comfortable bedrooms has been run for the last seven years by the husband & wife team, Trevor Toner and Jackie Kennedy. Their elegant and professionally run restaurant offers the diner a wonderful choice of innovative, modern Irish and European dishes with a strong emphasis on local and seasonal produce. Cheese is sourced from local cheese makers. Fresh fish is delivered daily from the port of Duncannon and fruit and vegetables are purchased locally - with chef Michael Thomas responsible for homemade breads, chutneys, soups, sauces and ice creams. Why not try their acclaimed 'Foie Gras' complemented by a glass of Muscat as the owners recommend. Indeed, a lot of attention has gone into their carefully chosen and comprehensive wine list and this really does not disappoint on any level. If you are in an indecisive mood try the 'Lacken House Platter', which is unusually, but pleasantly, portioned for one person - perfect for sampling a selection of their appetisers. Vegetarian diners need not be concerned as their needs are also met - why not try the 'Truffle roast globe artichoke, sweet potato and smoked gubbeen ravioli, red pepper coulis'. There is attention to detail once again when you visit Lacken House dessert menu. Leave the calorie counting for another day, and try their wonderful 'Chocoholic' - a speciality of the house that is made to order, and consists of home baked chocolate cake, white chocolate mousse, and chocolate crunch ice cream - need we say more!

Rooms: 10 ensuite. Double from €150. Single from €75. Family from €225 (based on 3 sharing). Dinner, bed & breakfast from €125 pps
Prices: Main course dinner from €28.50. Set menu €59. House wine from €21.
Food served: 18.30-21.30 Tue-Sat. 18.00-21.00 Sundays of bank holiday weekends.
Closed: 24-27 December.
Cuisine: Modern Irish, European.
Other Points: Non-smoking house. Children welcome. Car park. Private dining room. Highly Commended - Guesthouse with Restaurant of the Year 2003. Winner - Host of the Year 2005.
Directions: In Kilkenny city on the main Carlow to Dublin road (N10).

Lacken House & Restaurant

Ireland South

www.goodfoodireland.ie

Cashel Co Tipperary

Horse & Jockey Inn
Hotel, restaurant & leisure centre

Near Cashel, Co Tipperary
Tel. +353(0)504 44192
Email. horseandjockeyinn@eircom.net
www.horseandjockeyinn.com

This famous inn at the heart of Ireland's horse country has been trading continuously for over 250 years and is a popular meeting spot for jockeys, trainers and anyone involved in this cherished industry. The interior, which recently underwent extensive renovation, is spacious and welcoming, and the plentiful racing memorabilia contributes to the elegantly sporting atmosphere. The menu reflects the earthy roots of the establishment; a Sunday lunch of prime roast sirloin of beef and Yorkshire pudding followed by sherry trifle will please traditionalists, but there are also appealing chicken, fish and vegetarian options. Elsewhere, classics such as Irish oak smoked salmon salad, duck à l'orange and grilled lamb cutlets provide further robust sustenance. There's a good range of hot sandwiches, including Hot Joint of the Day, and grilled Cashel Blue and ham on homemade soda bread with cranberry preserve. The thirty comfortable, contemporary bedrooms are individually furnished.

Rooms: 30 ensuite. Double from €140. Single from €85. Family from €170.
Prices: Set Sunday lunch €25. Lunch main course from €9.50. Dinner main course from €14.10-€23.80. Bar snack from €7.50. House wine from €16.
Food Served: Daily in bar 10.30-22.00. Lunch last orders 15.30 Mon-Sat. 14.30 Sun. Dinner last orders 21.30 Mon-Sat. 20.30 Sun.
Closed: 25 December.
Cuisine: Traditional Irish & European.
Other Points: Garden. Children welcome. Car park. Gift shop. Leisure centre. Treatment rooms.
Directions: Midway 'tween Cork & Dublin on the N8. Five miles north of Cashel.

At the time of going to print the hotel was due to open a new leisure centre with pool, sauna, steam room, jacuzzi, gym and spa with hydro-therapy pool, together with an additional 35 deluxe bedrooms.

Thurles Co Tipperary

Inch House
Country house and restaurant

Thurles, Co Tipperary
Tel. +353(0)504 51348/51261
Email. mairin@inchhouse.ie
www.inchhouse.ie

Historic Inch House is almost 300 years old, and remained in the same family until it was taken over in 1985 by the current owners, the Egans, who have lovingly restored it. Relax before dinner in the comfortable William Morris-style drawing room, with stained glass windows and an open log fire. The grand dining room has a classic décor, with red walls, polished wooden floor and large picture windows, and serves modern Irish dishes with a European influence. Chef Kieran O'Dwyer has been at Inch House since 1996. Dinner could feature his take on Caesar salad: avocado, bacon and pine nut salad with wholegrain mustard and Caesar dressing. This might be followed with grilled fillets of seabass with nibbed almonds, served with a lemon and pesto butter sauce. A well-annotated international wine list

Rooms: 5 ensuite. Double from €110. Single from €65.
Prices: Set dinner from €47-€50. House wine from €17.
Food served: 19.00-21.30 Tue-Sat.
Closed: One week at Christmas.
Cuisine: Modern Irish.
Other Points: Garden. Car park. Children welcome.
Directions: From Thurles take Nenagh road, travel for 4 miles, pass the "Ragg" and Inch House is on the left 200 yards further on.

offers excellent value for money. Each of the five guest bedrooms has its own colour scheme and is furnished with elegant antiques. The surrounding area boasts views of the Devils Bit mountain and the Glen of Aherlow, and Inch House is convenient for trips to the Rock of Cashel, Cahir Castle and Holycross Abbey.

for online reservations

Ireland South

Ballymacarbry Co Waterford

Glasha Farmhouse
Farmhouse accommodation

Glasha, Ballymacarbry, Via Clonmel,
Co Waterford
Tel.+ 353(0)52 36108
Email.glasha@eircom.net
www.glashafarmhouse.com

Olive and Paddy O'Gorman have run this attractive guesthouse, on a working dairy farm, since 1995, although the place has been in the family for several generations. The nineteenth-century farmhouse has been sensitively modernised, and has a lovely landscaped garden of rose beds and water features. The O'Gormans are excellent hosts, and Olive's homecooking is a real treat. Magnificent breakfasts include scrambled eggs wrapped in smoked salmon and garnished with fresh flowers; pancakes with bacon and maple syrup; farmhouse cheeses; fresh berries and homebaked apple and raisin muffins and a variety of homebaked breads including courgette and walnut bread and cheddar and bacon loaf. There are tea-and-coffee making facilities in the spacious bedrooms, little chocolates to nibble by the bedside and jacuzzi baths in some rooms. The views of the surrounding mountains are stunning. A typical five-course dinner might bring smoked haddock with cream egg sauce, cream of homemade smokey bacon and potato soup, Rack of Comeragh lamb and rosemary sauce, orange gateau and cream, with petit fours and coffee to finish.

Rooms: 8 ensuite. Double from €100. Single from €60. Family from €120.
Prices: Set dinner €25-€35.
Food Served: 19.30-20.00 Mon-Sat.
Closed: 1 Dec - 28 Dec.
Cuisine: Modern Irish.
Other Points: Large garden and patio area. Car park. Children welcome over 12 years old. Winner - Bed & Breakfast of the Year 2005.
Directions: Glasha is situated off the R671 between Clonmel and Dungarvan. There are three signs for Glasha on the R671.

Cheekpoint Co Waterford

McAlpins Suir Inn
Waterside seafood restaurant and bar

Cheekpoint, Co Waterford
Tel. +353(0)51 382220/182
Email. frances@mcalpins.com
www.mcalpins.com

The historic McAlpin's faces the Suir river in the fishing village of Cheekpoint. Dunstan and Mary McAlpin attract big crowds with their fresh seafood. The inn itself goes back to the 17th century, and has been in the McAlpin family since 1971. The smart black and white bar and restaurant keeps an old-world feel on the inside with low ceilings and wooden tables. Try hot smoked mackerel with salad, then the famous seafood pie, with salmon, cod, prawns, shrimps, served with crisp cheese and potato crust. There are options for the non fish-lovers: perhaps pan-fried beef fillet or a vegetarian dish. All meals come with brown soda bread, butter and a side salad. The delicious home-made desserts change daily. The small wine list features New and Old World choices at good value.

Prices: Dinner main course from €12.50. House wine from €16.
Food served: 17.30-21.45 Tue-Sat.
Cuisine: Seafood and meat dishes.
Other Points: Children welcome over six years old. Winner - Dining Pub of the Year 2003.
Directions: From Waterford City follow the signposts to Dunmore East passing the hospital. Continue for two miles until you reach the Passage East turn off; follow signs for Cheekpoint. Continue straight down to the harbour and McAlpin's is on the left hand side facing the river.

Ireland South

www.goodfoodireland.ie

Dungarvan Co Waterford

Powersfield House
Country house bed & breakfast & cookery school

Ballinamuck, Co Waterford
Tel. +353 (0)58 45594
Email. powersfieldhouse@cablesurf.com
www.powersfield.com

With its gracious, Georgian-style lines, lovely mature gardens, on-site cookery school - offering lots of invaluable tips, and location just outside Dungarvan in one of the prettiest and most golfer-friendly areas of West Waterford, Eunice Power's delightful, five-year-old guesthouse boasts many of the comforts of a much grander establishment. Its warm, inviting lounge is antiques-furnished and decorated in restful beige and gold, while each of the 6 light-filled bedrooms are individually designed using tasteful colours with fresh floral arrangements. Smart bathrooms feature fluffy towels, spacious showers (some have baths), and a tempting basket of toiletry "goodies." Don't miss Eunice's delectable breakfasts and dinners, which might include Greek yoghurt with granola, bananas and Cappagh Runny Honey; local

Rooms: 6 ensuite, Double from €110. Single from €60. Family from €120.
Prices: Set dinner from €28-€38.
Food served: Dinner by arrangement for residents.
Closed: Christmas to mid Jan.
Cuisine: Contemporary Irish food, focusing on local organically grown ingredients.
Other Points: Non-smoking bedrooms. Garden. Children welcome. Car park. Cookery school.
Directions: Take the main Killarney road R672 from Dungarvan, second turn left, first house on the right.

Helvic smoked salmon with scrambled eggs; mussels and monkfish in a Thai broth with wild rice; and hot chocolate pudding with vanilla ice cream. Powersfield House offers a great escape at excellent value.

Grannagh Castle Via Waterford

The Thatch
Country pub

Grannagh Castle, Kilmacow,
via Waterford, Co Waterford
Tel. +353(0)51 872876

David Ryan's small, thatched pub is scenically situated opposite the seventeenth-century Grannagh Castle, on the banks of the river Suir, just two miles from Waterford City. Inside, it's a cosy spot, offering traditional music once a week, live music at weekends and decent pub food, prepared fresh every day using Irish produce. A blackboard lists daily specials, and homemade starters might include paté of the day with melba toast and Cumberland sauce, or soup with freshly baked brown bread. There's a choice of steaks, including prime Irish sirloin, and red meat is the theme of the Thatch Mixed Grill, a generous plate of bacon, egg, sausage, tomato, black and white pudding, steak and potato cake; smaller appetites can take on the Mini Grill. Fish of the day comes with Thatch salad and baked potato, and there's a range of sandwiches and paninis, including a vegetarian special of roast pepper, sun-dried tomato,

Prices: Lunch main course from €9. Bar snack from €3.50. Dinner main course from €11.50. House wine from €16.
Opening hours: 10.30-23.30 Mon-Thur, 10-30-00.30 Fri & Sat, 12.30-23.00 Sun.
Food served: Morning coffee 10.30-12.30. Lunch 12.30-15.00. Bar menu 15.00-21.00.
Closed: Good Friday, 25 December.
Cuisine: Modern & Traditional Irish.
Other Points: Car park. Beer garden.
Directions: Located two miles from Waterford City on the Limerick road opposite the River Suir and Grannagh Castle.

Cashel Blue, pesto and mayo, with many familiar dishes such as soup of the day, omelettes, salads and open sandwiches also available.

for online reservations **Ireland South**

Lismore Co Waterford

Barça Wine & Tapas Bar
Wine bar and restaurant

Main Street, Lismore, Co Waterford
Tel. +353(0)58 53810
Email. barcawine@eircom.net

Barca is a smart, modern wine and tapas bar, but also much more. Owners Ciara and Jane Gormley place their emphasis on quality ingredients, organic where possible. Organic salad leaves and vegetables are grown in nearby Glenribbon, and the Gormleys plan to grow some of their own soon. They use beef from Lismore butcher Michael McGrath, a family-run operation that has raised their own cattle for generations. Another famous supplier is Cork-based Frank Hederman, who sends Barca his smoked fish. Ahern's organic chickens come from outside Lismore. But as well as local produce, customers get a taste of Spain: Barca imports Spanish cured meats and olives from specialist Spanish companies. For lunch, try the fish cake or spinach tortellini. The restaurant is ideal if some of your companions just want nibbles but others are ravenous. The tapas menu includes hummus with cumin toasts, marinated anchovies or chorizo hash browns. Dinner is full of variety, with weekly seasonal specials in addition to the menu. Chef Debbie Shaw could offer main courses such as pan-fried seabass adobe on a bed of rocket, and tempting favourites such as rhubarb and apple crumble with home-made custard.

Prices: Lunch main course from €7.50. Bar snack from €3.50. Dinner main course from €12.50. House wine from €19.
Opening hours: 11.00-late Tue-Sat. 12.00-22.00 Sun.
Food served: 12.30-14.30 & 18.00-22.00 Tue-Sat. Sunday Brunch 12.30-16.00. Tapas 16.00-20.00.
Closed: January. Generally closed Mon but subject to seasonal changes. Please check in advance.
Cuisine: Tapas and continental.
Other Points: Garden. Winner - Special Award 2005. Regular wine tastings or special event evenings - enquire in advance. Winner - Wine List of the Year 2006.
Directions: Barça is on the main street in Lismore, which is on the N72 Waterford to Killarney road.

The international wine list features ports and sherries by the glass, which you can sip by the fireplace. choice of cavas, ports and sherries.

135

Ireland South

www.goodfoodireland.ie

Waterford City

Arlington Lodge Country House Hotel
Georgian hotel and restaurant

John's Hill, Waterford
Tel. +353(0)51 878584
Email. info@arlingtonlodge.com
www.arlingtonlodge.com

When Arlington Lodge was built in 1760, it was in the heart of the country. Of course, over the years, the city has come to meet it, but the house retains its private parkland setting in the grounds of St John's College, so it offers the benefits of country life on the city's doorstep, a real oasis. Originally the home of the Paul family of Waterford merchants, Maurice Keller opened for business in 2001 after careful restoration, and has been making his mark in the south-east since then with this Georgian gem. Individually decorated bedrooms are furnished with antiques, all feature king-or queen-sized beds, and some have four-posters and fireplaces. Great emphasis is placed on fresh, local produce in the stylish Robert Paul restaurant. Here the à la carte dinner menu features Dunmore East scallops tossed in parsley and garlic butter, served in puff pastry shells, followed by Ballykelly blackcurrant granita and grilled Stradbally lobster or slow-braised lamb shank, all presented with flair. For dessert there's the tempting mille feuille of chestnut mousse and nougatine tuile with hazelnut coulis. Maurice's attention to detail extends from his warm welcome to the special wine list he has built up, influenced by his own choices as well as those of customers, and the many independent producers he has met. Freshly prepared steak and seafood are served in the cosy red William Morris bar and you can enjoy afternoon tea in the drawing room. Breakfast at Arlington Lodge brings fresh fruit and fruit compote, home-made breads and jams, the full Irish breakfast and the special Waterford Blaa, a locally produced bun, toasted and served with poached eggs and melted Cheddar: delicious.

Rooms: 20 ensuite. Double from €150. Single from €110.
Prices: Dinner main course from €23.50. Set four course early evening menu-€28.50. Bar snack from €4.50. House wine from €19.
Food served: Restaurant 18.30-21.00 Mon-Sat. Bar 12.00-20.00 daily.
Closed: 25-27 Dec.
Cuisine: Modern Irish. Seafood and steak specialities.
Other Points: 5 mins. walk from city centre. Garden. Car park. Winner - Award for Excellence 2002.
Directions: Go over the bridge in Waterford, turn left down the quay. At third set of traffic lights from the Tower Hotel turn left. Continue to next set of lights, go straight through up John's Hill for approx. half a mile, the hotel is on your right. From Cork, straight through roundabout just after Waterford Crystal, take a right turn at the second set of lights straight up to John's Hill and at the lights turn left.

Arlington Lodge Country House Hotel

for online reservations **Ireland South**

Waterford City

Fitzpatrick's Manor Lodge Restaurant
City centre restaurant

Manor Lodge, Cork Road, Waterford
Tel. +353(0)51 378851
Email. fitzrestaurant@iol.ie
www.fitzpatricksmanorlodge.com

This restaurant, dating back to the Tudor period, was formerly the gate lodge of the Holy Ghost Hospital. The white and grey stone building has a warm interior, with soft yellow walls and wooden floors, and is divided into three sections. Head chef Garett Ryan brings his experience from working in New York's Plaza and Penninsula on 5th Avenue. His à la carte menu features pan-fried crab claws and fillet of beef with red onion marmalade. Fresh fish comes daily from the local port of Dunmore East. The dinner-for-two package, including a bottle of house wine, represents good value at €60. The menu could include smoked chicken risotto, followed by rainbow trout. But either way, save room for one of the stylish desserts made in-house - raspberry mousse, chocolate mocha tart or even passionfruit crème brûlée with macaroons. The international wine list is well annotated.

Prices: Early bird menu nightly to 20.00 (19.00 Sat) - €20. Dinner for two (incl wine) - €60 Excl Sat. À la carte main course from €16.50. House wine from €18.
Food served: 17.00-22.00 Mon-Sat. 17.00-21.00 Sun.
Closed: Good Friday, 24-25 Dec.
Cuisine: Modern Irish with international influences.
Other Points: Garden. Children's menu. Car park.
Directions: On the Tramore/Cork road (N25) in Waterford city.

Waterford City

Gatchell's Restaurant at Waterford Crystal
Daytime café and restaurant

Kilbarry, Waterford
Tel. +353(0)51 332575
Email.visitorreception@waterford.ie
www.waterfordvisitorcentre.com

Nicky O'Brien's restaurant, inside the sleek, modern Waterford Crystal visitors' centre, is named after Johnathan Gatchell, the original owner of Waterford Glasshouse in the 1800s. It serves traditional Irish food to the steady stream of guests who tour the bustling factory next door. The large, airy space is impressively contemporary in feel, and illuminated by natural light pouring through floor-to-ceiling windows. Everything is made on the premises and sourced locally where possible; vegetables come from a farm in Annestown, fish from Kilmore Quay and daily fresh Waterford 'Blas' from a nearby bakery. The concise menu brings soups such as Irish potato or turnip and bacon, while main courses include glazed loin of bacon with mustard mashed potato, cabbage and parsley sauce, Irish stew, and beef, Guinness and orange casserole.

Prices: Lunch main course from €9.75. House Wine from €5.
Food served: 8.30-17.30 daily from 18 Mar to 31 Oct. 9.00-16.30 daily from 1 Nov-16 March. Breakfast and afternoon tea served.
Closed: Christmas & St Patrick's Day.
Cuisine: Modern Irish.
Other Points: Children welcome, Car park.
Directions: Gatchell's Restaurant is located inside Waterford Crystal Visitor Centre, close to WIT on the main Cork Road (N25).

There's a fish option of salmon and prawn fishcake, and desserts such as Chocolate and Baileys roulade and rhubarb and orange crumble.

Ireland South

www.goodfoodireland.ie

Waterford City

Restaurant Chez K's
City centre restaurant

20-21 William Street, Waterford
Tel. +353 (0)51 844180
Email. info@chez-ks.com
www.chez-ks.com

Niall and Maria Edmondson have created a relaxing, ambient space for their contemporary style restaurant. The attractive dining room, complete with piano, is popular among locals and visitors alike, including the occasional celebrity. Diners can peruse the menu in the bar, or from comfy sofas in the reception area. Chef Shane Curtin uses only the freshest local seafood from Dunmore East, and all pastries, breads and desserts are homemade. Dinner might bring starters of caramelised scallops with shaved fennel and sweet peppers, lemon oil dressing or wild mushroom and smoked chicken risotto. Eclectic main courses include panfried black sole cooked on the bone with king tiger prawns, tomato, coriander and lime butter or for vegetarians Mediterranean vegetable quesadillas, guacamole and sour cream. Steaks from the grill are served with horseradish mash. All main courses are served with organic seasonal vegetables. Sweet treats include homemade chocolate chip cookies with vanilla ice cream and Valhrona warm chocolate sauce or Bailey's cheesecake with Amarula cream and to round off your evening there is a selection of house cocktails available.

Prices: Dinner main course from €18.25. House wine from €21.50. Early evening Menu available daily from 17.30-18.50.
Food served: 17.30-22.00 Mon-Sat. 16.00-21.00 Sun.
Closed: Middle 2 weeks of January.
Cuisine: Contemporary Irish, French and European flavours.
Other Points: Children welcome. Pianist every Saturday night.
Directions: Turn left at Tower Hotel to Dunmore East. The restaurant is located 400 yards on the left.

138

for online reservations — **Ireland South**

Waterford City

The Belfry Hotel
City centre hotel

Conduit Lane, Waterford
Tel. + 353(0)51 844800
Email. info@belfryhotel.ie
www.belfryhotel.ie

This comfortable, modern hotel in the centre of Waterford is owned and managed by the Reid family. It stands on the former grounds of Blackfriars Abbey, hence its name, and the smart cream and black exterior blends sympathetically with the surrounds. Inside, the hotel is decorated in low-key contemporary style, with 49 spacious ensuite bedrooms fully equipped with all mod-cons including internet access, satellite tv, large beds and bright, modern bathrooms. The Chapter House bar, with its stylish pillars of exposed brick, is a congenial place to meet for a drink; it also serves a tempting lunch and menu of dependable favourites. There's seafood chowder, or the hotel's homemade soup, and a good range of toasted sandwiches and panninis. More robust dishes include joint of the day, bangers and mash and fisherman's pie, as well as homemade lasagne. There are hard-to-resist desserts such as warm orange and chocolate chip bread and butter pudding. Dinner in the hotel's restaurant might include warm cajun salad or garlic and herb coated mushrooms with mains of fillet or sirloin steak, oven baked fillet of chicken or pan fried fillet of salmon with cherry tomatoes, red onion and basil compote, followed by chocolate biscuit cake and cream or bread and butter pudding with vanilla custard.

Rooms: 49 ensuite. Double from €100. Single from €75. Family room - rates on request.
Prices: Lunch main course from €8.50. Dinner main course from €14.95. Bar snack from €4.50. House wine from €16.50.
Hours: Bar 10.30-23.30. 10.30-00.30 Fri-Sat. 11.30-23.00 Sun.
Food served: Bar food 12.00-21.00 Sun-Thur. 12.00-19.00 Fri-Sat. Restaurant 18.30-21.30 Fri-Sat.
Closed: 24-30th December.
Cuisine: Modern Irish.
Other Points: Children welcome.
Directions: Follow the N25 along the quay, the hotel is located in Conduit Lane which is almost directly opposite the clock tower on the quay.

Symbols

- Accommodation
- Restaurant
- Café
- Pub/Bar
- Daytime opening only
- Deli
- Wine
- Bakery
- Gourmet/Farm Shop
- Leisure Centre/Spa
- CS Craft Shop
- VC Visitor Centre
- FP Food Producer

Good Food Ireland Awards

- 2002 Award Winner
- 2003 Award Winner
- 2004 Award Winner
- 2005 Award Winner
- 2006 Award Winner

Ireland South

Waterford Crystal

Place to Visit

Kilbarry, Waterford City, Co Waterford
Tel. +353(0)51 332500
Fax. +353(0)51 332716
Email. visitorreception@waterford.ie
www.waterfordvisitorcentre.com

Waterford City is the home of Waterford Crystal manufacturing plant and Visitor Centre, nestling on the South East coast of Ireland, The Visitor Centre has become one of the most popular tourist venues in the country, and its manufacturing plant gives visitors an opportunity to see first hand how Waterford Crystal is crafted, from molten crystal to the finished masterpiece.

The factory tour begins with a 'Living with Waterford' presentation, a short preview of Waterford's manufacturing and its products. The video presentation will have given you some idea of what to expect, but nothing compares with the atmosphere of the furnace room; the noise, the air, the heat and the activity. You will see red-hot molten crystal take shape, in a miracle of light, heat and skill. Watch carefully as our craftspeople transform glowing balls of crystal into elegant bowls & vases.

Your guide will then take you through our World Sports Dept. where a selection of our current most prized trophies are on display. There are many opportunities on this tour to have your photography taken, please remember to bring your camera. As you move to the cutting area, the atmosphere changes from the roar of furnaces to the whirr of diamond-tipped cutting wheels. It's an exciting sound which becomes all the more fascinating when you see the steady hand of our Master cutters. At the end of your factory tour, it's time to step back in time to meet our Master craftsmen in person and see them exercise their skills close up. The Workshop has been specially created to provide a relaxed atmosphere for our visitors to meet these Masters.

The Waterford Crystal Gallery is home to the world's largest display of Waterford Crystal, beautifully displayed in a bright, elegant showroom. In addition, you can see displays of Wedgwood, John Rocha at Waterford Crystal and Marquis by Waterford Crystal. The Gallery also includes a Craft and Jewellery Gift Store. We look forward to welcoming you to Waterford Crystal.

Other Points

Guided Tours, Craft & Jewellery Store, Restaurant and Car & Coach Parking. For group reservations please contact reception.

Hours

Visitor Centre Retail
Jan to Feb: daily 9.00 - 17.00
Mar to Oct: daily 8.30 - 18.00
Nov to Dec: daily 9.00 - 17.00
Factory Tours
Jan to Feb: Mon - Fri 9.00 - 15.15
Mar to Oct: daily 8.30 - 16.15
Nov to Dec: Mon - Fri 9.00 - 15.15

Admission Charged

Directions

Our visitor centre is approximately a five-minute drive from Waterford City on the N25 to Cork.

for online reservations

Ireland South

Bridgetown Co Wexford

Ballycross Apple Farm
Apple farm, farm shop & café

Bridgetown, Co Wexford
Tel. +353(0)53 9135160
Email. cve@indigo.ie

There is no doubting the main focus at Ballycross - apples don't get much more of a star billing than they do here. The orchards are a delight, but so too are the farm buildings with their well manicured courtyard, farm shop and café. The Irish climate is particularly well suited to growing apples and Ballycross does it all with considerable style. The apples here eat well and make the most fantastic juice - a good balance of sweetness with acidity and a depth of flavour not always found in other juices. You may choose to settle in for a glass of well chilled juice and a light lunch or to take a bottle or two home. A case is to be recommended, a bottle never quite seems to be enough.

Opening Hours: 2pm-6pm Sat&Sun.
Closed: Mid Feb-mid Aug.
Directions: Coming from Wexford in to Bridgetown go straight, through the railway crossing and take the next right. Ballycross Apple Farm is the 2nd turn on the right.

Duncannon Co Wexford

Sqigl Restaurant
Seaside restaurant

Quay Road, Duncannon, New Ross,
Co Wexford
Tel. +353(0)51 389188
Email. sqiglrestaurant@eircom.net

Located in a converted granite stone barn in the centre of Duncannon village, Sqigl (pronounced Squiggle) Restaurant is a modern and bright, contemporary restaurant run by Cindy Roche. The menu reads very well with an emphasis on seasonal products and local ingredients and particularly specialises in seafood - 'garlic marinated Wexford prawns served with warm asparagus and saffron aioli' or 'creamy Duncannon seafood chowder'. Those leaning towards a vegetarian option could opt for 'warm sautéed Wexford wild mushrooms on a bed of mixed salad and raspberry dressing' and 'mixed vegetable cutlets served with a creamy mushroom and spinach sauce'. Not forgetting meat and poultry lovers, their needs are also met with 'tournedos of prime Irish beef fillet, Portobello mushrooms, sautéed spinach, port wine reduction and horse radish cream'. At Sqigl, they grow their own herbs, bake their own breads and make all their own chutneys and marmalades so quality and freshness remain high throughout. Their value menu includes a short but well picked and very well priced wine selection, which is also to be commended.

Prices: Dinner main course from €18.50. House wine from €15.50.
Food served: 19.00-21.00 Wed-Sat off season and Tues-Sat during summer.
Closed: Good Friday. 24-26 December. Closed for 6 weeks from 3 January.
Cuisine: Modern Irish & Seafood.
Other points: Al fresco dining on balcony weather permitting.
Directions: From Wexford take the R733 (22 miles). From New Ross take the R733 (14 miles).

141

Ireland South

Rosslare Co Wexford

Kelly's Resort Hotel & Spa
Resort hotel and spa

Rosslare, Co Wexford
Tel. +353(0)53 9132114
Email. kellyhot@iol.ie
www.kellys.ie

This has been a family-run hotel for four generations, since it was founded in 1895. Despite its extensive leisure facilities, the hotel manages to retain a personal touch, under owner/manager Bill Kelly. It is situated along five miles of safe sandy beaches, and guests return regularly because there really is something for everybody at Kelly's. One recent addition to the facilities is the tranquil SeaSpa, offering everything from relaxing facials and massage to seaweed baths and aqua aerobics. Activity midweek breaks in spring and autumn include wine-tasting, cookery demonstrations, gardening and painting workshops. There is also a supervised playroom. Accommodation is of a high standard: the bright, spacious bedrooms are luxuriously decorated, and many have sea views. The food is but one of several ways to pamper yourself at Kelly's. Beaches restaurant head chef Jim Aherne may treat you to his terrine of Wexford game, followed by grilled ostrich steaks on braised lentils with mushroom and Madeira sauce, or perhaps grilled Kilmore shark with herb butter, and for dessert, dark chocolate and praline Feuillantine with vanilla custard. The extensive lunch menu could include broccoli and smoky bacon soup and grilled, home-made turkey burgers with onions, mushrooms and French fries. The more casual La Marine, run by chef Eugene Callaghan, offers lunch and snacks throughout the day, and dinner here might bring prawn and crab cake with baby spinach and Oriental dressing, followed by fillet of hake with

Rooms: 117 ensuite. Double from €175. Single from €88. Family room - rates on request.
Prices: Set lunch €25. Set dinner €45. Lunch main course from €16. Dinner main course from €22. Bar snack from €7. House wine from €22.
Hours: Bar 11.00-23.30. 11.00-00.30 Fri-Sat. 12.00-23.00 Sun.
Food served: Restaurant 13.00-14.00 & 19.30-21.00 daily.
Bar food 12.00-17.00. 12.00-16.00 Sun.
Cuisine: Irish, French and Italian.
Closed: Mid Dec-mid Feb.
Other Points: SeaSpa-thermal spa, holistic treatment and pure relaxation. Health and fitness programmes - a range of indoor and outdoor pursuits. Children welcome. Tennis courts. Snooker, bowls, croquet. Car park. Two indoor swimming pools, sauna and steam room. Three local golf courses. Car park. Garden. Special activity breaks. Winner-Hotel of the Year 2003. Winner - Wine List of the Year 2005.
Directions: Follow the N25 from Rosslare Europort (5 miles) turning off at the sign for Rosslare Strand. The hotel is located in the centre of the holiday resort.

spring vegetables and orange salsa cotta with fruit salad. Wines are directly imported from top French and Italian producers.

Wexford Town

La Dolce Vita
Daytime Italian café, restaurant, deli and wine bar

6/7 Trimmers Lane, Wexford
Tel. +353(0)53 9170806
Email. bigpons@eircom.net

Is La Dolce Vita really the best Italian restaurant in the country? The locals certainly seem to think so - you need to get there early to beat them to a table at lunchtime. With its green, white and red canopies, it's easy to spot. Ligurian-born Roberto Pons and his wife Celine keep things simple inside, with light wooden furniture and shelves stacked with pasta, oils and chocolates. You can also take away salamis, Parmesans and best of all, the home-made tiramisu. The menu will help you brush up on your Italian, but you do get English descriptions. Share an antipasto misto before your spinach and ricotta gnocchi, or follow home-made Italian bread with the great-value grilled fillet of sole with salad. The wine list - Italian, naturally - will get you in relaxed mood.

Prices: Main course from €8.50. House wine from €14.50.
Food served: 9.00-17.30 Mon-Sat. Hot food 12.00-16.00
Closed: Sundays. Closed Christmas for 4 days.
Cuisine: Italian.
Other Points: Children welcome. Winner - Café Restaurant of the Year 2005.
Directions: Located off Main Street, facing ruin of Selskar Abbey.

Of course, not everyone has the luxury of being free to drink a bottle of wine with lunch, so La Dolce Vita has no fewer than 14 interesting choices by the glass. Buon appetito!

Kelly's Resort Hotel & Spa

Cottage Delight

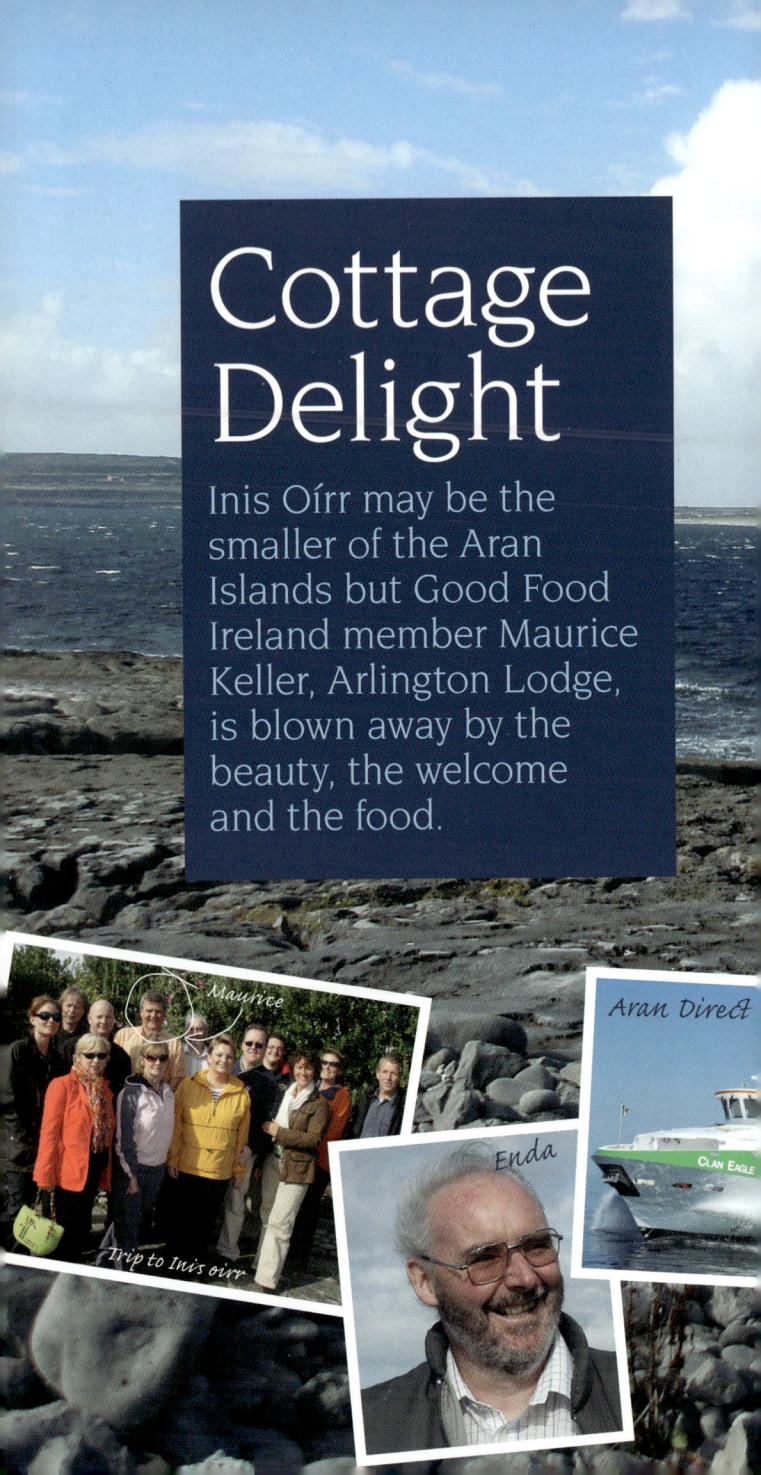

Inis Oírr may be the smaller of the Aran Islands but Good Food Ireland member Maurice Keller, Arlington Lodge, is blown away by the beauty, the welcome and the food.

Trip to Inis oirr — Maurice

Enda

Aran Direct — Clan Eagle

Rossaveal looked brilliant. If only because we were finally there after five and a half hours in the car. It was 5.30pm and the dusk was falling. Karen from Aran Direct, the new ferry company, lifted our spirits and we all felt excited about our island venture.

Aboard the ferry all seemed so different. This was my first time to Inis Oírr, the smaller of the three Aran Islands. The group for the trip, 15 in all, were all hoteliers or restaurateurs. We alighted on the pier at Inis Oírr to be greeted by an excited Enda Conneely with his magical blue van. Luggage aboard, itineraries handed out - we set off on foot to our various abodes for the night with instructions to meet for dinner at 8.30 in Enda's restaurant, Fisherman's Cottage.

I walked up the hill and the higher I went the more I had a sense of the beauty and difference of being on an island as the stone walls outlined the tiny fields and dropped away to the Atlantic Ocean and the Clare coastline in the distance. In that moment I understood the pride of the islanders.

And so it began, a brief introduction and a welcome by Enda and his wife Marie. It was obvious he loves food, loves good food and talked with passion of fishing in the morning and cooking with local vegetables in the evenings. A glass of wine or sherry followed, all very genteel, which quickly went out the window as we sat down at the dinner table.

What an experience - we were here to sample the best of the Aran Island's local food. Introduced by Enda course by course we started with Kombu Consomme, a revelation with a bonus and a description of all the nutrients it contained - a healthy start.

Local crab meat on potato cakes with chilli jam followed and then an introduction to the main local delicacy wrasse which came as brandade of salt wrasse with Parmesan. Bowls of salad and the most wonderful homemade soda breads followed.

I also tasted limpets for the first time, cooked with garlic. They were very pleasing. Enda also served dulse, a type of seaweed which was extremely good and cooked like I had never tasted before. A little drop of Pouilly Fuisse or red Bordeaux, Chateau Passe Craby accompanied.

The conversations around the table concentrated on food and the wonders of what we were eating topped the list. Enda's team never tired as they told us about traditions like how to eat our next course, salted wrasse with boiled potatoes and onion sauce. The secret was to eat the three ingredients together from a communal bowl using your fingers. Mixed reaction; different, striking but always interesting.

Strips of pink lamb with a selection of summer leaves tested our appetites and finally an Aran apple tart with an amazing blackberry coulis to finish. The dinner was a triumph.

Slowly the party made their way to Neds, pints of Guinness and various other concoctions flowed. Neill and Roisin McGrory, from McGrory's in Culdaff with fiddle and guitar accompanied by Patrick, a friend of Enda's from Inis Meáin on the whistle provided the entertainment, and what an evening ensued. Mirco from Farmgate Café in Cork city sang his mother's favourite song

147

Fisherman's Cottage

Dinner Menu
Local Aran Specialties
On request in advance for groups

Consommé with Kombu, Jamari & Lemon

Aran Potato Cakes with Fresh Crab & Chilli Jam

Limpets with Garlic

Brandade of Salt Wrasse with Parmesan & Salad

Boiled Aran Potatoes, Salted Wrasse &
Sweet Onion Sauce

Dulse

Connemara Lamb with Wild Garlic, Rosemary
& Mashed Aran Potatoes

Aran Apple Tart with Blackberry Coulis

in Italian and brought tears to our eyes. Songs and stories went on into the small hours and really the evening ended too quickly. Through a haze we set off into the darkness to find our beds.

Monday morning, sun blistering down, we wandered sheepishly to Enda's meeting room for a 10.30 rendezvous and a hearty breakfast. The session was a discussion on food, a topic we are all passionate about. A coffee break with warm homemade scones, tea brack, crab apple jelly and blackberry jam was followed by a tour of the island and a visit to the basket weavers. Inis Oírr was resplendent in the sunshine and all of us sorry that our stay was not longer.

As I sat in the car and headed east the memories, experiences and meaningful exchanges gave me renewed vigour and fresh ideas to bring home. ■

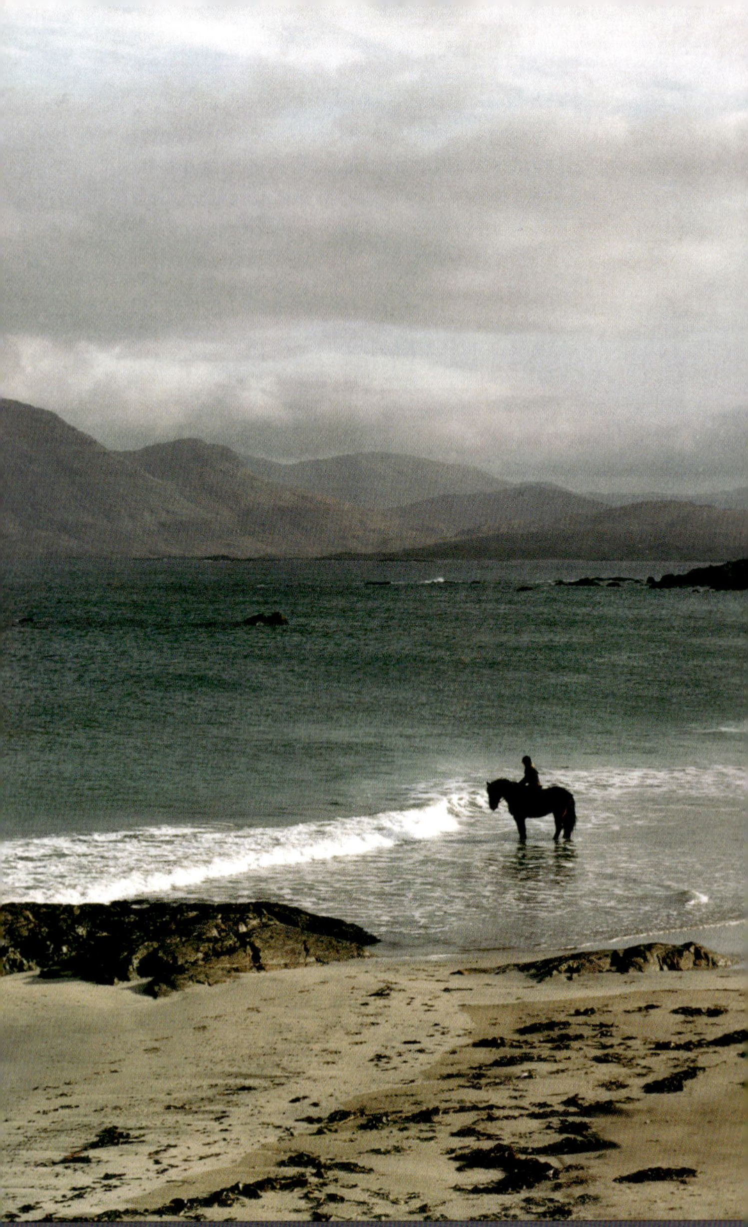

Ireland West

Ireland West Touring Route

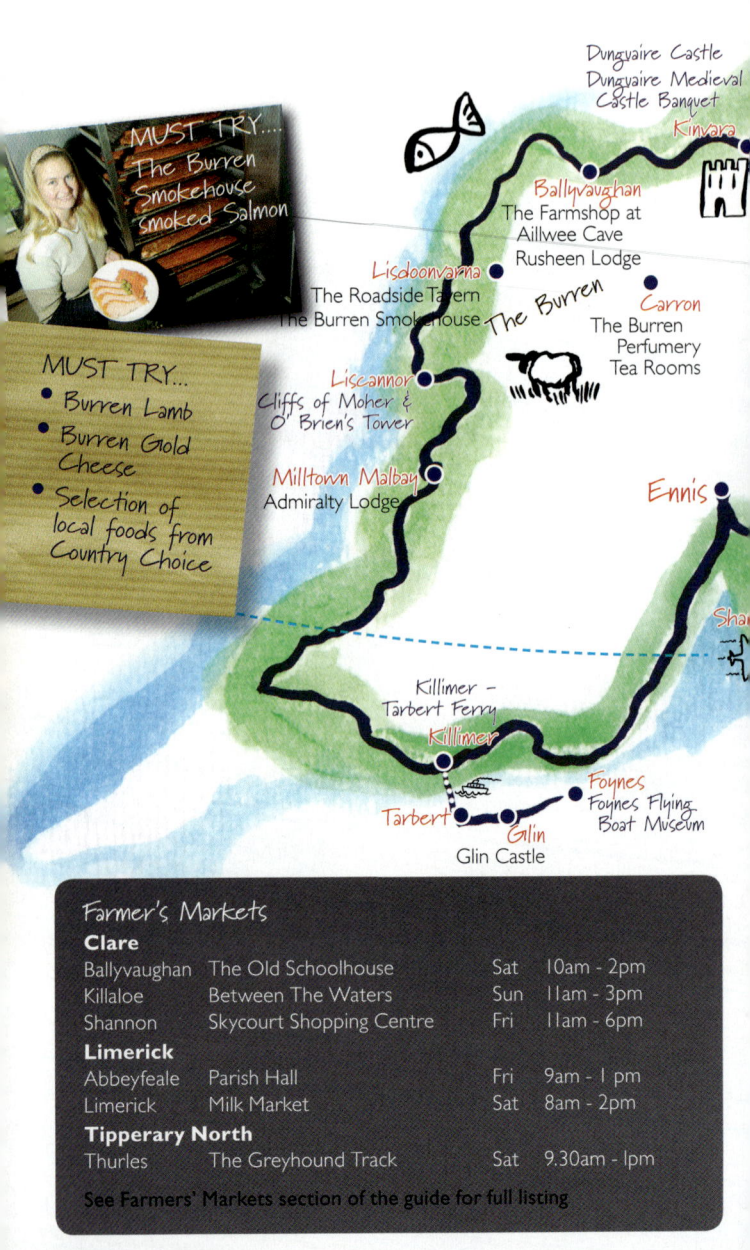

MUST TRY....
The Burren Smokehouse smoked Salmon

MUST TRY...
- Burren Lamb
- Burren Gold Cheese
- Selection of local foods from Country Choice

Dunguaire Castle
Dunguaire Medieval Castle Banquet
Kinvara

Ballyvaughan
The Farmshop at Aillwee Cave
Rusheen Lodge

Lisdoonvarna
The Roadside Tavern
The Burren Smokehouse

The Burren

Carron
The Burren Perfumery Tea Rooms

Liscannor
Cliffs of Moher & O'Brien's Tower

Milltown Malbay
Admiralty Lodge

Ennis

Shan

Killimer – Tarbert Ferry
Killimer

Tarbert **Glin** **Foynes**
Glin Castle   Foynes Flying Boat Museum

Farmer's Markets

Clare
Ballyvaughan	The Old Schoolhouse	Sat	10am - 2pm
Killaloe	Between The Waters	Sun	11am - 3pm
Shannon	Skycourt Shopping Centre	Fri	11am - 6pm

Limerick
Abbeyfeale	Parish Hall	Fri	9am - 1 pm
Limerick	Milk Market	Sat	8am - 2pm

Tipperary North
Thurles	The Greyhound Track	Sat	9.30am - 1pm

See Farmers' Markets section of the guide for full listing

LOOK OUT FOR......
Mossfield organic cheese

Emma's Café Deli
Birr Castle Demesne
Birr

Gort

Lough Derg

Nenagh
Country Choice

The Gallery Restaurant
Knappogue Medieval CastleBanquet
Knappogue Castle & Walled Gardens
Quin

Kilmurry
Craggaunowen, The Living Past

market-on-Fergus
Ferrygerry Country House

Killaloe
Brian Boru
Heritage Centre

Bunratty
Bunratty Castle &
Folk Park
Bunratty Medieval
Castle Banquet
Bunratty Folk Park
Traditional Irish Night

Limerick
King John's Castle

Bruff
Lough Gur
Visitor Centre

LOOK OUT FOR......
Cocoa Bean Artisan
Chocolates

MUST TRY....
St. Tola Cheese, Inagh Farmhouse

Ireland West

Ballyvaughan Co Clare

Rusheen Lodge
Guesthouse

Ballyvaughan, Co Clare
Tel. +353(0)65 7077092
Email. rusheen@iol.ie
www.rusheenlodge.com

Pretty Rusheen Lodge is set in a valley of the Burren limestone mountains. Overlooking Galway Bay, the village of Ballyvaughan is within easy access of the Aran islands, Connemara and Galway city. Also close by are Lahinch and Galway Bay golf courses. Colourful shrubs and rockeries surround this immaculate guesthouse. Karen McGann's considerate touches include fresh flowers, spacious, elegantly decorated bedrooms and suites with generous-sized beds, and a wet room for anglers. In the residents' lounge, visitors can read up on the area or watch TV. Breakfast is a very important part of the Rusheen Lodge experience and is taken in the dining room overlooking the spectacular Burren mountains, and you can choose from a buffet of juices, fruit and cereals before a hot meal which might include scrambled egg (from Ballyvaughan farmers' market) wrapped in Burren smoked salmon, accompanied by home-made brown and fruit soda bread. Rusheen Lodge operates on a bed and breakfast basis, but Ballyvaughan has several pubs and restaurants.

Rooms: 9 ensuite. Double from €76. Single from €68. Family from €90.
Closed: Mid Nov - mid Feb.
Other Points: Non-smoking house. Garden. Children welcome. Car park. Winner - Guesthouse of the Year 2006.
Directions: Situated 0.75km outside the village of Ballyvaughan on the N67 Lisdoonvarna road.

Ballyvaughan Co Clare

The Farmshop at Aillwee Cave
Farmshop and cheese makers

Ballyvaughan, Co Clare
Tel. +353(0)65 7077036
Email. barbara@aillweecave.ie
www.aillweecave.ie

Visitors to the two-million-year-old cave at Aillwee, in the spectacular limestone landscape of the Burren, should make time for the splendid farm shop alongside. Ben Johnson, cheesemaker and apiarist, is responsible for the production of award-winning Burren Gold, a Gouda-type cheese which you can watch being made before tasting. If inspiration strikes, you can sign up to one of Ben's cheesemaking courses. A wide range of other local cheeses - Poulcoin goat's cheese, Cratloe sheep's cheese - as well as pickles, homemade jams, pestos, oil and spiced vinegars fill the shelves. Ben dons his beekeeping hat to produce honeycombs and wildflower honey. The shop also stocks up to 20 varieties of homemade fudge, ranging from triple chocolate to maraschino cherry. There's a potato bar, with attractive stone seating and outsize images of local wildflowers, as well as a tea room for freshly made soups, sandwiches, quiches and ginger bread, and a kiosk selling hot dogs and muffins in peak season only.

Hours: Open daily.
10.00-18.30 April-September.
10.00-17.00 October-March.
Other Points: Car Park. Children welcome. Cheese making.
Directions: Located 5km south of Ballyvaughan on the R480.

The Burren Perfumery Tearoom

Ireland West

www.goodfoodireland.ie

Carron Co Clare

🍽 ✕ 🍴 ◉ CS VC

The Burren Purfumery Tea Rooms
Daytime café, visitor centre, craft shop, perfumery

Carron, Co Clare
Tel. +353 (0)65 7089102
Email. burrenperfumery@eircom.net
www.burrenperfumery.com

Set in a quiet valley in the heart of the Burren, this Purfumery is surrounded by some of the most spectacular scenery in the west. Owned by Sadie Chowen for the past five years, her philosophy is to create products inspired by the landscape and environment. And this carries through to the food served in the tearooms. Food is fresh, local and mostly organic, bought at the wonderful Galway market. The centre has its own beehives and organic herb garden. The rose-covered tearooms serve a mouth-watering selection of organic scones with homemade jam, cakes and pies. Choose from apricot and almond tart, porter cake with Guinness, layered chocolate Green and Blacks cake. Gluten free orange and almond summer cake is delicious. Sip an elderflower cordial, fresh apple juice or choose from the wide range

Prices: Lunch main course from €8.
Food Served: 9.00-17.00 daily.
Closed: Oct to Mar.
Cuisine: Organic, local produce.
Other Points: Visitor Centre. Perfumery. Craft shop. Wine licence. Children welcome. Garden. Car park.
Directions: Located 2km from Carron, in the centre of the Burren. The nearest towns are Kinvara (to the North East), Ballyvaughan (to the North West), Corrofin (to the South) and Ennistymon (to the South West).

of organic teas, coffees and herbal tea on the menu. Try freshly made organic tomato and herb soup or pea, mint and coriander with delicious bread from the kitchen. Choose fresh herb garden tea and the herbs are picked straight from the garden. Local Burren cheese is accompanied by homemade chutney and garden organic salads.

Lisdoonvarna Co Clare

● ◉ CS VC FP

The Burren Smokehouse
Smoked fish/gourmet store & craft shop

Lisdoonvarna, Co Clare
Tel. +353(0)65 7074432
Email. info@burrensmokehouse.ie
www.burrensmokehouse.ie

With over 30,000 visitors a year, this traditional stone smokehouse with its visitor's centre and gourmet shop have become something of a landmark in the heart of the Burren country. The shop itself sells everything from music, books and maps to crafts and kitchen utensils, but it is the food that takes centre stage, much of it local: Clare jams and Burren honeys, Cocoa Bean chocolates and award-winning cheeses such as the locally made St Tola's Goat Cheese and Burren Gold. They also smoke the local Kilshanny cheese, but Birgitta and Peter Curtin are most famed for their award-winning smoked fish: their cold smoked Irish salmon recently won them yet another Gold in the Great Taste Awards 2005. They also smoke their own trout, and mackerel. A great place to stock up

Opening hours: 9.00-17.00 & 9.00-18.00 Jun & Aug and weekends. 10.00-16.00 Jan to Mar.
Closed: Good Friday. 25, 26 Dec.
Other Points: Video presentation on smoking of fish. Craft shop. Children welcome. Car park.
Directions: Eight kilometres from the Cliffs of Moher. Five hundred metres from the square in Lisdoonvarna on the Doolin side of the town. Two hundred metres from The Roadside Tavern.

for gourmet gifts or treats for yourselves: make up your own selection from the various smoked fish available or pick up one of the cane picnic baskets brimming with specially selected goodies.

Ireland West

Lisdoonvarna Co Clare

The Roadside Tavern
Traditional pub and restaurant

Lisdoonvarna, Co Clare
Tel. +353(0)65 7074084
Email. info@burrensmokehouse.ie
www.burrensmokehouse.ie

This family-run pub is one of the oldest in the Burren, having been overseen by the Curtins for more than 100 years. Its famously laid-back atmosphere and guaranteed craic makes it as attractive to visitors as it is to the locals. It has a particular draw for the musicians of the region; at its summer peak, there is live music seven nights a week. The unpretentious menu is short and gets straight to the point with winning dishes like traditional Irish bacon, cabbage and parsley sauce and a slightly less traditional rendition of Irish stew (featuring local Burren beef in place of the more typical lamb). Pride of place, quite rightly, is given to several dishes featuring smoked fish and eel from the family's award-winning Burren Smokehouse (worth a visit while you're in the area); try the Burren smoked fish platter which is served with organic leaves from nearby Newquay. And for dessert? Apple pie and cream of course. What else would you be wanting in this sort of a home-from-home place?

Prices: Main course from €9. Bar snack from €3.50. House wine from €15.
Opening hours: 10.00-23.30
Food served: 12.00-21.00 May-Sept. 12.00-15.00 rest of year.
Closed: Good Friday & 25 Dec.
Cuisine: Modern and traditional Irish .
Other Points: Car park. Traditional Irish music nightly during the summer months and Friday & Saturday nights rest of year.
Directions: Eight kilometres from the Cliffs of Moher. Two hundred metres down from the square of Lisdoonvarna on the Doolin road.

The Burren Smokehouse

Ireland West

www.goodfoodireland.ie

Newmarket-on-Fergus Co Clare

Carrygerry Country House
Country house and restaurant

Newmarket-on-Fergus, Co Clare
Tel. +353(0)61 360500
Email. info@carrygerryhouse.com
www.carrygerryhouse.com.

Gillian and Niall Ennis' beautiful country house is set in seven acres of mature woodlands with lovely views over the Shannon estuary, just three miles from Shannon airport. Built in 1793, it was carefully restored in the late 'eighties. The restaurant is a handsome space in shades of warm plum with chairs upholstered in matching fabric. The same colours predominate in the drawing room, where period furniture adds gracious charm. Niall's modern Irish menu - using organic fruit and vegetables, home-grown herbs and the best local meat and seafood - includes classics such as baked goat's cheese and fresh tomato relish puff, leaf salad and pesto dressing, and a creamy seafood chowder scented with garden dill. Main courses bring satisfying dishes such as fillet of lemon sole, coated in spicy Cajun breadcrumbs, chunky chips, sweet chilli mayo, dressed salad or oven roasted rack of Clare lamb, herb crust, minted jus. To finish, there are delicious homemade desserts, perhaps creamy honeycomb and chocolate cheesecake with butterscotch glaze or a duo of freshly churned sorbets (raspberry and pear) with crisp tuile biscuits. Twelve ensuite bedrooms are luxuriously furnished, some with four-posters.

Rooms: 11 ensuite. Double from €110. Single from €65. Family from €165.
Prices: Set dinner (5-course) €45. House wine from €18.50.
Food Served: 18.30-21.30 Tue-Fri. 18.30-22.00 Sat.
Closed: 24-26 December.
Cuisine: Modern and traditional Irish.
Other Points: Children welcome. Car park. Non-smoking house. Wnner - Country House of the Year 2006.
Directions: Take slip road for airport, then take first exit for airport at next roundabout, take fourth exit for Newmarket, next roundabout take second exit, continue for two miles to T-junction, turn right, Carrygerry House quarter mile on the right.

Carrygerry Country House

Ireland West

Quin Co Clare

The Gallery Restaurant
Village restaurant

Main Street, Quin, Co Clare
Tel. +353(0)65 6825789
Email. marian@thegalleryquin.com
www.thegalleryquin.com

Situated in a charming historic village, a short distance from Ennis, Shannon, Dromoland, Knappogue & Bunratty, Gerry and Marian Walsh's restaurant is located by the bridge and opposite the Abbey. Tastefully refurbished in 2005, the attractive stone exterior is softened by window boxes overflowing with flowers and two smart, potted trees. Gerry is the chef and his menus are an appetising list of dishes which make good use of fresh local seasonal produce. For Sunday lunch, there are homemade soups, roast and fish of the day and some traditional puddings. Evening meals bring signature dishes such as rack of Burren lamb with rosemary and garlic, roast duckling with orange sauce and fresh fish in season, carefully cooked to perfection. The varied and well

Prices: Set Sunday lunch €20. Dinner main course from €17.50. House wine from €18.95. Winter & summer specials - ask for details.
Food served: Sunday Lunch 12.00-16.00. Evening meals 17.00-22.00 Tue-Sun incl.
Cuisine: Traditional Irish.
Other Points: Children welcome. Groups catered for. Available for private use. Winner - Host of the Year 2006.
Directions: Located in Quin village, six miles from Ennis on the R469.

presented menu is complemented by a well selected wine list. Ask about the excellent value Early Bird specials.

Spanish Point Co Clare

Admiralty Lodge
Seaside country house & restaurant

Spanish Point, Milltown Malbay, Co Clare
Tel. +353 (0)65 7085007
Email.info@admiralty.ie
www.admiralty.ie

Pat and Aoife O'Malley's lovely country house stands in a peaceful setting overlooking the beautiful beach at Spanish Point, forty minutes from Shannon airport. It's ideally situated for golfing guests, with the Spanish Point Links course just minutes away, and the Doonbeg and Lahinch championship courses a short drive. Inside, pretty wallpaper in shades of dark pink, plenty of comfortable, brown leather armchairs, antique prints and ornate ceilings lend an elegant, slightly clubby feel to the interior. Twelve spacious, individually designed bedrooms with four-poster beds, marble en-suites and flat screen tvs, provide guests with comforts both traditional and modern. The smart restaurant, complete with grand piano and white, wood-panelled walls, offers sophisticated country house cooking. Croquettes of duck confit, foie gras & roots served with a warm salad of lentils and espelette pepper is a typical starter, while mains might include pan fried fillet of Irish beef, sweet potato dauphinois gratin, baby

Rooms: 12 ensuite. Double from €160. Single from €135. Family from €200.
Prices: Dinner main course from €20. Bar Snack from €6. House Wine from €24. Set dinner from €39.
Food served: Afternoon tea & Lounge menu served daily. Dinner served from 18.30-21.30. Sun lunch 12.30-15.00.
Closed: Mid-week in Jan & Feb. Restaurant closed Mondays.
Cuisine: (European) Contemporary Mediterranean.
Other Points: Non-smoking bedrooms. Garden. Car Park. Helipad. Children over 3 years welcome.
Directions: On the main Galway/Kerry coastal Road. 10 mins drive from Lahinch.

onions caramelised and red wine reduction. Finish with a delicious dessert which might include millefeuille of raspberries, mousseline cream with lime and white chocolate.

The Gallery, Quin

for online reservations   Ireland West

Brian Boru Heritage Centre   *Place to Visit*

Killaloe, Co Clare
Tel. +353(0)61 360788
Fax. +353(0)61 361020
Email. reservations@shannondev.ie
www.shannonheritage.com

The lake town of Killaloe is picturesquely situated at the southwest tip of Lough Derg. The 11th. century High King of Ireland, Brian Boru who was one of the most influential and colourful figures in Irish history was born here.

The heritage centre, which is located within the Tourist Information Centre, reveals the story of Brian Boru through a series of colourful exhibits, graphic illustrations and an interactive audio-visual presentation.

Other Points
Gift/souvenir shop, parking.

Admission charged

Hours
May to Sept: daily 10.00 - 18.00
(last admission to exhibition 17.30)
Times may be subject to change.

Directions
Situated off the N7 between Limerick and Nenagh - take the R 494 route to Killaloe & Ballina.

Bunratty Folk Park Traditional Irish Night   *Place to Visit*

The Corn Barn, Bunratty Folk Park,
Bunratty, Co Clare
Tel. +353(0)61 360788
Fax. +353(0)61 361020
Email. reservations@shannondev.ie
www.shannonheritage.com

Experience the magic of Irish music, song and dance. The Corn Barn is the perfect setting for a celebration of the best traditions of Ireland today. You are invited to enjoy the company of the finest singers, dancers and musicians of the local villages and experience the homeliness, friendship and warmth of a true traditional Irish evening. This evening has something to offer everyone: stories of life in Ireland in bygone days, traditional and contemporary dancing and Irish music that will have your feet tapping and your hands clapping. Dine on home cooked food and excellent wine while enjoying lively entertainment.

Hours
Apr to Oct: Nightly at 19.00
(reservations necessary).

Admission charged

Directions
Located just off the N18 between Limerick City and Ennis, 7.4 miles from Shannon Airport and 8 miles from Limerick City.

Ireland West

www.goodfoodireland.ie

Bunratty Castle & Folk Park

Place to Visit

Bunratty, Co Clare
Tel. +353(0)61 360788
Fax. +353(0)61 361020
Email. reservations@shannondev.ie
www.shannonheritage.com

At Ireland's premier visitor attraction, enjoy two wonderful experiences - the acclaimed 15th century Bunratty Castle and 19th century Folk Park. The Castle is the most complete and authentic medieval fortress in Ireland thanks to its splendid restoration. At night time it is the impressive setting for medieval banquets which are held year round. Bunratty Folk Park is where 19th century Irish life is recreated, in a 'living' village and rural setting. The folk park features farmhouses, a watermill, a church, a village street and a magical walled garden. Enjoy the tastes, scents, sights and sounds of this enchanting place.

Other Points
Gift/souvenir shop, parking, toilets, picnic area, wheelchair access.

Admission charged

Hours
Open year round
Jan, Feb, Mar, Nov. & Dec 9.30-17.30
(Last Admission to Folk Park 16.15)
Apr, May, Sept & Oct - 9.00-17.30
(Last Admission to Folk Park 16.15)
June, July & Aug - 9.00 - 18.00
(Last Admission to Folk Park 17.15)
Last Admission to the Castle - 16.00 Year round.
Closed Good Friday & Dec 24th, 25th, 26th.
Times may be subject to change

Directions
Located just off the N18 between Limerick City and Ennis, 7.4 miles from Shannon Airport and 8 miles from Limerick City.

Bunratty Medieval Castle Banquet

Place to Visit

Bunratty, Co Clare
Tel. +353(0)61 360788
Fax. +353(0)61 361020
Email. reservations@shannondev.ie
www.shannonheritage.com

Join the Earl of Thomond for a glorious banquet at this majestic 15th century castle. The Earl's Butler welcomes guests from the four corners of the world toasting an era of great Irish taste with excellent food, fine wine and honey mead. You will be entertained by the world famous Bunratty Singers with enchanting melodies to harp and violin accompaniment. For over 40 years the Ladies of the Castle along with the Earl's Butler have entertained guests in time honoured tradition. The Castle Entertainers have toured extensively, appeared on top television shows and entertained many well known dignitaries and celebrities.

Hours
Twice nightly, year round (reservations necessary) at 17.30 and 20.45.

Admission charged

Directions
Located just off the N18 between Limerick City and Ennis, 7.4 miles from Shannon Airport and 8 miles from Limerick City.

for online reservations

Ireland West

Cliffs of Moher New Visitor Experience

Place to Visit

Near Liscannor, Co Clare
Tel: +353 (0)65 7086140
Fax: +353 (0)61 7086145
Email: info@cliffsofmoher.ie
Website: www.cliffsofmoher.ie

The Cliffs of Moher, one of Ireland's top visitor sites, stretching for 8 kms and 214 metres over the waters of the Atlantic Ocean. Unchanged for millennia the landscape of the Cliffs of Moher has, for centuries, welcomed visitors who come to marvel at their splendour and be at one with nature. They are also the largest mainland colony for nesting seabirds in Ireland, where visitors can see Puffins, Kittiwakes, Fulmar, Guillemot among many others. A new Visitor Centre, including a state of the art interpretation centre – the Atlantic Edge, with extensive visitor facilities opens early in 2007, which has been subsumed into the contours of the local terrain and covered by the grass hillside. New facilities include extension of pathways, development of viewing platforms and seating areas as well as ecological reconstruction of the eroded cliff edge habitat. The new visitor centre includes a Coffee Shop, Tourist Information Desk, Retail Shop, Restaurant, Public Toilets and a Major Interpretation Area, the Atlantic Edge and two Audio Visual displays, The Clare Journey and the Virtual Reality Cliff Face adventure, The Ledge. The Ledge provides a WOW factor to visitors and is a must for visitors of all ages.

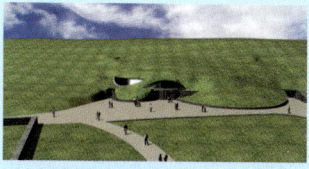

Hours
Oct - Apr: 9.00 - 17.30
May - Sept: 8.30 - 21.00
Opening times are subject to change. Please visit our website to confirm times and admission rates. O'Brien's Tower opening is weather dependent and is capacity controlled.

Directions
From Ennis: N85 to Ennistymon, turn left onto N67 (signpost Lahinch). In Lahinch turn left onto R478, through Liscannor onto the Cliffs of Moher. From Galway: N18 to Kilcolgan, turn right onto N67 (signpost Ballyvaughan) and on to Lisdoonvarna. Turn right onto the R478 to the Cliffs of Moher.

Craggaunowen - The Living Past

Place to Visit

Near Kilmurry, Co Clare
Tel: +353 (0)61 360788
Fax: +353 (0)61 361020
Email. reservations@shannondev.ie
www.shannonheritage.com

Craggaunowen - the Living Past Experience is Ireland's original award winning Pre-historic Park. Situated on 50 acres of wooded grounds, it features a stunning recreation of some of the homesteads, animals and artefacts, which existed in Ireland over 1,000 years ago. Explore the Crannog, the Ring Fort, and the 'Brendan Boat' - a leather hulled boat used to re-enact the Atlantic voyage of St. Brendan and the early Christian monks reputed to have discovered America centuries before Columbus. Enjoy the fresh air and lake walks in a most enjoyable rural setting. Savour the wonderful home made fare in the charming farmhouse tearoom.

Other Points
Gift/souvenir shop, tearoom, parking, toilets, picnic area, wheelchair access.

Admission charged

Hours
Mid Apr to Sept: daily 10.00 - 18.00
(Last admission 17.00)
Opening times may be subject to change.

Directions
Located off the R469 near Quin, Co Clare.

Ireland West

www.goodfoodireland.ie

Knappogue Medieval Castle Banquet
Place to Visit

Knappogue Castle, Quin, Co Clare
Tel. +353(0)61 360788
Fax. +353(0)61 361020
Email. reservations@shannondev.ie
www.shannonheritage.com

Enjoy a night of musical splendour and entertainment at historic Knappogue Castle. Once the splendid home of Sean MacNamara, a medieval Lord, it is now the imposing venue for a memorable evening of the feast of kings. Here the ladies of the Castle welcome guests with a programme of music, song and dance taking you on a musical journey from medieval times to the present day. This colourful and vivid show will enthral and delight from the moment of arrival through an entire evening of good food and wines, as the Earl's Butler ensures that everything proceeds in time-honoured tradition.

Hours
Apr to Oct: 18.30.
(Reservations necessary).

Admission charged

Directions
Located on R469 near the village of Quin, Co Clare.

Knappogue Castle & Walled Gardens
Place to Visit

Quin, Co Clare
Tel. +353(0)61 360788
Fax. +353(0)61 361020
Email. reservations@shannondev.ie
www.shannonheritage.com

Don't miss this truly magnificent medieval Castle in the unspoilt landscape of idyllic Quin, Co Clare. Knappogue Castle was built in 1467 by Sean MacNamara, son of Sioda (who built Bunratty Castle) and has a long and varied history. It has been host to two Irish Presidents as well as other heads of state including General de Gaulle. Visit the magical setting of the recently restored Walled Garden - a romantic oasis to sit and muse or just escape the 'madding crowd'. The castle also plays host to the famous medieval banquet and is available for hire as an exclusive wedding venue.

Other Points
Gift/souvenir shop, parking, toilets.

Admission charged

Hours
May to Mid Sept: 9.30 - 17.00
(last admission 16.15)
Times may be subject to change.

Directions
Located on R469 near the village of Quin, Co Clare.

for online reservations

Ireland West

Killimer-Tarbert Car Ferry

Local Amenity

Shannon Ferry Group Limited
Killimer, Kilrush, Co Clare
Tel. +353 (0)65 905 3124
Fax. +353 (0)65 905 3125
Email. enquiries@shannonferries.com
www.shannonferries.com

Killimer-Tarbert Car Ferry, "Bridging the Best of Ireland's West", links the main tourist routes of the West of Ireland from Killimer, Co. Clare to Tarbert, Co. Kerry as part of the N67. With scheduled sailings every day, this pleasant twenty minute journey across the Shannon Estuary will save 85 miles /137 km from ferry terminal to ferry terminal providing a staging point for the many attractions of Clare, Kerry and adjoining counties. Take some time to enjoy our visitor centre, which stocks an extensive range of books, souvenirs, music, tea, coffee, sweets and ice-creams.

Timetable
Service every day of the year except Christmas Day (weather permitting)

1st April to 30th September

	Departure	Mon-Sat	Sun
1st Ferry	Killimer every hour on the hour	7.00 - 21.00	9.00 - 21.00
	Tarbert every hour on the 1/2 hour	7.30 - 21.30	9.30 - 21.30

Mid May - end Septmber (Additional Sailings)

2nd Ferry	Killimer every hour on the 1/2 hour.	10.30 - 17.30	
	Tarbert every hour on the hour.	11.00 - 18.00	

1st October to 31st March

	Departure	Mon-Sat	Sun
1st Ferry	Killimer every hour on the hour	7.00 - 19.00	9.00 - 19.00
	Tarbert every hour on the 1/2 hour	7.30 - 19.30	9.30 - 19.30

Ireland West Touring Route

Fred & Molly at Rathmullan House

MUST TRY...
McSwynes Bay blue lobster
Inishowen seafood
Bunagee Harbour crab
Mallin Head mussels & oysters
Foyle mussels
Fish from Donegal Bay

MUST VISIT... Kate's Kitchen for a selection of local foods

MUST TRY...
- Carrigeen Moss
- Dulse & Kombu
- Local seaweeds

Farmer's Markets

Donegal

Donegal	Diamond	Saturdays Monthly
Letterkenny	McGinley's Car Park, Pearse Rd	1st & 3rd Sat 9am - 3pm

Leitrim

Carrick-on-Shannon	Market Yard Centre	Thur 10am - 2pm
Manorhamilton		Fri

Sligo

Sligo	Sligo IT car park	Sat 9am - 1pm

See Farmers' Markets section of the guide for full listing

Map of Ireland Route

- **Culdaff** — McGrory's of Culdaff
- **Ballyliffin** — Ballyliffin Lodge & Spa
- **Rathmullan** — Rathmullan House
- **Gweedore**
- Derryveagh Mts.
- **Derry** — Brown's Restaurant Bar & Brasserie; The Tower Museum
- Bluestack Mts.
- Killeter Forest
- **Dunkineely** — Castle Murray House Hotel
- **Donegal**
- **Bundoran**
- **Belleek** — Belleek Pottery
- Lough Erne Lower
- **Enniskillen** — Castle Coole
- Darty Mts.
- Lough Erne Upper
- **Sligo** — Kate's Kitchen
- Slieve Gamph Mts.
- **Carrig-on-Shannon**

167

Ireland West

www.goodfoodireland.ie

Ballyliffin Co Donegal

Ballyliffin Lodge & Spa
Seaview hotel, restaurant & spa

Shore Road, Ballyliffin, Co Donegal
Tel. +353(0)74 9378200
Email: info@ballyliffinlodge.com
www.ballyliffinlodge.com

Cecil Doherty's luxurious new hotel, set on a 2.5 acre site in the village, boasts commanding views of Malin Head, Pollan Bay and Ballyliffin Golf Club, designed by Nick Faldo. The hotel's artwork, unique to the hotel, has been specially commissioned from local artist Sharon McDaid, drawing inspiration from local bronze-age rock art. The 40 beautifully designed rooms include a bridal and executive suites which feature large jacuzzi baths set into the bedrooms, as well as hand-painted feature walls. This is a wonderful place to unwind and get away from it all. Service is friendly and efficient and whether you want to relax in the 17-metre pool, indulge in some spa treatments or play a round of golf at the local golf club, there is something for everyone. In the intimate atmosphere of the Holly Tree Restaurant, Chef Kwanghi Chan uses fresh local produce, including fish from Malin and Greencastle, and Slaney Valley beef. Start with venison sausage served on a rosti potato with spiced apple compote, and follow with fillet of monkfish with ginger and lemongrass with buttered spinach, basil mash and deep-fried leeks: all beautifully presented. For dessert, you may be tempted by the panna cotta with mango, lime and coconut confit, served with fruits of the forest ice cream. The competitively priced wine list leans toward France.

Rooms: 40 ensuite. Double from €160. Single from €115. Children from €30 per child sharing with 2 adults.
Prices: Lunch main course from €8.95. Dinner main course from €17.50. Bar snack from €4.90. House wine from €18.
Closed: Christmas Day.
Food Served: Restaurant: 18.00-22.00. Bar food: 12.00-22.00 Mon-Sat, 16.00-22.00 Sun. Sunday carvery 12.00-16.00.
Cuisine: Modern Irish with French influence.
Other Points: Children welcome. Non-smoking bedrooms. Dogs welcome. Car park. Leisure facilities - pool, sauna, steam room, jacuzzi, aerobic studio, gym. Rock Crystal Health and Beauty Spa.
Directions: Ballyliffin is 25 miles (40km) from Derry, 98 miles (160 km) from Belfast and 172miles (280km) from Dublin. Travelling from Derry (and Belfast), cross the Foyle bridge and take the A2 towards Moville, turning off for Carndonagh at Quigleys point (Carrowkeel). Ballyliffin is six miles (10km) beyond Carndonagh.

for online reservations

Ireland West

Dunkineely Co Donegal

Castle Murray House Hotel
Clifftop hotel and restaurant

St John's Point, Dunkineely, Co Donegal
Tel. +353(0)74 9737022
Email. info@castlemurray.com
www.castlemurray.com

Set against the Donegal mountains and overlooking McSwyne's bay and the floodlit ruins of McSwynes Castle, the stunning location of this friendly, family-run, country hotel offers an idyllic setting to enjoy the exceptional unspoilt views that Co. Donegal is blessed to offer. Run by Marguerite and Martin Howley there is a relaxed atmosphere from which to explore the nearby highest sea cliffs in Europe - Slieve League, Glenveigh National Park and Fintra Beach. The location of the hotel restaurant maximises the fantastic panoramic views, which adds to this romantic setting where you can also enjoy fine wine and the culinary delights of Remy Dupuis who has been chef there since 1994. There is a strong emphasis on local produce and seasonality determines what the menu may offer.

The house special starter is 'prawns & monkfish in garlic butter' and there is their acclaimed 'McSwyne's bay blue lobster 'from the tank' which can be grilled or steamed and served with bolet mushroom sauce'. Alternatively, there was a 'roasted pheasant breast, stuffed with Serrano ham, fresh herbs and truffle sauce' or 'stuffed rabbit saddle with black pudding and calvados sauce', which might catch the eye for those of you preferring a non-seafood option. All the rooms are ensuite with seaviews and along with the bar and reception area have recently been refurbished.

Rooms: 10 ensuite. Double from €120. Single from €80. Family from €120.
Prices: Set Sunday lunch €27. Bar snack from €5-€8.50. Dinner main course from €25. House wine from €21.
Food Served: Bar snacks 12.00-15.00 Mon-Sat(high season only). Sunday lunch 13.30-15.30. Dinner 18.30-21.30 daily.
Closed: Mid Jan to mid Feb. Mon & Tue during low season.
Cuisine: Modern Irish & French.
Other Points: Non-smoking. Children welcome. Garden. Car park. Small dogs welcome.
Directions: Fifteen minutes from Donegal town in Killybegs direction. One mile off the main road for St John's Point.

Symbols

- Accommodation
- Restaurant
- Café
- Pub/Bar
- Daytime opening only
- Deli
- Wine
- Bakery
- Gourmet/Farm Shop
- Leisure Centre/Spa
- CS Craft Shop
- VC Visitor Centre
- FP Food Producer

Good Food Ireland Awards

- 2002 Award Winner
- 2003 Award Winner
- 2004 Award Winner
- 2005 Award Winner
- 2006 Award Winner

Ireland West
www.goodfoodireland.ie

Inishowen Penninsula Co Donegal

McGrorys of Culdaff
Hotel, pub and restaurant

Culdaff, Inishowen, Co Donegal
Tel. +353(0)74 9379104
Email. info@mcgrorys.ie
www.mcgrorys.ie

McGrory's makes for a great base to explore the Inishowen Peninsula. This family-run hotel, established in 1924, underwent a major refurbishment in recent years, almost doubling the number of rooms. You can be sure of a warm welcome: McGrory's plays host to renowned music sessions for every taste in its two stone-walled bars. If you're lucky enough to coincide with one of the hotel's wine and gourmet evenings, you could enjoy skewered monkfish with honey, soya and sesame dressing, followed by chateaubriand and dark chocolate tart from Head chef Roland Houston, who once worked in the London House of Commons. Dinner in the restaurant, which features distinctive cherrywood panelling, could start with Bunagee crab with tangy mayonnaise and rocket. Main courses range from grilled halloumi with sesame seeds and Moroccan couscous to fillet steak with rocket and Parmesan. Fresh organic vegetables come from nearby Malin. There is also an extensive bar-food menu available throughout the day, including goats' cheese bruschetta, vegetable curry and smoked salmon ravioli. The carefully selected wine list has a good international mix.

Rooms: 17 ensuite. Double from €110. Single from €60.
Prices: Lunch main course from €9.90. Dinner main course from €16. Bar snack from €6.75. House wine from €15.
Food served: Bar 12.30-20.00.daily. (check for seasonal changes) Restaurant 18.30-21.00 Tue-Thu. 18.30-21.30 Fri-Sat. 13.00-15.30 &18.00-20.30 Sun.
Closed: 23-27 December. Restaurant : Mondays (and Tuesdays in low season).
Cuisine: Modern Irish.
Other Points: Car park. Children welcome.
Directions: On the R238 between Moville and Malin Head.

for online reservations **Ireland West**

Rathmullan Co Donegal

Rathmullan House
Country house hotel and restaurant

Rathmullan, Co Donegal
Tel. +353(0)74 9158188
Email. info@rathmullanhouse.com
www.rathmullanhouse.com

This beautiful country house hotel is a luxurious base from which to explore Donegal's Fanad Peninsula. Glenveagh National Park and the Glebe Gallery make for a fine day trip, and also nearby is the stunning Ballymastocker bay. Built in the 1800s, it was once the home of the Batt banking family, the house is now run by brothers Mark and William Wheeler, with their wives Mary and Yvonne. Their award-winning gardens run down to Lough Swilly's sandy beaches. Guests have the best of both modern and traditional worlds: there is an in-door, heated swimming pool, and the three elegant sitting rooms are furnished with antiques. The Wheelers are great supporters of small artisan food producers and use fresh local produce where possible. It's worth a stay for their sumptious breakfast alone, featuring Carrigeen moss (collected themselves) poached in milk, Dongeal baked ham, homemade wheaten and Guinness breads, speciality cakes and much more from their buffet as well as the full Irish. Fruit, vegetables and herbs come from the garden, and the Wheelers also keep their own hens. Head chef Tommi Tuhkanen features the best of local seafood, meat and game. Try Thornhill Farm duck three ways to start, followed by Greencastle landed halibut

Rooms: 32 ensuite. Double from €170. Single from €85. Family from €85 per adult with rates for children available on request.
Prices: Lunch main course from €15. Dinner main course from €30. Bar snack from €10. House wine from €21.
Food served: 13.00-14.30 and 19.30-20.45 daily.
Closed: 7 Jan - 7 Feb, 24-27 Dec.
Cuisine: Modern Irish with emphasis on seasonality and produce from artisan suppliers.
Other Points: Garden. Children welcome. Swimming pool. Tennis courts. Dogs welcome by prior arrangement. Dog friendly bedroom available. Highly Commended - Hotel of the Year 2003. Winner - Hotel of the Year 2004.
Directions: From Letterkenny take the R245 to Ramelton, turn right at bridge to Rathmullan (R247), go north through village, gates on the right.

and then lime and ginger pannacotta. Wines include several organic and biodynamic options. A carefully chosen children's menu features smaller portions of a large variety of simple, delicious food. All in all, a special and unforgettable treat.

171

Ireland West

www.goodfoodireland.ie

Aran Islands Co Galway

Fisherman's Cottage
Coastal café/restaurant

Inishere, Aran Islands, Co Galway
Tel. +353(0)99 75073
Email. foodwise@eircom.net
www.southaran.com

Overlooking Galway Bay on the island of Inishere, Fisherman's Cottage is surrounded by a beautiful garden where chef proprietor Enda Conneely and his wife Maria grow some vegetables and herbs for use in the kitchen. Fish from the island and Rossaveal is used in their delicious fish pie, a popular item on the evening menu. Irish beef from Finnerty's in Eyre Square and smoked fish from the Burren Smokehouse in Lisdoonvarna bring a very high standard to the dishes on both the lunchtime and evening menus. Lunchtime specialties include potato and chive soup with homemade brown bread, smoked salmon platter, open steak sandwich and fresh mackerel salad. Relax during the afternoon with an espresso and a slice of one of the selection of delicious home cooked cakes - coffee, carrot, banana and walnut and lemon squares. If you're dining in the evening, start with a mushroom and thyme leaf tart or smoked mackerel pate, followed by sirloin steak or Thai-style bean cassoulet with coconut and coriander, served with basmati rice. This is quality food in a casual dining atmosphere.

Prices: Lunch main course from €4. Dinner main course from €16. House wine from €15.
Food Served: 10.30-16.00 & 19.00-21.00 daily during July and August. Other months closed Mondays. Phone for dinner reservations.
Closed: October to May.
Cuisine: Eclectic.
Other Points: Garden. **Directions:** Turn right at pier, continue for 400 metres.

Aran Islands Co Galway

Tigh Ned
Coastal pub

Inishere, Aran Islands, Co Galway
Tel. +353(0)99 75004
Email.tighned@eircom.net

For 20 years, Paraic O'Conghaile has been at the helm of this delightful pub on Inishere, the smallest of the Aran Islands. It was originally established in 1987 and has retained much of its original character. The walls inside are covered with photographs and artefacts that show traditional island life. Outside, the beer garden has magnificent views over Galway Bay. During the summer, visitors can enjoy nightly traditional music, while sipping a pint. Visiting musicians are especially welcome to join in. Home cooked food is available from May to September; an island crab special uses fish straight from the port. The closest island to the mainland, Inishere gained popularity in the nineties - it appeared as Craggy Island, home to Father Ted. It's reached by ferry from either Rossaveal or Doolin.

Prices: Lunch main course from €3.90. Bar snack from €3.90.
Opening Hours: 10.30-23.30 Mon-Thurs & Sun. 10.30-00.30 Fri & Sat.
Food Served: 12.00-16.30 daily.
Closed: Food service closed October to April.
Cuisine: Modern Irish.
Other Points: Children welcome. Garden. Credit cards not accepted-
Directions: Turn right at the pier, continue for 200 metres.

Ireland West

Clifden Co Galway

Abbeyglen Castle
Seaview hotel

Sky Road, Clifden, Co Galway
Tel. +353(0)95 21201
Email. info@abbeyglen.ie
www.abbeyglen.ie

This 19-century castle has a fairytale setting, by the sea beneath Connemara's scenic Sky Road. Set in 12 acres of sheltered parkland and well-tended gardens, it has been owned and loved by the Hughes family since 1969. Here you can relax by open fires and cosy couches - you'll be treated like royalty by Paul and Brian Hughes, and their staff. The 45 individually decorated bedrooms have all the comforts you could possibly need. The castle has its own outdoor heated swimming pool, sauna, jacuzzi and tennis court, or you could try pony trekking and shore angling. If you catch your own fish, chef Kevin Conroy will prepare it for your dinner. If you're not so lucky, there's sure to be some other local delight to tempt you - starting with Kevin's chicken liver paté, then fresh sea halibut or supreme of guinea fowl, and finishing with a choice of home-made desserts. It's difficult

Rooms: 45 ensuite. Double from €258 (including dinner bed and breakfast). 12.5% service charge will apply.
Prices: Bar lunch main course from €11. Dinner main course from €23. Set dinner €49. House wine from €22.95.
Food Served: Bar lunch 12.30-14.00 daily. Restaurant dinner 19.00-21.00 daily.
Closed: 4 Jan to 1 Feb.
Cuisine: French, International.
Other Points: Garden. Children welcome over 12 years old. Car park. Leisure facilities - outdoor heated swimming pool, sauna, jacuzzi, tennis court.
Directions: N59 west, 50 miles from Galway.

to choose from the reasonably priced international wine list, but it is divided by style, which helps.

Connemara Co Galway

Connemara Smokehouse
Fish smokery and shop

Bunowen Pier, Aillebrack, Ballyconneely, Co Galway
Tel. +353(0)95 23739
Email. info@smokehouse.ie
www.smokehouse.ie

The setting is one of the most beautiful areas in Ireland, the ingredients some of the purest; fish, salt, smoke, herbs, sugar, honey and Irish whiskey. The Connemara Smokehouse is the oldest in the region and for over 25 years the family have been perfecting this ancient craft. What you get are well balanced foods, the smoking always playing a supporting role; enhancing rather than dominating so the sweetness of the salmon, for example, comes through gently. Not content to work with salmon only however, you can also buy smoked mackerel, tuna, cod and

Opening Hours: 9.00-17.00 Mon-Fri. Closed 13.00-14.00
Closed: Sat. & Sun. Seasonal & bank holidays.
Directions: About 5 miles south of Clifden on the L102.

kippers. While the company specialises in wild salmon it also smokes farmed and organic salmon and if you are a fisherman yourself you can have your own catch treated to this ancient gentle process. All the products are widely available or you can order directly on line.

Ireland West

Connemara/Renvyle Co Galway

Renvyle House Hotel
Coastal hotel and restaurant

Renvyle, Connemara, Co Galway
Tel. +353(0)95 43511
Email. info@renvyle.com
www.renvyle.com

Set on 200 acres of woodland and lakes at the foot of the Twelve Bens, historic Renvyle House is on the Connemara loop, so you can easily fit in trips to Kylemore Abbey, Killary Fjord or the Connemara National Park. The hotel, once the home of Oliver St John Gogarty, offers several activity packages, such as murder mystery weekends, golfing and fly-fishing breaks, professionally guided walks and adventure activities at the nearby Killary activity centre such as scuba diving and water-skiing. The 68 spacious and comfortable ensuite rooms are all tastefully furnished. Build up your energy with the extensive Renvyle breakfast menu, which includes pan-seared lamb's liver, grilled fillets of Cleggan plaice and crêpes filled with fresh fruit. Enjoy the open turf fires with a tasty afternoon tea, that features crabmeat, smoked salmon and seafood chowder, as well as home-made desserts and scones. For dinner, head chef Tim O'Sullivan might serve roasted quail with beetroot mash and red wine jus. Fish-lovers are well catered for with main courses here, and there's also Connemara lamb and a vegetarian option such as aubergine fritters with cous cous and ratatouille. Afterwards, tiramisu is served with home-made biscuits. Classification by area helps guide you through the large wine list and there is a great half-bottle selection.

Rooms: 68 ensuite. Double from €60. Single from €30. Family (2 adults & 2 children) from €110.

Prices: Lunch main course from €19.50 (13.00-14.00). 5-Course dinner from €47.50. Bar snack from €5. House wine from €20.50

Food Served: Breakfast 8.30-11.00. Bar Food/Afternoon Tea 12.00-17.30. Dinner from 19.00. Last orders 21.00 daily.

Closed: Mid-week in Dec. 7 Jan - 8 Feb '07.

Cuisine: Modern Irish, International. Specialising in fresh seafood and Connemara lamb.

Other Points: Non-smoking bedrooms. Garden. Children welcome. Dogs welcome. Car Park. 9-hole golf course. Lake for boating and fly fishing. Tennis courts. Lawn Bowls. Croquet. Outdoor swimming pool (summer months). Clay pigeon shooting. Childrens' playground. Winner - Ireland West Regional Award 2006.

Directions: From Galway take the N59 towards Clifden. Go straight through the towns of Moycullen, Oughterard and Maam Cross. At Recess (one mile past Joyce's Craft Shop) take a right (signposted) and drive through the Inagh Valley. At the end of the Inagh Valley take a left towards Kylemore. Pass Kylemore Abbey and when you reach the crossroads at Letterfrack take a right. Go through the village of Tully Cross (veer left at the church) and through Tully and you will arrive at the gates of Renvyle House. Entire journey is approx 55 miles.

Ireland West

for online reservations

Galway City

McDonagh's Seafood House
Seafood bar, fish and chip bar & fish shop

22 Quay Street, Galway
Tel. +353(0)91 565001
Email. fish@mcdonaghs.net
www.mcdonaghs.net

Four generations of experience has gone into McDonaghs, and it shows: it's sheer heaven for fish-lovers. Since 1902, the company's tradition has been to buy whole catches from local fishermen, which guarantees a great variety. Under the management of Colm McDonagh, the restaurant smokes its own fish on the premises, and if you catch a fish on your trip to the west, they will smoke it for you to bring home. McDonagh's is divided in two, with a takeaway for traditional fish and chips in one part and table service at the Seafood Bar on the other. The menu here brings starters such as Clarenbridge oysters and marinated herring from the Orkney islands served with fresh beetroot. Follow with any of several grilled fish options, served with a choice of sauces and accompanied by the obligatory mushy peas. House specials include salmon baked with layers of tomatoes, basil leaves and buffalo Mozzarella, and sautéed monkfish with garlic, chilli and ginger butter, served with coriander rice. Dessert might be chocolate fudge cake or rhubarb crumble. The compact wine list is great value.

Prices: Seafood Bar main course from €11.00-€24.00. Fish and Chip Bar prices from €7.35. House wine from €16.
Food Served: Seafood Bar: 17.00-22.00 Mon-Sat. Closed Sun. Fish & Chip Bar 12.00-00.00 Mon-Sat. 17.00-23.00 Sun. Fish shop: 10.00-17.30 Tue-Thurs. 9.00-18.00 Fri. 9.00-17.30 Sat. Closed Sun & Mon.
Closed: 25, 26 Dec & 1 Jan.
Cuisine: Traditional Irish seafood.
Other Points: Children welcome.
Directions: At the bottom of Quay St.

Galway City

Sheridan's Cheesemongers
Gourmet cheese, food and wine shop

14 - 16 Churchyard Street, Galway
Tel. +353(0)91 564829
Email.
galway@sheridanscheesemongers.com
www.sheridanscheesemongers.com

Sheridans Galway is more than a cheese shop. You step into a world of good food, all sourced with care, love and attention. You can pick from salamis and cold meats from Italy, cheeses from all over Europe and endless vinegars, oils and good things in jars, not to mention the biscuits, jams and bars of chocolate. If you visit on Saturday the market will be in full swing outside. This is picnic paradise. At the right time of year you can pick from endless stalls selling vegetables and then concentrate on the meats and cheeses this fine retailer does best. The business of retailing cheese is somewhat more complicated than many other foods. Buy here and you are very likely to be eating something deep, staisfying, complex and rewarding. The short wine bar menu includes a charcuterie, cheese, and smoked fish plate or try the tempting short bites of boquerones & caperberries, salted Almonds, marinated olives or quail eggs & cumin salt. A delicious choice of soup and sandwiches is available for takeaway from the cheese shop from 11am - 6pm Monday to Friday. These can also be taken upstairs to consume with a glass of their extensive range of wines.

Opening Hours: Cheese Shop: 9.30-18.00 Mon-Fri. 9.00-18.00 Sat. Closed Sundays except in summer months then open 13.00-18.00. Wine Shop: 14.00-21.00 Tue-Fri. 12.00-20.00 Sat. Closed Sun & Mon.
Closed: 25, 26 Dec. 1 Jan.
Food served: Wine bar - 14.00-20.30 Tue-Fri. 12.00-19.30 Sat.
Directions: Located on the Square in front of St Nicholas' Church.

175

Ireland West

www.goodfoodireland.ie

Galway City

Sheridan's on the Docks
Waterfront pub

3 New Docks, Galway
Tel. +353(0)91 564905

Ownership of this pub is enough to give you confidence. Kevin & Seamus Sheridan have built up both a business and a reputation for local and artisan products with shops in Galway and Dublin. This establishment, the birthplace of Padhraic O'Conaire, is a first foray into the sector but things look promising. The focus is on uncomplicated unfussy food served in simple surroundings with stone flagged floors, lots of wood and restrained decoration. With the Sheridan pedigree it is no surprise to find the likes of local and organic salad, good cheese, both from Ireland and futher afield. There is also local bread. A good Irish stew was forthcoming and proper rare roast beef sandwich. Top producers like Gubeen and Woodcock smokery get star billing and there are the likes Galway Hooker ale, O'Hara's stout,

Prices: Bar snack from €6.
Opening hours: 16.30-23.30 Mon-Thur. 12.30-00.30 Fri. 10.00-00.30 Sat.
Food Served: until 21.00 each day.
Closed: Sundays. 25 Dec. Good Fri.
Directions: Located opposite the Docks.

Curim Beer and Kinsale Larger all on top. Lest you be concerned that this is a pub in the old-fashioned sense, wine is given equal attention. This is a welcome new entry to the guide, the kind of establishment we hope to see much more of in years to come.

Leenane Co Galway

Blackberry Café
Waterside café & restaurant

Leenane, Co Galway
Tel. +353(0)95 42240

Sean and Mary Hamilton's small café and restaurant in the pretty village of Leenane is a real find. It's poised on the edge of Killary harbour, Irelands' only genuine fjord, and a stunning sight for the first-time visitor. For over a decade, it has offered a deliciously simple, seafood-dominated menu - available in high season from midday until 9pm - to walkers, tourists and locals. Dinner might begin with a tian of crab with an avocado cream or a plate of Connemara smoked salmon, followed by steamed mussels in garlic and wine, roast cod on a bed of creamed spinach, with salad and fries or a seafood platter with a selection of local fish. Meat options include traditional Irish stew with Connemara lamb, vegetables and potatoes, or homemade beef burgers with a delicious mushroom or pepper sauce. Open sandwiches, panini and wraps can be had

Prices: Snack from €4.50-€10.95. Dinner main course from €13.95-€25. House wine from €19.
Food Served: 12.00-16.30 and 18.00-21.00 Wed-Mon. Open daily July/August.
Closed: 30 Sept - Good Friday.
Cuisine: European.
Directions: 40 miles from Galway. 20 from Westport, 20 from Clifden. Situated on Killary Harbour.

at lunchtime, as well as salads of local seafood, fresh crab or salmon. A concise list of French and New World wines offers two house wines by the half bottle and a minicellar of wines by the generous glass. Service is friendly and prompt.

Ireland West

Leenane Co Galway

Delphi Lodge
Lakeside country house

Leenane, Co Galway
Tel. +353(0)95 42222
Email. info@delphilodge.ie
www.delphilodge.ie

Peter and Jane Mantle run this fine sporting lodge, built in the 1830s and set in a serene valley with Connacht's highest mountains as its backdrop. Downstairs are the cosy library and a large drawing room, which overlooks the lake. Many of the 12 comfortable bedrooms also have lake views. The 1,000-acre estate owns many fine salmon-fishing waters. Delphi Lodge is not a hotel: it is a private country home that aims to capture the relaxed atmosphere of an old-fashioned house party. Dinner is served at one large oak table, presided over by either Peter himself or the captor of the day's biggest salmon. Game is from the Lodge's own shoots, and they also serve their own smoked fish. The chef team, Gareth Reid and Cliodhna Prendergast, might serve a set dinner of lightly grilled oysters with wild garlic, followed by home-made wood pigeon ravioli with a light Parmesan sauce. Their main course could be roasted monkfish with tomato and basil salad and an anchovy and parsley dressing, and for dessert, ice nougat parfait with Irish coffee sauce. Peter's wine list is truly extensive, featuring more than 300 carefully selected bottles, and showing the ratings of wine critics where possible. Finish your interesting evening with coffee, chocolates and conversation in the Piano Room.

Rooms: 12 ensuite. Double from €150. Single from €105.
Prices: Set dinner €50. House wine from €22.
Food served: Dinner 20.00 daily (residents only).
Closed: 20 Dec-10 Jan.
Cuisine: Combination of traditional and new wave.
Other Points: Flyfishing. Non-smoking. Garden. Car park. Snooker. Library. Food and Wine weekends offered in autumn and winter. Picnic lunch baskets can be provided. Winner - Country House of the Year 2005.
Directions: 8 miles northwest of Leenane on the Louisburgh road.

Ireland West

www.goodfoodireland.ie

Moycullen Co Galway

Killeen House
Country house bed and breakfast

Killeen, Bushypark, Galway
Tel. +353(0)91 524179
Email. killeenhouse@ireland.com
www.killeenhousegalway.com

Comfort, individuality and hospitality - these are the hallmarks of this charming 19th-century country house. Set in 25 acres of grounds by the shores of Lough Corrib, it is just outside Galway, so makes an ideal starting point for a trip to Connemara. If you have more time to enjoy the moment, take a walk to the water's edge or make yourself at home in the elegant drawing room. Killeen House is furnished with carefully chosen antiques, and bedrooms reflect different styles - Victorian, Edwardian, Regency and Art Nouveau. Owner Catherine Doyle ensures guests get that personal touch, with afternoon tea served on arrival. This is a luxurious retreat with very grown-up appeal. But Killeen House fortifies you for the real world with an outstanding breakfast, featuring pinhead oatmeal porridge or home-made muesli, followed by the traditional Irish fry or scrambled free-range egg and wild salmon, and also including home-made bread and marmalade, served with silver cutlery and fine china.

Rooms: 6 ensuite. Double from €140-€180. Single from €100-€140. Family from €180-€220.
Other Points: Garden. Children welcome over 12 years old. Car park. Winner - Guesthouse of the Year 2003.
Directions: On the N59, the main Clifden road. Killeen House is 4 miles from Galway city centre and half way between Galway city and Moycullen village.

Moycullen Co Galway

White Gables Restaurant
Cottage restaurant

Moycullen Village, Co Galway
Tel. +353(0)91 555744
Email. info@whitegables.com
www.whitegables.com

Outside, White Gables is an old stone cottage with red window frames that's straight from a fairytale. Inside, the stone walls, fresh flowers and warm red tones create a cosy atmosphere. Here they use plenty of local, seasonal ingredients, such as vegetables and cheese from the Galway Saturday market. The menu is bursting with traditional favourites. Start with McGeough's smoked Connemara lamb served wafer-thin with mixed pickles and follow with onion soup and a fillet steak. Fish lovers can opt for poached fresh turbot with martini sauce or lobster from their sea-water tank. The dessert menu features classics: strawberry pavlova or bread and butter pudding, as well as the simple but tempting poached pear with chocolate sauce or fresh pineapple with Kirsch and ice cream. The dinner set menu is good value at €44, which might include home-made chicken liver pâté with Cumberland sauce, followed by clear beef consommé, their famous roast half duck with orange sauce and a choice of desserts. An elegant wine list takes in both New and Old World. Sunday lunch becomes a real occasion at White Gables: it's best to book ahead.

Prices: Set Sunday lunch €26.50. Dinner main course from €25. House wine from €20.
Food Served: Dinner 19.00-22.00 Tue-Sun. Lunch 12.30-15.00, Sunday.
Closed: Mondays (except early August). 23 Dec - 14 Feb.
Cuisine: Traditional, with seafood specialities.
Other Points: Children welcome. Car park. Bar waiting area for guests.
Directions: Situated at the crossroads in Moycullen Village. Located on the N59 8km from Galway City.

for online reservations — **Ireland West**

Aran Direct
Local Amenity

29 Forster Street, Galway and
Rossveal Harbour, Co. Galway
Tel. +353 (0)91 566535
Fax. +353 (0)91 534315
Email. info@arandirect.com
www.arandirect.com

Cruise to the Aran Islands off the coast of Galway in the West of Ireland. Aran Direct offers daily sailings to all 3 Aran Islands (Inis Mór, Inis Meáin and Inis Oírr) on Galway's newest luxury ferries. There is also an Island Hop service during the summer months. Aran Direct ferries are brand new state-of-the-art vessels, and are the only ferries with electronic stabilisers to ensure a smooth, safe and comfortable crossing. The ferries leave from Rossaveal in County Galway, and there is an optional private bus transfer from Galway City. Discount for online bookings.

Known as "The Islander's Choice", Aran Direct is owned and operated by Islanders.

Timetable
Every day except 25th & 26th Dec.

Going Out
Rossaveal to Inis Mór:	10.30am, 1.00pm*, 6.30pm
Rossaveal to Inis Meáin / Inis Oírr:	10.30am, 6.30pm

Coming Back
Leaving Inis Mór:	8.00am, 12.00pm*, 5.00pm
Leaving Inis Oírr:	9.15am, 4.45pm
Leaving Inis Meáin:	9.25am, 4.55pm

* *Every day from 1st Apr - 31st Oct, Sat & Sun only from 1st Nov to 31st Mar*

Timetable correct at time of print. Timetable may be subject to change - please check before travelling by phoning +353 (0)91 566535 or logging on to www.arandirect.com.

Brigit's Garden
Place to Visit

Roscahill, Co Galway.
Tel. +353 (0)91 550905
Fax. +353 (0)91 550491
Email. info@galwaygarden.com
www.galwaygarden.com

Brigit's Garden offers a touch of magic at the gateway to Connemara. The 11-acre site brings Celtic heritage to life through nature, art and unique gardens themed on the Celtic festivals. This is a place to find relaxation and inspiration as you explore the gardens and nature walks, the Wind Chamber and fairy fort, the Roundhouse and the Calendar Sundial, the largest sundial in Ireland. This is a family-friendly place that appeals to all ages. The delicious lunch and tea menu in the Garden Café features home-baking and produce from the gardens.

Admission charged

Hours
Daily 10.00 am to 5.30 pm from mid-April to the end of September, and by appointment at other times.

Directions
Well signposted, 2 kms from the N59 between Moycullen and Oughterard, 20 minutes from Galway city.

Other Points
Garden Café, Gift Shop, Guided Tours, Wheelchair access,
Toilets and Free Parking.

Ireland West

Dunguaire Castle

Place to Visit

Kinvara, Co Galway
Tel. +353(0) 61 360788
Fax. +353(0)61 361020
Email. reservations@shannondev.ie
www.shannonheritage.com

Visit Ireland's most photographed and picturesque Castle in the idyllic location of Kinvara, Co. Galway. It has for hundreds of years stood proudly on the site of the 7th. century stronghold of Guaire, the King of Connaught, its majesty dominating the shore of Galway Bay. The Castle bridges almost 5 centuries of Irish history, from the skirmishes, battles and sieges that characterise its colourful past, through to the literary revival of the early 20th century. In 1924, Oliver St. John Gogarty, surgeon, poet, and author, a contemporary and friend of WB Yeats and Lady Gregory, acquired the Castle as a place of quiet retreat.

Admission charged

Hours
Mid Apr to Sept: 9.30 - 17.00
(Last admission 16.30)
Opening times may be subject to change.

Directions
Located near Kinvara, Co Galway, off the N18 (Limerick/Galway road).

Other Points
Gift/Souvenir Shop, Parking, Toilets.

Dunguaire Medieval Castle Banquet

Place to Visit

Dunguaire Castle, Kinvara,
Co Galway
Tel. +353(0) 61 360788
Fax. +353(0)61 361020
Email. reservations@shannondev.ie
www.shannonheritage.com

Enjoy an enchanting evening at 500-year-old Dunguaire Castle, on the shores of Galway Bay - one of Ireland's most picturesque locations. Following the tradition of medieval 'King Guaire' who resided at Kinvara, we invite you to savour a delicious four-course dinner with wines - food to please the palate and entertainment to lift the soul. In a truly intimate setting, the castle's superb artists will inspire you with extracts chosen from works of great literary writers such as Synge, Yeats, Shaw and O'Casey, chosen to lighten the heart and performed by artists perfectly moulding themselves into their parts.

Admission charged

Hours
Apr to Oct: Twice nightly at 17.30 and 20.45 (reservations necessary)

Directions
Located near Kinvara, Co Galway, off the N18 (Limerick/Galway road).

Ireland West

Glin Co Limerick

Glin Castle
Historic country house

Glin, Co Limerick
Tel. +353(0)68 34173
Email. knight@iol.ie
www.glincastle.com

Glin Castle, which is still the private home to Madam Fitzgerald and The Knight of Glin, Desmond Fitzgerald, is one of Ireland's most historic properties - it has been in the FitzGerald family, for over 700 years! With just fifteen individually decorated, luxurious bedrooms each with its own private bathroom, one can enjoy a warm and intimate atmosphere in this stunning castle. The staff are professional and provide little touches along the way which all adds to the wonderful experience of a stay at Glin Castle, which is only open for seven months of the year. The whole atmosphere seems to combine elegance and grace, and evoke a feeling of times gone by with its stunning décor and exceptional collection of Irish antique furniture and paintings. It is located on the bank of the river Shannon only one hour's drive from Shannon airport and is surrounded by formal gardens and parkland in the middle of 500 acres of woodland and dairy farm. The exquisite castle gardens provide an environment in which visiting gardeners can investigate the plants, flowers and trees. Dining at Glin Castle is an experience to be treasured with fine country cooking using fresh produce from it's own walled garden adds to the simple, seasonal and wonderful dishes. Start perhaps with a 'roulade of smoked salmon and crab with horseradish dressed leaves' and follow with 'pan seared scallops with garlic and lemon butter' or perhaps 'slow braised lamb shank and to finish hot chocolate gateau with Blackberry compôte and softly whipped cream'.

Rooms: 15 ensuite. Double from €310.
Prices: Set dinner from €53 (residents only.) House wine from €23.
Food served: 18.00-21.30.
Closed: November to March.
Cuisine: Country house.
Other Points: Non-smoking. Garden. Car park. Tennis. Croquet. Winner - Country House of the Year 2004.
Directions: On the N69 between Foynes and Tarbert. From Shannon follow the signs for Cork and Tralee and the N69 for 32 miles. Turn left off the main road in Glin village and right at the top of the square.

Glin Castle

Ireland West

www.goodfoodireland.ie

Foynes Flying Boat Museum

Place to Visit

Foynes, Co Limerick
Tel. +353 (0)69 65416
Fax. +353 (0)69 65600
Email. famm@eircom.net
www.flyingboatmuseum.com

Re-live the pioneering aviation era from 1939 to 1945 when Foynes was the centre of the aviation world. The famous flying boats were frequent visitors, carrying a diverse range of passengers, from celebrities to refugees. The Museum is situated in the original Terminal Building with its Radio and Weather Room. The exhibits feature an introduction to the first transatlantic passenger service and Foynes during the war years. It also features different airline exhibits, memorabilia and a 1940's style cinema, showing the award winning film 'Atlantic Conquest'. Go on board the World's ONLY Boeing B314 full size replica Flying Boat or fly it on one of our flight simulators. Enjoy an Irish Coffee in the building where it was first invented by Chef Joe Sheridan in 1942.

Other Points
Coffee Shop and Souvenir & Gift Shop, Picnic Area and Free Car & Coach Parking.

Hours
Mar 31 to Oct 31: daily 10.00 - 18.00
Last Admission 17.00.

Admission Charged

Directions
Located on the N69 Coastal Route from Limerick to Kerry, 23 miles from Limerick City.

King John's Castle

Place to Visit

Kings Island, Limerick City
Tel. +353(0)61 360788
Fax. +353(0)61 361020
Email. reservations@shannondev.ie
www.shannonheritage.com

King John's Castle is a 13th century Castle on 'King's Island' in the heart of medieval Limerick City overlooking the majestic river Shannon. Explore 800 years of history brought to life in the imaginative historical exhibition, excavated pre-Norman houses, fortifications, siege mines and the battlement walks. King John, as "Lord of Ireland" minted his own coins at this very location. The sights, scenes and sounds of the Castle and its environs all combine to recreate the atmosphere of the era.

Other Points
Gift/souvenir shop, parking, toilets, picnic area, wheelchair access. Car park open May - Sept.

Admission charged

Hours
Open Year round
Jan, Feb, Nov, Dec - 10 - 16.30
last admission 15.30
Mar, Apr & Oct - 9.30 -17.00
last admission 16.00
May - Sept - 9.30 -17.30
last admission 16.30
Closed Good Friday & Dec 24th, 25th, 26th.
Times may be subject to change.

Directions
Located on Kings Island in Limerick City.

Lough Gur Visitor Centre

Place to Visit

Near Bruff, Co Limerick
Tel. +353(0)61 360788
Fax. +353(0)61 361020
Email. reservations@shannondev.ie
www.shannonheritage.com

The story is told of the pre-Celtic settlers of Ireland who farmed and lived in this peaceful valley. Over time, the lake, which dominated the everyday lives of the people, became sacred and valuable offerings were made to the gods of the lake. The Visitor Centre houses an audio-visual show, exhibition of artefacts and display panels which interpret the story of man from the Stone Age. This story stretches back over 5,000 years and continues in the people who still farm and dwell in the valley. You will be captivated by the beauty, charm and tranquillity of this ancient place.

Other Points
Gift/souvenir shop, parking, toilets, picnic area.

Admission charged

Hours
May to Mid Sept: daily 10.00 - 18.00
Last admission 17.30
Opening times may be subject to change.

Directions
Leave Limerick taking the Tipperary roundabout. Drive to Ballyneety, Grange, and Holycross turning left at Holycross on R514 and arrive at Lough Gur.

Ireland West

www.goodfoodireland.ie

Ballinrobe Co Mayo

JJ Gannon's Hotel
Hotel, restaurant & winebar

Main Street, Ballinrobe, Co Mayo
Tel. +353(0)94 9541008
Email. info@jjgannons.com
www.jjgannons.com

The setting is magical, the feel stylish, contemporary and sophisticated. This area of south Mayo is popular both with anglers and walkers. Indeed anyone keen on the outdoor life. Step inside Niki and Jay Gannon's hotel however and you are soothed and pampered. Rooms are generous, many with good views and all with lots of natural light and well chosen muted colours. The restaurant, although with a contemorary interior, is in a building dating back to 1838. The menu changes daily, shadows the seasons and concentrates on local produce. Herbs, vegetables and fruits come from the kitchen garden, and local producers provide free range and organic poultry and meat. Fresh fish is delivered daily. Fresh breads, jams and desserts are all made in the kitchen.

Rooms: 11 ensuite. Double from €120. Single from €70. Family from €200.
Prices: Lunch main course from €9.50. Dinner main course from €22.50. Bar snack from €8.50. House wine from €18.
Food Served: 7.00-21.30 daily.
Closed: Open all year.
Cuisine: Restaurant: French style. Bar: modern Irish.
Other Points: Non-smoking bedrooms. Garden. Children welcome. Dogs welcome. Car park.
Directions: Town centre location

If you'd like something a little more informal you can also eat in the bar. Or simply sit and enjoy a drink before or after eating in the main restaurant.

JJ Gannon's Hotel

Ireland West

Knock Co Mayo

Knock House Hotel
Hotel and restaurant

Ballyhaunis Road, Knock, Co Mayo
Tel. +353(0)94 9388088
Email. info@knockhousehotel.ie
www.knockhousehotel.ie

Knock House Hotel is set in 100 acres of parkland right beside the world-famous Knock Shrine, a site of pilgrimage for more than 100 years. Indeed, the modern hotel takes this as its inspiration: each room is simply decorated with a unique print inspired by the gardens around the shrine. The striking limestone building itself curves around the hill. Close by is Knock International Airport, and both Galway and Westport are less than an hour away. The hotel is just a short distance from some of the best golf courses the West of Ireland has to offer, and it runs regular golf packages. The substantial and great-value lunch includes options such as deep fried Brie, roast rib of beef and warm peach rice conde. The lobby menu of soup and paninis runs all day. Dinner in its Four Seasons restaurant might start with a seasonal fruit platter, followed by beef consommé and seared tender lamb cutlet. The dessert menu sticks to old favourites done well: homebaked apple and rhubarb crumble, summer flan or Irish cheeses. At breakfast, enjoy grilled kippers with a basket of brown bread.

Rooms: 68 ensuite. Double from €77. Single from €55.
Prices: Lunch main course from €10.25. Dinner main course from €14.50. Bar snack from €4.80. House wine from €21.50.
Food Served: 7.30-22.00.
Cuisine: Traditional and modern.
Other Points: Non-smoking. Garden. Children welcome. Car park.
Directions: 1 hour from Galway city, 1 hour from Sligo on N17 road.

Westport Co Mayo

Quay Cottage
Waterside restaurant

The Harbour, Westport, Co Mayo
Tel. +353 (0)98 26412
Email. quaycottage@eircom.net
www.quaycottage.com

Quay Cottage sits on the Westport waterfront, in view of Croagh Patrick. Outside it appears to be a modestly sized, traditional cottage. Inside, however, it's actually a large high-ceilinged restaurant, divided into three parts. It prides itself on a friendly atmosphere, as well as great attention to detail: owners Kirstin and Peter McDonagh even grow the flowers that decorate your table. They have chosen a nautical theme for the interior, with photos, shells and compasses adorning the walls. Starters might include fish chowder, using a selection of the day's fish, or calamari served with a Greek salad. Main courses feature baked whole seabass served with a red onion, chilli, tomato and basil salsa, and there are daily specials. But non-fish lovers are also well looked after: for them there's vegetarian puff pastry parcel or baked breast of chicken with a spinach and sun-dried tomato filling, wrapped in Parma ham and served with a creamy garlic and chive sauce. The wine list is an interesting selection, reasonably priced, and specially chosen to accompany the menu.

Prices: Dinner main course from €17.90. House wine from €17.50.
Food Served: from 18.00-22.00.
Closed: 3 days at Christmas. January, also Sun & Mon during the winter season.
Cuisine: Modern Irish
Other Points: All children welcome.
Directions: On Westport Harbour at the entrance gates to Westport House.

Ireland West

www.goodfoodireland.ie

National Museum of Ireland - Country Life

Place to Visit

Turlough Park, Castlebar, Co Mayo
Tel. +353 (0) 94 90 31755
Fax. +353 (0) 94 90 31628
Email. tpark@museum.ie
www.museum.ie

This award-winning Museum, a branch of the National Museum of Ireland, is set in the spectacular grounds of Turlough Park. It brings to life the traditions of rural life throughout Ireland from 1850–1950 through the innovative combination of artefacts and displays, archival video footage and interactive screens. Fascinating artefacts deal with domestic life, agriculture, fishing and hunting, clothing and textiles, furniture and fittings, trades and crafts, transport, sports and leisure and religion. Over four floors, the Museum treats visitors to a taste of how our ancestors lived their daily lives, in both difficult and joyful times. This is history truly come to life. Admission to the Museum is free.

Other Points
Free car and coach parking, Museum shop and café, Family Programme and events for all ages, wheelchair accessible, Audio-visual presentation, garden walks and daily guided tours. Groups must book guided tours in advance.

Hours
Open all Year. Tue -Sat 10.00 -17.00.
Sun 14.00 -17.00
Closed Mondays (incl. Bank Holiday Mondays).
Closed Good Friday & Christmas Day.

Directions
Access is from Turlough Village, which is situated off the N5, 8 kms east of Castlebar, Co. Mayo.

Ireland West

Birr Co Offaly

Emma's Café Deli
Town centre café, restaurant, deli

31 Main Street, Birr, Co Offaly
Tel. +353(0)57 9125678
Email. emmascafedeli@eircom.net

This newly opened café in the heart of the Georgian town of Birr is a great place to stop for lunch if you're visiting the beautiful castle gardens - as, indeed, TV gardener Diarmuid Gavin found on a recent visit. Owner Emma Ward is a genuine foodie and produces some fine examples of homecooking on her contemporary Irish menu. The daily changing soup is made from local organic vegetables - there's a child's portion, too - and Emma's Salad deli plate comes with homemade bread, relish and cheese. Breakfast treats include homemade muffins, cherry scones, muesli with organic yoghurt and fairtrade coffees. A small deli counter offers a range of Irish cheeses, fresh pesto and good quality hams. Brightly painted walls surround a large wooden table with soft leather seating in the separate dining area.

Prices: Main course lunch from €6.
Food served: 9.30-18.00 Mon-Fri. 10.00-18.00 Sat. 12.30-17.00 Sun (Mar to Oct).
Closed: Bank Holidays.
Cuisine: Modern Irish.
Other Points: Children welcome. Credit Cards not accepted. Piano in shop so feel free to play if the mood takes you!
Directions: In the centre of town. On the left hand side half way down the Main Street.

Mossfield Organic Farm

Ireland West

www.goodfoodireland.ie

Birr Castle Demesne

Place to Visit

Birr, Co Offaly
Tel. +353 (0)57 91 20336
Fax. +353 (0)57 91 21583
Email. mail@birrcastle.com
www.birrcastle.com

Birr Castle Demesne with unique and fascinating 120 acres of gardens and parkland providing a lovely backdrop for an afternoon stroll amongst its formal gardens; wildflower meadows; river walks and fernery. A visit in spring or summer is rewarded with splashes of colour and heady scents from the different flowers. The grounds, which are open to the public, are also home to the Great Telescope, which for 70 years held the title of the world's largest telescope. There are other interesting features on display in the Science Centre, which takes the story from the terrestrial problems of constructing the telescope to the celestial rewards of all it revealed in the heavens. Birr Castle Demesne offers an excellent way to spend an afternoon in relaxing surroundings, as well as learn of the important scientific achievements of the Irish in the 18th century.

Hours
Mid Mar to Oct 31 daily 9.00-18.00
Nov 1 to Mid Mar daily 10.00-16.00

Admission Charged

Directions
Birr Town is in the centre of Ireland and can be easily reached from the N6 via Tullamore, or the N7 via Roscrea. In Birr Town Centre Square, take the exit beside Bank of Ireland and after 200m take left at high castle wall. The entrance is on right, car parking 50m further on left.

Inagh Farmhouse Cheese

Connemara Smokehouse

Ireland West Touring Route

Nephin Beg Range

Castlebar
National Museum of Ireland – Country Life

Louisburg

Westport
Quay Cottage

Ballinrobe
JJ Gannons Hotel

Renvyle
Renvyle House Hotel

Leenane
Blackberry Café
Delphi Lodge

Clifden
Abbeyglen Castle

Maam Cross

Lough Corrib

Connemara

Ballyconeely
Connemara Smokehouse

Roscahill
Brigit's Garden

Moycullen
Killeen House
White Gables Restaurant

Inveran

Aran Direct

Aran Islands

Inis Oirr
Fisherman's Cottage
Tigh Ned

Must Try...

LOOK OUT FOR...
- Wrasse – local Aran Island fish
- Aran apples & potatoes
- Dulse
- Limpets

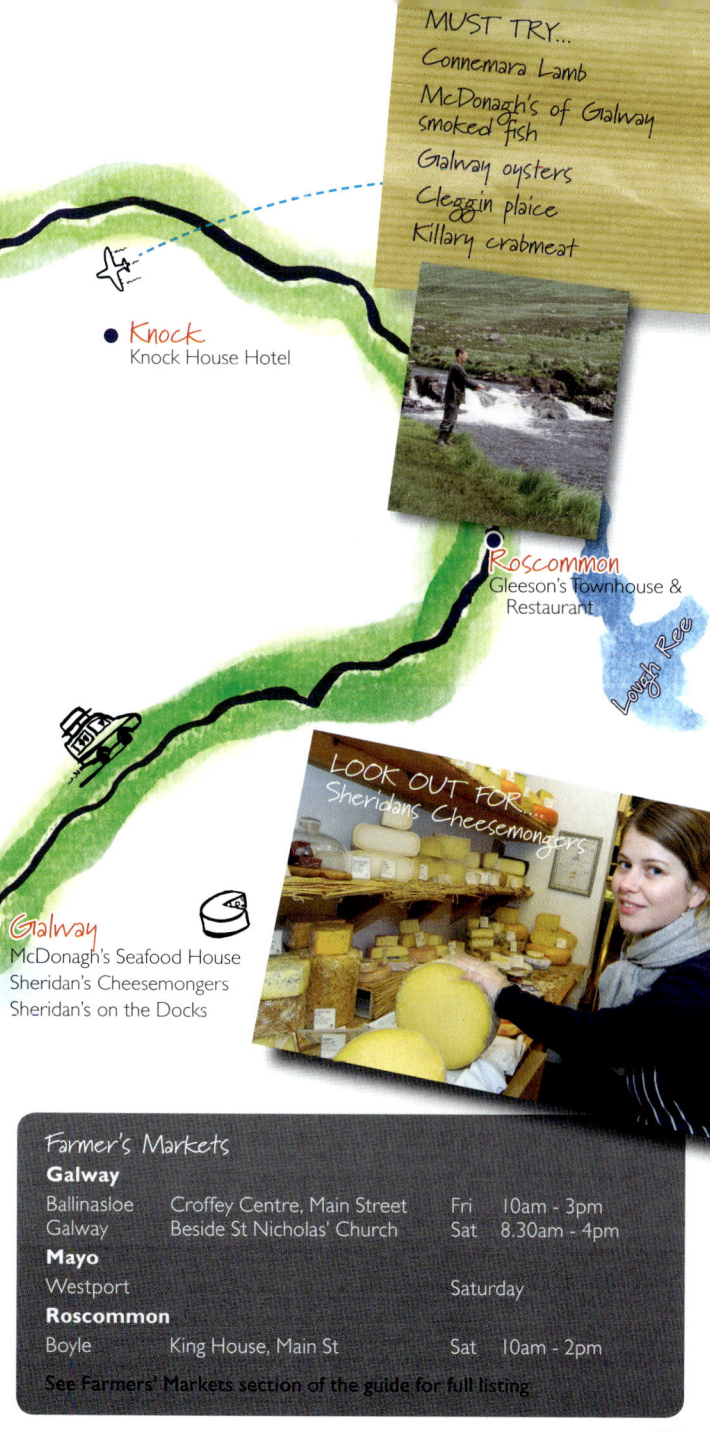

MUST TRY...
Connemara Lamb
McDonagh's of Galway smoked fish
Galway oysters
Cleggin plaice
Killary crabmeat

● **Knock**
Knock House Hotel

Roscommon
Gleeson's Townhouse & Restaurant

Lough Ree

LOOK OUT FOR....
Sheridans Cheesemongers

● **Galway**
McDonagh's Seafood House
Sheridan's Cheesemongers
Sheridan's on the Docks

Farmer's Markets

Galway

Ballinasloe	Croffey Centre, Main Street	Fri	10am - 3pm
Galway	Beside St Nicholas' Church	Sat	8.30am - 4pm

Mayo

Westport		Saturday

Roscommon

Boyle	King House, Main St	Sat	10am - 2pm

See Farmers' Markets section of the guide for full listing

Ireland West

Roscommon Town

Gleeson's Townhouse & Restaurant
Townhouse, restaurant and café

Market Square, Roscommon
Tel. +353(0)90 6626954
Email. info@gleesonstownhouse.com
www.gleesonstownhouse.com

Gleesons is a beautifully restored nineteenth-century guesthouse with restaurant, located approximately one hour from Galway and two hours from Dublin in the centre of Roscommon town overlooking the historic town square. Owned and run by Eamonn and Mary Gleeson, there is attention to detail throughout, with friendly and welcoming staff. There are nineteen comfortable bedrooms including an executive suite with hydrotherapy bath and junior suite. The Manse Restaurant prides itself in providing quality country cooking using local produce and organic ingredients where possible. Ideally situated next door to the weekly Roscommon Farmers Market they are perfectly poised to source local fresh ingredients from local suppliers. They also grow their own herbs and make there own delicious bread, scones, quiches and desserts. For dinner you could try the 'Leitrim organic farmers beefburger, which is served with Mossfield organic garlic and basil cheese on homemade onion foccaccia with frizzled onion' or perhaps their 'herb crusted rack of Roscommon lamb with garlic whipped potato, red onion confit and port wine glaze. Finish with a moreish hot apple and pecan tart with maple syrup and custard. Their wine list offers a good selection, which is very competitively priced. All in all, this is a place that people return to year after year and we understand why.

Rooms: 19 ensuite. Double from €110. Single from €55. Family from €150. Suite from €150.
Prices: Lunch main course from €9.50-€13.95. Dinner main course from €14.95-€24.95. House wine from €15.50.
Food served: Café 8.00-21.00 daily. Restaurant 18.30-21.00 Sun-Thur. 18.30-22.00 Fri-Sat.
Closed: 25, 26 Dec.
Cuisine: Modern Irish/European.
Other Points: Garden. Children welcome. Car park. Dogs welcome. Winner - Host of the Year 2004.
Directions: From Dublin take N6 to Athlone, then take the N61 to Roscommon. From Sligo, N4 to Boyle, then the N61. Located in Roscommon Town Centre, next door to tourist office.

Eamonn and Mary Gleeson

for online reservations **Ireland West**

Sligo Town

Kate's Kitchen
Town centre gourmet food and wine shop

3 Castle Street, Sligo
Tel. +353(0)71 9143022
Email: info@kateskitchensligo.com
www.kateskitchensligo.com

Located in Sligo's town centre near to Sligo Abbey, 'Kate's Kitchen' is definitely worth a 'stop, look and purchase'! An unusual concept, this 'twin shop' with it's old fashioned, black painted frontage complete with red and gold lettering and large bay windows was established in 1982 by Kate Pettit and Frank Hopper. 'Hopper & Pettit' to one side stocks the 'best of the best' from the world of cosmetic and toiletry products, for both men and women, while 'Kate's Kitchen' to the right is a Gourmet Food and Wine Shop/Delicatessen. It is a real Aladdin's Cave with an array of Gourmet delights and fine foods. Following Kate's own recipes loyal customers enjoy sampling home made produce like salads, patés, glazed hams, tea-bracks or carrot cake.

Opening Hours: 9.00-18.00.
Closed: Sundays and bank holidays.
Directions: Town centre location near Sligo Abbey.

They also stock a vast selection of Irish and European cheeses and chocolates eg. Waterford's Gallweys luxury handmade Irish Whiskey Chocolates. You will always find gift inspiration from one of the crammed wooden shelves, which are full of tempting bottles, jars and packages of all shapes and sizes. It really is Sligo's charming and delightful food & wine version of 'Willie Wonka's chocolate factory' for all you 'foodies' out there - Enjoy!

Nenagh Co Tipperary

Country Choice
Coffee shop, deli and gallery

25 Kenyon Street, Nenagh, Co Tipperary
Tel. +353(0)67 32596
Email: peter@countrychoice.com

What can be said that hasn't already been said about Peter and Mary Ward's wonderful delicatessen and café in Nenagh? Only that it is a 'must' for any travellers from home or abroad - perhaps if you are visiting Lough Derg or travelling between Limerick and Dublin you could pop in for some real delights! It is at this welcoming wine-coloured café that you will be treated to wholesome home-cooked meals where only the finest regional farm produce sourced locally is used. Perhaps try a 'local free-range pork and apple casserole with Devil's Bit cider' or 'Irish stew of slow cooked gigot with champ'. You will not be disappointed even if you only have time for a coffee and 'homemade bread and butter pudding' but do take the time to bring some goodies home for later - choose between their home made jams and chutneys, or a perhaps a selection of Tipperary cheese. Why not sample one of their specially chosen wines that they import exclusively for their loyal clientele.

Prices: Lunch main course from €9.
Food served: 9.00-17.00 Mon-Sat.
Closed: Sunday, Good Friday & 25 Dec.
Cuisine: Modern Irish.
Other Points: Art Gallery. Winner - Special Award 2004.
Directions: Leave N7 for Nenagh. Go to traffic lights, turn left at Bank of Ireland. Country Choice is half-way down the street on right hand side.

There is always a special offer on and usually wines purchased from the shop to enjoy with your meal incur only €5 corkage. Established in 1982, Country Choice has gained a well-deserved respect from locals and holiday makers alike for it's fresh home made food, organic fruit and vegetables, wholemeal breads, stunning cheeses and artisan food products.

PLAIN AND ARTY

What you get may not be fancy, but it can certainly be good. Caroline Workman seeks out the best of what Good Food Ireland members are championing all the time in Northern Ireland - local, fresh and seasonal

Caroline Workman is a speciality food consultant and food writer. She spent five years working in the restaurant trade before setting up her own company, Food Stuff Ireland, a marketing and training consultancy dedicated to the speciality food trade.

Soft batch bread with chewy crusts sandwiching succulent baked ham. Earthy soda farls, buttered and sticky with local raspberry or strawberry jam. Dappled potato bread, fried crisp and served with thick and salty dry cured bacon, or folded to enclose stewed Armagh apples. This is the 'plain' food that characterises Northern Ireland, a predominantly rural region with honest, traditional tastes.

Traditional butchers and home bakeries are numerous here. They have a loyal following for their excellent, trustworthy meat and champion sausages - beef sausages in particular - or the unique vernacular breads, which must be eaten fresh from the griddle on the day they are made, or fried in lard for a big Ulster fry.

Prawn cocktail and steak are the most popular restaurant dishes and with good chefs, the prawns will be super sized, sweet beauties from the tidal waters of places like Strangford Lough and Dundrum Bay. There is practically no question that the beef will be grass fed and properly matured as long as they shop with a trusty butcher. Co Tyrone farmers, with their small farm holdings and 'soft' rain seem to breed particularly fine stock.

Salmon is almost everyone's favourite fish, and here it's not that surprising to find rural convenience stores or restaurants supplied by local salmon fishermen. However, when you can't get wild salmon, organically farmed fish from Glenarm exercised by the almighty currents off the Antrim coasts make a very acceptable alternative.

As with any region spoilt for a particular foodstuff, locals have traditionally tended to ignore the fantastic seafood from our clean coastline and freshwater loughs. Oysters and mussels from Dundrum, Strangford and Carlingford are exported to London and beyond. Silver or brown eel from the River Bann and Lough Neagh are shipped off to Holland.

Again, however, we're catching ourselves on: dedicated seafood restaurants are more numerous than ever before, and fish such as ling, mackerel, turbot and brill are making appearances on their

Paul Arthurs, Kircubbin

menus. Eel, as well as salmon, is being smoked by a new generation of artisans, to be served with buttered wheaten bread, another local food icon. You'll find areas where there's always been an uncommon enthusiasm for ancient recipes. Ardglass potted herrings, found in butcher's shops and at the stalls of fish traders in Co Down, are marinated in vinegar, rolled with bay leaf and baked with breadcrumbs to be eaten as a snack.

Eels mostly found in mid Ulster are dipped in flour and fried, leaping as if alive in a hot buttered pan, and then served up with oniony white sauce and creamy mash. Alternatively they suit a long, slow stew.

Vegetable roll – sliced 'sticks' of fatty but flavoursome boned out brisket chopped and combined with onion, leek carrot and lots of white pepper are served with buttery swede or turnip and more mash.

It's unfortunate that these are often only domestic dishes, beaten to the restaurant or pub tables by equally comforting liver & bacon, bacon & cabbage, lamb or stout enriched beef stews or pies, or 'modern' recipes of lamb shank, pork belly, and Co Down venison carpaccio.

There's also a lot more experimentation with salads, vegetables and soft fruits, which grow brilliantly in our warm microclimate. But it's hard to beat a plate of dark green Pamphrey leaves, braised cabbage or leeks, squeaking in butter, or sweet carrots mashed with parsnip. And let's not forget potatoes - often served three ways: big, boiled 'balls of flour', champ (mashed with milk and scallions) and golden sautéed fries.

Nor should we ignore the north's sweet tooth. It starts at 'Elevenses' when wee buns, tray bakes or short breads are bought out to accompany cups of tea, and continues through the afternoon with fruit-studded cakes, buttered barmbrack, or a slice of cake. Sugary hits of fudge or 'yellow man', a bubbly golden confection, are also popular.

At 'High Tea' bread, butter and jam will be served alongside savoury food and followed by desserts – say lemon meringue pie or a piece of apple & rhubarb crumble. 'Supper' - just before you go to bed - might be sandwiches and another wee bun or a nightcap of Black Bush. ∎

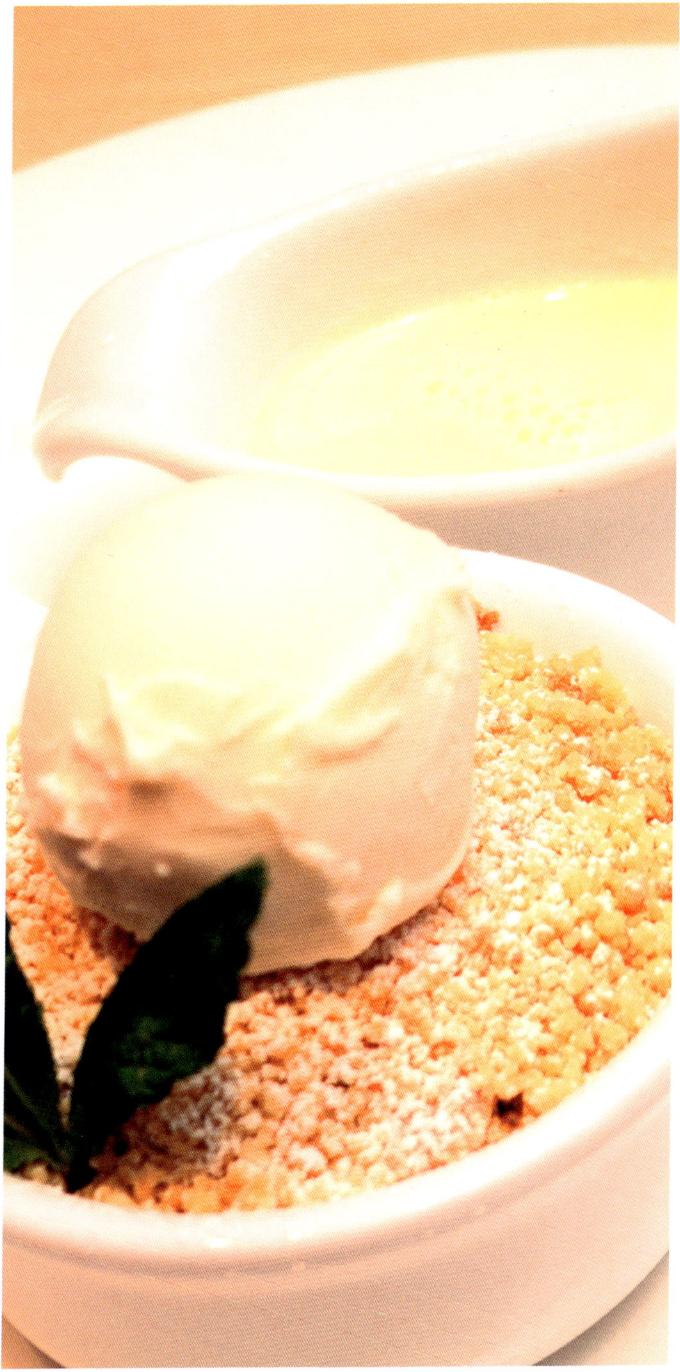

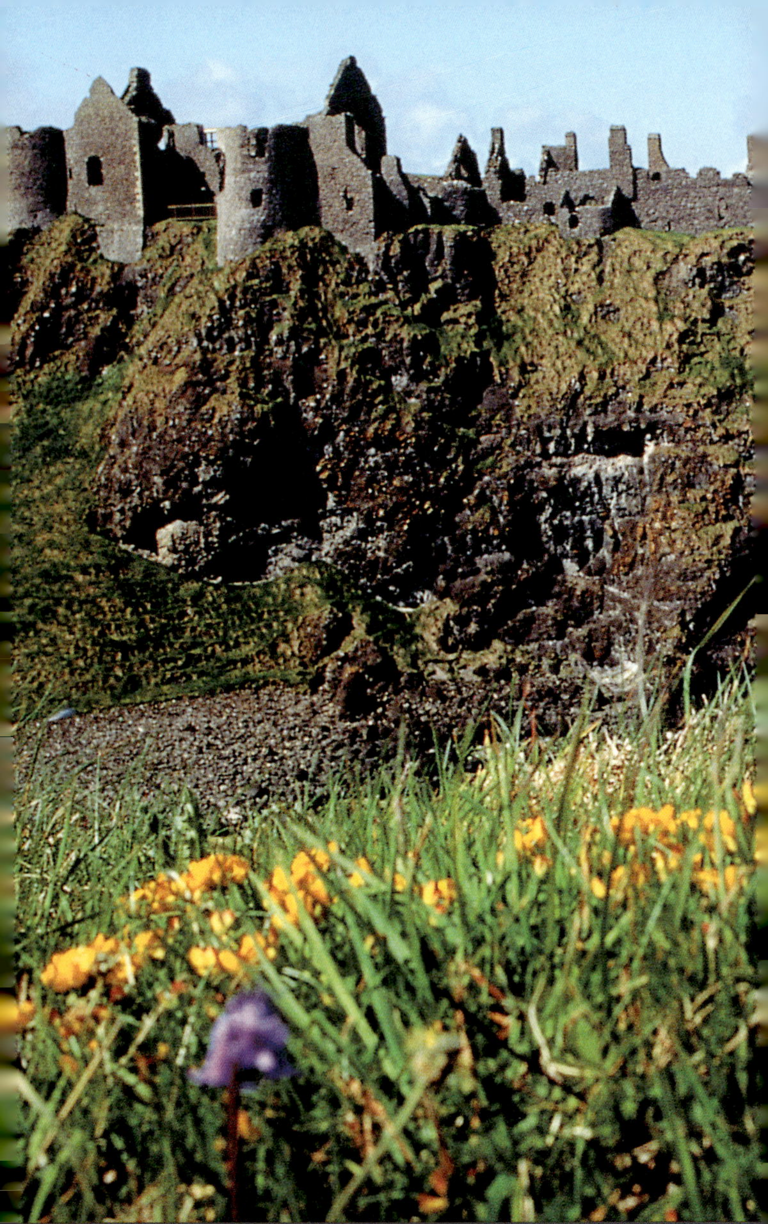

Ireland North

Ireland North Touring Route

Bushmills — Bushmills Garden Centre Café

Coast Road

Coleraine

Limavaddy

Derry
Brown's Restaurant Bar & Brasserie
The Tower Museum

MUST TRY......
Ditty's potato farls, griddle breads, oatcakes, "wee buns"

Ditty's Home Bakery & Coffee Shop
Laurel Villa

Magherafelt

Moneymore
Springhill

MUST TRY......
- Mourne Lamb
- Armagh Apples
- The Ulster Fry
- From Moyallen: pork & dry cured bacon, sausages

Omagh

Cookstown

Belleek Pottery 40 miles west of Enniskillen

Dungann
Grange Loc

Enniskillen
Castle Coole

Armagh
Armagh County Museum

Farmer's Markets

Antrim

Belfast	St Georges Market 12-20 East Bridge St	Fri 6am - 1pm Sat 9am - 3pm
Lisburn	Lisburn market	Every Sat
Templepatrick	Templepatrick	4th Sun 11am - 6pm

Armagh

Portadown	Portadown market	Last Sat of every month

Tyrone

Dungannon	Tesco's carpark	1st Sat 8.30am - 1pm

See Farmers' Markets section of the guide for full listing

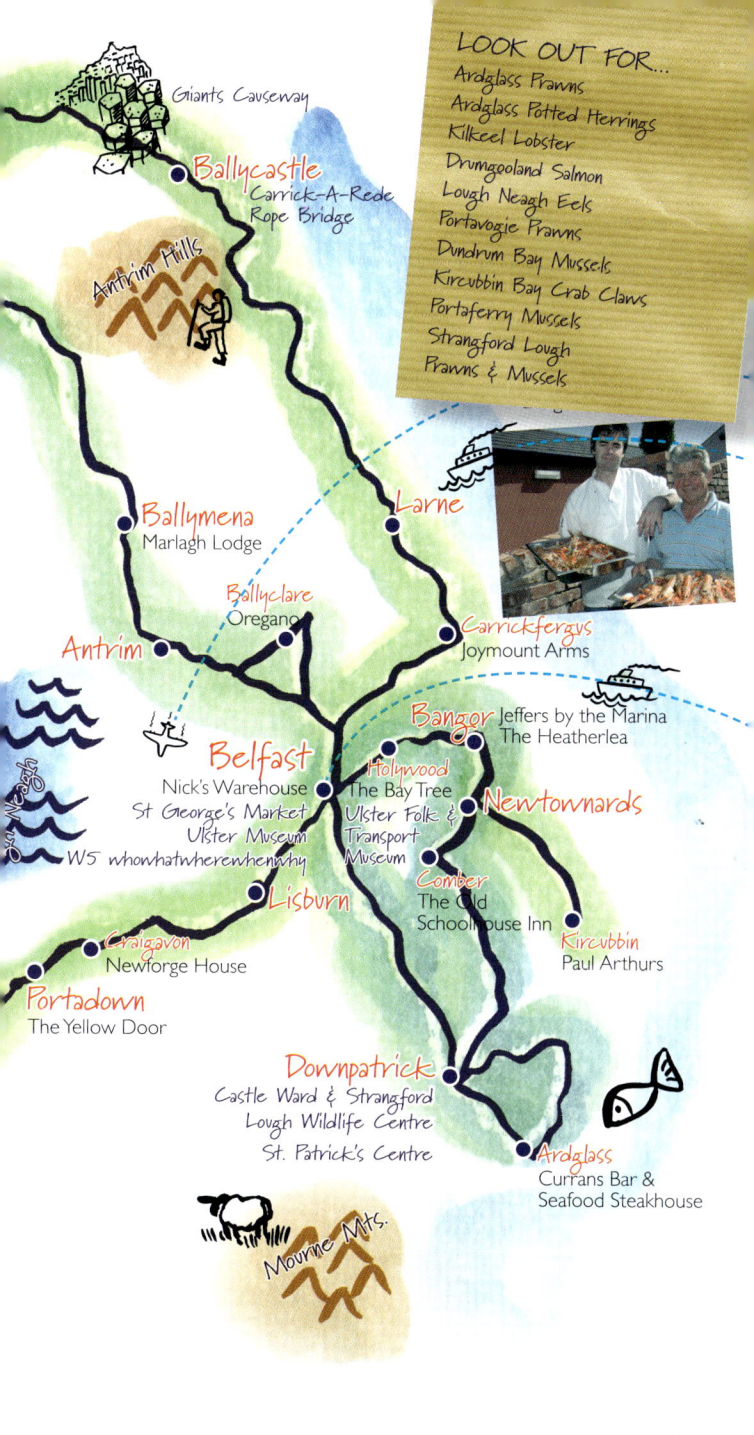

LOOK OUT FOR...
Ardglass Prawns
Ardglass Potted Herrings
Kilkeel Lobster
Drumgooland Salmon
Lough Neagh Eels
Portavogie Prawns
Dundrum Bay Mussels
Kircubbin Bay Crab Claws
Portaferry Mussels
Strangford Lough
Prawns & Mussels

Giants Causeway

Ballycastle
Carrick-A-Rede Rope Bridge

Antrim Hills

Ballymena
Marlagh Lodge

Larne

Ballyclare
Oregano

Antrim

Carrickfergus
Joymount Arms

Bangor Jeffers by the Marina
The Heatherlea

Belfast
Nick's Warehouse
St George's Market
Ulster Museum
W5 whowhatwherewhenwhy

Holywood
The Bay Tree
Ulster Folk & Transport Museum

Newtownards

Lisburn

Comber
The Old Schoolhouse Inn

Craigavon
Newforge House

Kircubbin
Paul Arthurs

Portadown
The Yellow Door

Downpatrick
Castle Ward & Strangford Lough Wildlife Centre
St. Patrick's Centre

Ardglass
Currans Bar & Seafood Steakhouse

Mourne Mts.

Ireland North

www.goodfoodireland.ie

Ballyclare Co Antrim

Oregano Restaurant
Rural restaurant

29 Ballyrobert Road, Ballyrobert,
Ballyclare, Co Antrim BT39 9RY
Tel. +44(0)28 9084 0099
Email. oregano.rest@btconnect.com
www.oreganorestaurant.co.uk

You'll have to go a bit off the beaten track to find Oregano - but it's worth it. Dermot and Catherine Regan, a young couple who have the right ethos with regard to sourcing local foods, run the restaurant. Victorian architecture outside results in a high-ceilinged, spacious and bright dining room. The modern menu uses flair and imagination, combining ingredients not normally seen together. An example is seared hake and scallops with a chorizo, tomato and flat parsley risotto and crispy fried leeks. Or try seared fillet of seabream with soft polenta and slow roast tomatoes. Belfast fishmonger Walter Ewing supplies fish. Beef comes from Jenkins local farm and Finnebrogue in Downpatrick supplies venison. Pork, fruit and vegetables are from Ballylagan Organic Farm in Straid. All breads are home baked. The lunch menu offers 'bangers & mash' pork and leek sausages with wholegrain mustard mash and onion gravy. Evening mains have venison with fondant potato or roast breast of duck with thyme scented roasted sweet potatoes and Asian greens. Desserts are irrestible - try coffee and caramel crème brûlée or rhubarb and fig tart. Irish cheeses are accompanied by grape chutney. There's a global wine list and six excellent house wines at a reasonable price.

Prices: Lunch main course from £6.75. Dinner main course from £10.95. House wine from £13.95. Set 2/3 course menu £14.95/£17.95 available 12.00-14.30 & 17.30-19.30 Tue-Fri.
Food served: 12.00-14.30 and 17.30-21.30 Tues-Fri. 18.00-22.00 Sat. Sunday lunch 12.00-15.00.
Closed: Mondays. 24-26 December. 1 Jan. 11-13 July.
Cuisine: Modern Irish
Other Points: Children welcome. Garden. Car park.
Directions: From Belfast take the M2 north, then A6 to Sandyknowes roundabout. Take the Larne exit to Corrs corner roundabout, take a left turn to Ballyclare and Oregano is one and a half miles on right hand side.

Ireland North

Ballymena Co Antrim

Marlagh Lodge
Country house and restaurant

71 Moorfields Road, Ballymena
Co Antrim BT42 3BU
Tel. +44(0)28 2563 1505
Email. info@marlaghlodge.com
www.marlaghlodge.com

Robert and Rachel Thompson have restored this listed nineteenth-century house with immense good taste. It was built for the rebellious heir to the now-destroyed Crebilly castle and his headless ghost is said to haunt the grounds. The light, well-proportioned rooms are full of original Victorian features, with open fireplaces, antique pianos and beautiful William Morris wallpaper. The Thompsons are keen musicians with eclectic tastes, which are reflected in the plentiful reading matter throughout the house. Evening meals - available to non-residents (Fri/Sat) with notice - are dinner-party style, with a typical menu taking in Prosciutto wrapped roasted asparagus with sun-dried tomato pesto and Parmesan crisps for starters followed by roasted fillet of Finnebrogue venison with plum and chilli jam or thyme and orange marinated poussin. Finish with dark and white chocolate marquise with creme anglaise, freshly made coffee and homemade goodies! Breakfast brings a 'tummy warmer' of porridge with whisky, cream and brown sugar while eggs are free range and jams and brown bread are homemade. Three bedrooms - blue, chintz and print - have luxurious sheets and antique dressers. Splendid bathrooms, two en-suite, come with roll-top baths and salvaged sinks.

Rooms: 3(2 ensuite). Double from £80. Single from £40.
Prices: Set dinner £31.50 (non residents). House wine from: £14.50.
Food Served: Dinner served daily for residents - book by noon.
Non-residents Fri & Sat only.
Closed: Christmas & New Year.
Cuisine: Modern Irish.
Other Points: No-smoking house. Garden. Children welcome. Car park. Winner - Guesthouse & Restaurant of the Year 2004.
Directions: A26 to Ballymena. One mile after "Line Bridge" turn right to "Country Garage", cross two crossroads to Rankinstown Road, house at end on the right (gravel drive).

205

Ireland North

www.goodfoodireland.ie

Belfast City Co Antrim

Nicks Warehouse
City centre restaurant & wine bar

35-39 Hill Street, Belfast,
Co Antrim BT1 2LB
Tel. +44(0)28 9043 9690
Email. info@nickswarehouse.co.uk
www.nickswarehouse.co.uk

This red-brick building, originally built for the Bushmills whiskey company in 1832, draws the discerning Belfast crowd. The menus at Nick Price's "warehouse" are enough get the juices flowing: there are so many delicious combinations you'll want to come back to try more. Lunch at the Anix restaurant includes parsnip and turnip soup, local smoked salmon on a chunky guacamole salad with dill mayonnaise or maple-cured bacon with vegetable ratatouille. Dinner could be grilled sweet potato with St Tola Feta cheese and baby spinach salad, followed by duck breast with a warm noodle salad and soy, pickled ginger and lime dressing, or Kilkeel lobster with a pineapple and avocado salad and lemon mayonnaise. The kitchen makes three different types of bread every day, and Nick keeps an extensive herb garden for the restaurant's use. The wine bar has

Prices: Lunch main course from £6.25. Dinner main course from £9.25. House wine from £12.50.
Food served: 12.00-15.00 Mon-Fri. Dinner 18.00-21.30 Tue-Thurs. 18.00-22.00 Fri-Sat.
Closed: Sundays. Easter Sun & Mon. 12 July, 25, 26 December.
Cuisine: Modern Irish.
Other Points: Winner - Ireland North Regional Award 2006.
Directions: Near St Anne's Cathedral, off Waring Street.

recently been refurbished, and windows open out onto the street, giving a lively continental atmosphere on sunny evenings. The carefully chosen wine list regularly gets new and interesting additions, and there is a separate Spanish list, as well as fine wines that, with their flat bottle mark-up policy, are great value.

Bushmills Co Antrim

Bushmills Garden Centre
Coastal restaurant, café, bakery & gift shop

88 Ballyclough Road, Bushmills
Co Antrim, BT57 8XA
Tel. +44(0)28 2073 1287
Email. info@creativegardens.net
www.creativegardens.net

Close by the famous Bushmills Distillery, this traditional restaurant and teashop prides itself on cooking with the finest local ingredients. All the food is prepared daily on the premises, with Burns Butchers supplying meat and fresh fish arriving to the kitchen straight from the local port, Portovogie. The range of home baked scones is breath-taking - as well as the usual plain, cherry and fruit, the varieties include date and wheaten, blueberry, and raspberry and white chocolate. There is also fat free fruit cake and for coeliacs, gluten free coffee cake and Belgian chocolate brownies. For lunch, choose from gourmet soup, cottage pie, paupiette of salmon or chicken and broccoli bake. The evening menu offers beef au poivre, fillet of cod, chicken provencale, aromatic duck and pork fillet crevette. Finish with

Prices: Lunch main course from £6.50.
Opening hours: 10.00-17.00 Mon-Wed & Fri-Sat. 10.00-19.30 Thurs. 12.00-17.00 Sun.
Food served: 12.30-14.30 daily. Thurs 17.30-19.30.
Cuisine: Traditional café home-cooked food.
Closed: 25, 26 Dec. Easter Sunday.
Other Points: Children welcome. Garden. Car park. Dogs welcome. Gluten free baking.

one of the hard-to-resist desserts - chocolate fudge cake, cheesecake or lemon drizzle cake and a cup of flavoured latte. Walk off all this delicious food with a visit to the near-by Giant's Causeway.

Ireland North

Carrickfergus Co Antrim

The Joymount Arms
Waterfront traditional pub & restaurant

16-18 Joymount Street,
Carrickfergus, Co Antrim
Tel. +44(0)28 9336 2213
Email. joymountarms@aol.com
www.joymountarms.co.uk

You can't miss Jack Creighton's Joymount Arms in Carrickfergus - it's painted a beautiful raspberry-red. The original building was built about 1830 when it was a spirit grocer (you could have a jar while buying the groceries.). The pub was established in 1846 and continues to be a popular meeting place for wining and dining. It faces onto Belfast Lough so offers visitors spectacular views of the County Down coastline. Everything is cooked from scratch in the kitchen, using fresh, local ingredients. Irish beef comes from McMurrays butchers; pheasant, fish and wild salmon are also sourced in the area. Traditional pub fare includes beef and Guinness in a rich mushroom gravy, slow roast shoulder of Irish lamb served with buttery champ and cabbage and bacon. Ownies Bistro offers such delights as herb crusted fillet of salmon, Portovogie scampi, rib eye steak, wok fried sizzlers and pasta dishes. Special teenage menu has paninis, pasta, or strip steak. There's a small, but decent wine list that includes a good selection of quarter bottles.

Prices: Lunch/dinner main course from £5.25. Bar snack from £2.95. House wine from £8.95.
Opening Hours: 11.30-23.00 Mon-Thurs & Sun. 11.30- 0020 Fri-Sat.
Food Served: 12.30-14.30 and 17.00-20.30 Mon-Thurs. 12.00-15.00 and 17.00-21.00 Fri-Sat. 12.30-20.30 Sun.
Closed: Bistro closed 25, 26 Dec and 1 Jan. 12 July holidays.
Cuisine: Traditional/modern Irish.
Other Points: Private function room. Sunken beer garden. Children welcome. Children/teenage menu.
Directions: From Belfast follow signs to Carrickfergus. At the castle go through two sets of traffic lights. After second set, turn left. Turn right at mini roundabout. Joymount Arms is 100 yards on the left, just past the library.

Nick's Warehouse

Ireland North

www.goodfoodireland.ie

St. George's Market

Place to Visit

12-20 East Bridge Street, Belfast,
Co Antrim BT1 3NQ.
Tel. +44 (0)28 9043 5704
Fax. +44 (0)28 9027 0501
Email. markets@belfastcity.gov.uk
www.belfastcity.gov.uk

If you want to enjoy a real taste of Belfast, visit St. George's Market, one of the most colourful and vibrant destinations in Belfast. There has been a Friday market on the St. George's site dating back to 1604. The present St. George's Market, built 1890-1896, is one of Belfast's oldest attractions and still maintains its status today as one of the best markets in the UK. Since its £4.5m refurbishment in 1997, this charming Victorian building offers one of the most vibrant and colourful destinations that Belfast has to offer. St. George's Market has just been voted one of the top 5 UK markets in 2006 by the National Association of British Market Authorities. As well as being home to some of the finest fresh produce, with customers travelling from near and far to sample the delights of the Friday and Saturday markets, it has quickly become one of the City's most popular places to visit.

The Friday Variety Market opens at 6.00am every week and runs until approximately 1.00pm. This is a hugely vibrant retail experience of 248 market stalls selling diverse wares from Atlantic Shark to zips, old antiques to fresh fruit. The fish section alone contains 23 fish stalls and holds the reputation for being the leading retail fish market in Ireland. It is this eclectic mix that attracts thousands of people along each week to probably the best market in Northern Ireland. It's easy to get caught up in the excitement as you barter with the friendly local stallholders for a bargain.

The City Food & Garden Market takes place in St George's every Saturday from 9.00am to 3.00pm. Enjoy the best food tastes and smells brought by local producers, including beef from Armagh, award winning Irish Farmhouse Cheeses, free range eggs from Limavady, venison, pheasant in season and local organic vegetables from Culdrum Farm and Millbrook Farm. In addition to these local delicacies, there is also a fusion of tempting continental and speciality foods from around the world. Included are such delights as wild boar, cured meats, venison, Spanish tapas, Caribbean foods, Mexican and Slavonic foods, continental coffees and teas, Italian olive oils with traditional French Crepes and extraordinary French pastries to mention just a few. Added to this plethora of tempting foods the Saturday market also encompasses flower stalls ensuring this Saturday market is a kaleidoscope of colour.

St. George's City Food & Garden Market has something for everyone. More than just a shopping experience, customers can sample the produce, relax with a coffee and a newspaper against a backdrop of live jazz or flamenco music. This market is a real Saturday treat and a great outing for all the family. You'll never know who you'll meet on Saturdays at St. George's Market.

Transport
A free market bus runs every 20 minutes between the City Centre (outside Boots the Chemist, Donegal Place or HMV, Castle Place) and the market. Bus departs 8am on Friday and every 20 minutes thereafter. Bus departs 9.00am on Saturday and every 20 minutes thereafter. Nearest customer parking at Hilton car parks opposite the market.

Hours
Variety Market: Fri 6.00 - 13.00
City Food & Garden Market
Sat 9.00 - 15.00

Directions
St George's Market is located opposite Belfast Waterfront Hall and the Hilton Hotel in Oxford Street, which runs parallel to the River Lagan. From the rear of Belfast city Hall walk eastwards down May Street for a few minutes, cross over Victoria Street and St George's is directly in front of you.

Ireland North

The Giant's Causeway

Place to Visit

Causeway Road, Bushmills,
Co Antrim BT57 8SU
Tel. +44 (0)28 2073 1582 or 2972
Fax. +44 (0)28 2073 2963
Email.
giantscauseway@nationaltrust.org.uk

The North Antrim Coast is a designated Area of Outstanding Natural Beauty. Along its beautiful coast is the world famous Giant's Causeway, an icon of Northern Ireland and its only World Heritage Site.

Other Points

Guided tours by arrangement for groups over 15 (Tel. 028 2073 1582 for details). Country walk, Suitable for picnics, Shop, Refreshments, Available for functions, Programme of events, Access for visitors with disability, Facilities for families, Learning, Dogs welcome on leads.

Admission Charged

Hours

Stones & Coastal Path open all year
Trust Shop
Open all year -except 25 & 26 Dec
For opening times please contact property directly.
Tea Room
Open all year - except 25 & 26 Dec
For opening times please contact property directly.

Directions

On B146, 2ml from Bushmills.
Drive time: Belfast 1.15hr.

Ulster Museum

Place to Visit

Botanic Gardens, Belfast, BT9 5AB
Tel. +44 (0)28 9038 3000
www.ulstermuseum.org.uk

The Ulster Museum is the perfect place to explore art, history and the natural world.

The Museum holds a rich variety of Irish, British and International paintings and drawings, as well as ceramics, glass, silver and costume from a collection of thousands of works covering centuries of fine and decorative arts. The history collections illustrate the story of the north of Ireland from the end of the Ice Age 10,000 years ago to the present day. The sciences collections hold a wonderful variety of material relating to the natural world, from animals and plants to minerals, gemstones and fossils. From ancient and world cultures to contemporary art, the Museum offers something for everyone - young and old, new faces and regular visitors.

Redevelopment of the Museum
An exciting £12 million redevelopment of the Ulster Museum is taking place from autumn 2006.

The Museum is **closed from the end of August 2006 for approximately 2.5 years**, but visitors can find information on the collections, the redevelopment project and the Museum's outreach activities during closure on the website.

Ireland North

www.goodfoodireland.ie

W5 - whowhatwherewhenwhy

Place to Visit

W5 at Odyssey, 2 Queen's Quay,
Belfast, Co Antrim BT3 9QQ
Tel. +44 (0)28 9046 7700
www.w5online.co.uk.

W5 is Ireland's first and only purpose-built interactive discovery centre and is located at the Odyssey Complex, Belfast. As one of Northern Ireland's premier visitor attractions the centre has over 160 amazing unique, hands-on exhibits, which offer hours of fun for visitors of all ages. There are five action-packed interactive exhibition areas called WOW, START, GO, SEE & DO with attractions including a laser harp, animation stations, cloud rings, a lie detector and lots more! In addition to the exhibits, W5 also present live science shows and have a changing programme of special events. New for Summer 2006, Lovesport, an exhibition that lets you take part in a range of physical and computer-based sporting activities. Exhibition is free with admission to W5.

Other Points

W5 is fully accessible, educational workshops, corporate hire facilities, birthday party package, coffee shop available, admission charged, season pass, group and family ticketing options available.

Hours

Mon - Sat 10.00 - 18.00
Sun 12.00 - 18.00
Last admission 17.00
Please note, during school term time W5 will close one hour earlier Mon - Thur at 17.00 with last admission at 16.00.

Directions

From Belfast City Centre - follow signs for the A2 Bangor onto Queen Elizabeth Bridge. Keep in the left lane and immediately after crossing the River Lagan turn left onto Queen's Island. Follow the road for 1/4 mile, the car park is on your right.

Ireland North

Craigavon Co Armagh

Newforge House
Geogian country house

58 Newforge Road, Magheralin
Craigavon, Co Armagh, BT67 OLQ
Tel. +44 (0)28 9261 1255
Email. enquiries@newforgehouse.com
www.newforgehouse.com

Located in the country village of Magheralin, only a half hour drive from Belfast, this classic Georgian family-run guesthouse dates from around 1785. Currently run by John and Louise Mathers, it has been in the Mather family for six generations and is perfectly positioned to travel and explore Northern Ireland - particularly the historic city of Armagh or Lough Neagh. The house has been sensitively restored to reflect an elegant, luxurious and friendly 'home from home'. There are six double bedrooms with large en-suite bathrooms, which all contain period features and are complemented with the best modern conveniences. Open log fires and fresh flowers add to the lavish and luxurious yet relaxed atmosphere. The dining experience benefits from the owner's utmost attention as much as the décor and surroundings of this historic house. Where possible, local produce is sourced with particular emphasis on seasonal ingredients and organic produce. The diner could try 'hot-smoked Drumgooland Salmon & Isle of Skye Smoked Salmon with a chive crème fraîche' and follow with 'cutlets of Irish spring lamb with a redcurrant jus'and to finish a selection of Irish cheese or home grown raspberry & vanilla Mascarpone pot.

Rooms: 6 ensuite. Double from £100. Single from £65. Family room from £115.
Prices: Dinner (3 courses) from £27.50 incl coffee. Bar Snack from £3.50. House wine from £12.00.
Food served: Dinner 18.30-20.30 Tues-Thurs, 19.00-21.00 Fri-Sat. 24 hours notice required. Light meal available Sun & Mon on request.
Closed: Christmas & New Year, occasionally at other times.
Cuisine: Modern Irish.
Other Points: Garden. Children welcome. Car Park. Civil Wedding Licence. Small weddings catered for.
Directions: From Belfast M1 West, exit 9 for Moira/ Lurgan. Continue approx. 3 miles. In Magheralin take first left at Byrne's pub onto Newforge Road. Continue approx. 0.5 miles. First left after speed limit sign.

Newforge House

Ireland North

www.goodfoodireland.ie

Portadown Co Armagh

The Yellow Door
Bistro, deli, bakery and patisserie

74 Woodhouse Street, Portadown,
Co Armagh BT62 1JL
Tel. +44(0)28 3835 3528
Email. info@yellowdoordeli.co.uk
www.yellowdoordeli.co.uk

Simon Dougan's The Yellow Door has built its reputation by using free-range, local and organic produce wherever possible, smoking its own fish, making its own ice cream and, of course, baking all its own breads. Alongside this deli and patisserie is a licensed bistro and café, where you can treat yourself to any of several beautifully prepared and presented dishes. Breakfast here could be a simple bacon and egg ciabatta or a banana toastie with maple syrup. Chef Michael Donaghey's lunch options include Malaysian beef curry and wilted spinach on coriander egg noodles, or a gourmet sandwich such as Moyallon pork sausage with home-made apple chutney. A new casual lounge area with soft seating and coffee tables was due to open at time of going to press, and the main shop was set for a refurbishment to include library shelving containing hundreds of old cookery books, and lower shelves with Disney books for the kids. Before you leave, choose a mouth-watering dessert from the patisserie such as lemon and passionfruit tart or warm pear and honey upside-down cake.

Prices: Lunch main course from £5. House wine from £9.50.
Food served: 9.00-17.00 Mon-Sat.
Closed: Sundays. 25, 26 Dec. May day. 12, 13 July.
Cuisine: Modern Irish/French.
Other Points: No-smoking area. Children welcome. In-house bakery and French patisserie.
Directions: M1 exit 11 into town centre. On high street turn left only one street on left going downhill away from church, one way system.

The Yellow Door

Paul Arthurs

Ireland North

www.goodfoodireland.ie

Armagh County Museum

Place to Visit

The Mall East, Armagh BT61 9BE
Tel. +44 (0)28 3752 3070
Fax. +44 (0)28 3752 2631
Email. acm.info@magni.org.uk
www.armaghcountymuseum.org.uk

Strolling along the tree-lined Mall, near the centre of St Patrick's cathedral city, a visit to Armagh County Museum is an ideal way to experience a flavour of the orchard county. Built in 1834 to a classical design, its impressive columns dominate the entrance, making it one of the most distinctive buildings in the area. The Museum's extensive collections and displays reflect the lives of people who have lived and worked in Armagh or have been associated with the county. Discover a rich and varied legacy revealed in objects ranging from prehistoric artefacts to household items from a bygone age. There are military uniforms, wedding dresses, ceramics, natural history specimens and railway memorabilia. An impressive art collection includes works by many well-known Irish artists. The Museum also has an extensive reference library, rich in local archive material, along with photographic and map collections. With a range of changing exhibitions throughout the year, it is an ideal place to see and explore the fair county of Armagh.

Other Points
Museum Shop, Baby Changing Facilities, Access and Facilities for Disabled Visitors, Group Visits by prior arrangements for Adults, Community and School Groups, and Friends Association.

Admission is free

Hours
Mon - Fri 10.00 - 17.00
Sat 10.00 - 13.00 & 14.00 - 17.00

Directions
From Belfast exit and junction 11 from M1. Follow the signs through Portadown for Armagh. On entering the city the Museum is located about half way along the Mall, between the old gaol and the courthouse.

Ireland North

Londonderry Co Derry

Browns Restaurant, Bar & Brasserie
City centre restaurant & bar

1 & 2 Bonds Hill, Londonderry,
Co Derry BT47 6DW
Tel. +44(0)28 7134 5180
Email. eat@brownsrestaurant.com
www.brownsrestaurant.com

Ivan Taylor is known for his consistently original and adventurous menus that have attracted glowing reviews over the 22 years he's been open. Ingredients are local where possible with many supplies coming from the local 'walled city market', while all jams, chutneys, pickles, dressings and breads are freshly made in-house. Lunch starters might include pâté de campagne with home pickles & rustic bread, followed by seared lamb tagine with cous cous and flatbread while dinner starters might bring roast fillet of plaice with black grapes & a vermouth cream, and main course of char-grilled rare breed sirloin of beef with a balsamic onion jus and a salad of lardoons and petit pois. Puddings such as Yorkshire tart with a compote of blueberries and ice cream are luxury incarnate. The stylish interior, designed by Taylor himself, combines good lighting and comfortable seating with funky foliage and natural textures. There's a good-value, promptly served lunch menu, pre-theatre and children's menus, gluten-free dishes and a private dining room.

Prices: Lunch main course from £6.95. Dinner main course from £8.95. House wine from £12.95.
Food served: 12.00-14.15 Tue-Fri and 17.30 till late Tue-Sat.
Closed: Sun & Mon. First two weeks in August.
Cuisine: Modern Irish with a twist.
Other Points: Children welcome. Car park. A private dining/ function/ meeting room. Winner - Newcomer of the Year 2005.
Directions: In the Waterside area of town, opposite the old railway station.

Magherafelt Co Derry

Ditty's Home Bakery & Coffee Shop
Bakery and coffee shop

3 Rainey Street, Magherafelt,
Co Derry BT45 5AA
Tel. +44(0)28 7963 3944
Email. dittybky@aol.com
www.dittysbakery.com

With their emphasis on the handmade breads locally traditional to Northern Ireland, which range from wheaten and soda breads to griddle-baked fluffy soda farls (served toasted and topped with homemade jam) and earthy potato farls (crisp-fried in butter), it's no wonder Robert and Helen Ditty's local bakery is a popular spot for breakfast. They do also offer the likes of fresh fruit and berries with natural yoghurt to those customers who can resist the farls and fries. Lunch includes homemade soups, burgers and tartlets, alongside more substantial fare such as minute steak with red onion marmalade and fresh green salad. Their baking is in demand farther afield too; Ditty's oatcakes can be bought in prestigious delis throughout Ireland and the UK, and bespoke hampers and cakes for anniversaries and special occasions can be ordered directly from the bakery.

Prices: Main course from £5.
Food served: 8.00-17.30 Mon-Sat.
Closed: Sundays. 25, 26 Dec. 1 Jan. Easter Mon & Tue. First Mon in May. 12,13 July.
Cuisine: Traditional Irish.
Other Points: Non-smoking. Children welcome.
Directions: From Belfast: M22/M2 (by pass Toomebridge), follow A6 until you reach Derry/Magherafelt/Castledawson roundabout, take left to Magherafelt, go to centre of town, taking a right at top of hill in Rainey Street. The shop is located on corner roundabout.

215

Ireland North

Magherafelt Co Derry

Laurel Villa Townhouse
Town centre guesthouse

60 Church Street, Magherafelt,
Co Derry BT45 6AW
Tel. +44(0)28 7930 1459/7963 2238
Email.info@laurel-villa.com
www.laurel-villa.com

An elegant, climber-covered Victorian home in the centre of Magherafelt, Laurel Villa offers the best of both worlds: a traditional welcome with modern facilities. Eugene and Geraldine Kielt run this unique guesthouse as a team - she is a fine home baker, whose specialities include wheaten bread and soda bread, he is a qualified tour guide. A native of Magherafelt, Eugene offers several customised tours to local places of historical and cultural interest, including one inspired by the works of the region's Nobel Laureate, Seamus Heaney. Laurel Villa is decorated with literary memorabilia, and features an entire reference room devoted to books of genealogical and Irish interest. There is also an extensive collection of medicine bottles recalling the days when Laurel Villa was the home of a doctor. Rooms feature period furniture and antiques. The breakfast menu features the traditional Ulster fry as well as omelettes, French toast, cheeses served with oatcakes and home-made chutney, and of course Geraldine's breads and home-made jams. The Laurel Villa fresh fruit salad, served with organic yoghurt and topped with oat granola, is a speciality.

Rooms: 5 ensuite. Double from £60. Single from £35.
Closed: Christmas
Other Points: Non-smoking bedrooms. Garden. Children welcome. Car Park. Reference library with Genealogical and Local Studies source material.
Directions: Conveniently situated along A31 in Magherafelt Town Centre. From M2/A6/Belfast/Airports/Ports, take A31 into town. Straight through first mini roundabout. House is 50 yards further along on right opposite St. Swithin's Church. From A29/Moneymore/Tobermore go into town centre. Follow signs for Belfast/M2. House is 200 yards from Bridewell Tourist Information Office, on left opposite St Swithin's Church.

for online reservations **Ireland North**

The Tower Museum

Place to Visit

6 Union Place, Derry City, Co Derry, BT486AF.
Tel. +44 (0)28 7137 7331
www.derrycity.gov.uk/museums

The Tower Museum uniquely houses two exhibitions relating to the city's history and development. The award winning Story of Derry exhibition chronicles the City's history from it's geological formation to present while An Armada Shipwreck - La Trinidad Valencera, a new interactive exhibition, tells the story of the discovery and excavation of the many artefacts recovered from the sunken ship.

Other Points
Wheelchair accessible. Interactive facilities for children. Educational resources for schools and state of the art audiovisual presentation. Multiple language interpretation also available for the Armada Shipwreck exhibition.

Hours
For more information on opening hours, prices, events and programmed activities please view www.derrycity.gov.uk/museums or telephone 0044 (0) 28 71377331.

Directions
From Belfast follow the A6 route, via Dungiven, to Derry/ Londonderry and follow signs for City Centre. From Dublin follow the M1 route towards Belfast. Take turn off at Ardee, following N2 to Derry via Strabane. From Dublin follow the M1 route towards Belfast. Take turn off at Ardee, following N2 to Derry via Strabane. From Dublin follow the M1 route towards Belfast. Take turn off at Ardee, following N2 to Derry via Strabane.

Springhill

Place to Visit

20 Springhill Road, Moneymore,
Co Derry, BT45 7NQ
Tel. +44 (0)28 8674 8210
Email. springhill@nationaltrust.org.uk
www.ntni.org.uk

Springhill has a beguiling spirit that captures the heart of every visitor. Described as "one of the prettiest houses in Ulster", it's welcoming charm reveals a family home with portraits, furniture and decorative arts filling the rooms. It's a simple but very pretty 'plantation' house with over 300 years of intriguing history, as well as magnificent gardens. Expert guides will add to the mysterious allure with stories of the friendly ghost, Olivia.

The old laundry houses one of Springhill's most popular attractions, the Costume Collection. The collection has some exceptionally fine 18th to 20th century pieces and is a fascinating mix of colourful haute couture and everyday clothing and accessories. No visit is complete without also enjoying the beautiful walled gardens or the beech tree walk.

Other Points
Historic house, Garden, Shop, Refreshments, Guided tours, Suitable for picnics, Country walk, Available for functions, Programme of events, Access for visitors with disability, Facilities for families, Learning, Dogs welcome on leads in grounds/garden only, Caravan Site.

Hours
17 Mar – 30 Jun, 13.00 – 18.00 w/ends and BH/PH (incl. 6 Apr – 15 Apr)
1 Jul – 31 Aug, 13.00 – 18.00 daily
1 – 30 Sep, 13.00 – 18.00 w/ends
Last admission 1hour before closing.

Directions
Bus: Ulsterbus No 210 and 110 between Belfast and Cookstown, alight at Moneymore, 1ml walk. **Car:** 1ml from Moneymore on B18 to Coagh (5ml from Cookstown). Drive from Belfast 50 mins.

Ireland North

www.goodfoodireland.ie

Bangor Co Down

FP

The Heatherlea
Town centre daytime cafe, deli & bakery

90-96 Main Street, Bangor,
Co Down BT20 4AG
Tel. +44(0)28 9145 3157

Situated right in the heart of Bangor, this traditional café and bakery is run by Paul and Patricia Getty. There has been a bakery on the site since 1937 but the building today is bright, modern and airy. Although the food might be described as good, plain and traditional, there's an excellent choice offered throughout the day. Get a hearty breakfast early in the morning - the traditional Ulster fry is joined on the menu by a breakfast bap or bacon roll or, unusually, rich fruit loaf toasted with banana. Morning or afternoon shoppers and visitors drop in for a flavoured latte or cappuccino to accompany one - or two - of the delicious pastries. Scones, doughnuts, fresh cream pastries and pancakes are fresh from the bakery. The dessert range has regulars such as apple sponge, rhubarb tart, lemon meringue, butter sponge and pavlova. The children's' menu has home made soup and Irish stew. Lunch specials include deep-layered lasagne, chicken and ham pie and mango chicken.

Prices: Lunch main course from £4
Food Served: 8.30-16.30 Mon-Sat.
Closed: Sundays. 25,26 Dec. 1 Jan. Easter Mon & Tues. May Day. 12, 13 July.
Cuisine: Traditional/modern Irish.
Other Points: Children welcome. Parking nearby.
Directions: Follow A2 to Bangor from Belfast. Drive to Main Street. The Heatherlea is situated between the two town churches on left hand side facing the sea.

Bangor Co Down

Jeffers by the Marina
Waterside restaurant & café

7 Gray's Hill, Bangor, Co Down
Tel. +44(0)28 9185 9555
Email. info@stephenjeffers.com
www.stephenjeffers.com

The setting is pretty magical and the approach doesn't get much better than this: informal, stylish and well priced. Not many menus in Ireland start at £2.50 and work their way up but here that is exactly what does happen. You could nibble on some olives, dive straight into the charcuterie plate or choose pasta in two sizes. Sausages come with crisp onion rings and are local as is the slow cooked lamb. This is dining where you have control. You can have breakfast too, and afternoon tea. The options seem endless. Helped along with knowledgable staff who are clearly determined to make sure you have a good time. This is all something of a winning formula. Coupled with the seaside location, great views and the endless coming and going of boats its like being on holiday.

Prices: Lunch main course from £5. Dinner main course from £8. House wine from £10.
Food Served: 10.00-16.00 Mon. 10.00-22.00 Tue-Fri. 9.00-22.00 Sat. 11.00-20.00 Sun.
Closed: 25 & 26 Dec. 1 Jan. 12 & 13 July.
Cuisine: Modern/classical cooking.
Other Points: Children welcome.
Directions: From Bangor centre, turn left at traffic lights at bottom of Main St. Go along marina on Queen's Parade, straight ahead at mini roundabout at bottom of Gray's Hill. Restaurant on the left.

Ireland North

Chapeltown Co Down

Curran's Bar & Seafood Steakhouse
Traditional pub and resaurant

83 Strangford Road, Chapeltown,
Ardglass, Co Down BT30 7SP
Tel. +44(0)28 4484 1332
Email. info@curransbar.net
www.curransbar.net

Built in 1791, this traditional pub has passed through generations of the same family. Over the years, it has been noted for story-telling, music and singing. In 2003, present family members carried out extensive refurbishment and the result is one of the finest bars and restaurants in the area. The snug provides a cosy room with welcoming fire in winter. The outdoor beer terrace is a suntrap in the summer; in winter months patio heaters warm guests. The Stables is a conversion of the old milking houses and is used as a function room. Food is served in all areas of the bar as well as in the 60-seater restaurant. This elegant room has soft velvet drapes, wooden floors and family portraits. The menu - written in English, French and Spanish - offers a selection of fish fresh from S&P Mulligan in Ardglass. Prawns, mussels, cod, crab, salmon and haddock jostle for space with Downpatrick game, and ribeye, fillet and sirloin steak from local butcher McGreevy's. Good service, pleasant staff and a competent chef with firm commitment to using locally sourced produce combine to make eating here an experience to be savoured. A well-chosen wine list provides excellent notes.

Prices: Lunch/dinner main course from £5.95. Bar snack from £5.95. House wine from £11.
Food Served: 12.30-21.00 daily. Weekend specials. No food 25 Dec.
Opening Hours: 11.00-23.00 Mon-Thur & Sun. 11.00-01.00 Fri & Sat.
Cuisine: Modern Irish
Other Points: Baby-changing facilities. Car park. Children's play area. Function room. Beer garden. Dogs welcome.
Directions: From Downpatrick to Ardglass take first left out of village towards Strangford and drive for 2 miles. Opposite church.

Comber Co Down

The Old Schoolhouse Inn
Guesthouse and restaurant

100 Ballydrain Road, Comber,
Co Down BT23 6EA
Tel. +44(0)28 9754 1182
Email. info@theoldschoolhouseinn.com
www.theoldschoolhouseinn.com

Situated at Castle Espie, beside the beautiful scenery of Strangford Lough and only eight miles from Belfast, the Old Schoolhouse Inn is an ideal place to stay, eat and relax in Northern Ireland. Owners Avril and Terry Brown rescued the Ballydrain Primary school after it closed in 1985; the result is a charmingly atmospheric restaurant with 12 clean, comfortable and simply furnished ensuite rooms, each named after an American president of Ulster descent. Avril is committed to using seasonal produce from local growers, and her French-inspired menu is traditional and assured. Dinner, taken by candlelight, could include a delicious starter of lobster salad followed by fillet of venison with thyme and blueberry sauce or seared halibut with prawns and mushroom sauce. There are homemade puddings and locally grown strawberries for dessert. Set menus are reasonably priced, and there's a decent wine list, divided into an old, new and connoisseur's selection.

Rooms: 12 ensuite. Double from £70. Single from £50.
Prices: Dinner (2 courses) £19.95; (3 courses) £21.95. Set Sunday Lunch £15.95. House wine from £13.95.
Food served: Sunday lunch 12.30-15.00. Dinner 19.00-21.30 Mon-Sat.
Closed: 25 December.
Cuisine: French, Grande Mère.
Other Points: No-smoking area. Garden. Children welcome. Car park.
Directions: From Comber on the A22 turn left at the Brown signposts. The Old Schoolhouse Inn is well sign-posted; follow the signs for approximately 2 miles.

219

Ireland North

Holywood Co Down

The Bay Tree
Coffee shop, restaurant, craft shop & gallery

118 High Street, Holywood,
Co Down BT18 9HW
Tel. +44(0)28 9042 1419
www.baytreeholywood.com

Sue Farmer uses the best of local ingredients on her inventive menu for the Bay Tree. Pass through a craft shop, and you see the restaurant's classic interior features simple cream walls and is dotted with blackboard specials. Breakfast at the Bay Tree offers plenty to lift the spirits: as well as porridge with whiskey, they have recently introduced a special breakfast for two, with smoked salmon and champagne available in half bottles. Try a smoothie, or the Bircher muesli: oats soaked in apple juice served with fruit, honey and nuts, and don't forget the famous home-made cinnamon scones. For lunch, there's bacon and mustard croustade or a special such as the cheesey leek flan. Breads, jam, marmalade and chutneys are all home-made, and organic vegetables come from Helen's Bay Organics. On Friday nights, dinner brings many tempting and imaginative offerings: Hungarian chilled cherry soup, followed by lamb, halloumi and aubergine kebab with tomato and mint salad, and to finish, pecan shortbreads with raspberries and chocolate ice cream. The restaurant stocks traditional Armagh cider, or you can choose from eight varieties of tea. The craft shop sells designer pottery, and the upstairs gallery is dedicated to watercolours, prints, jewellery and ceramics.

Prices: Lunch main course from £4.95. Dinner 2 courses & coffee £19.50; 3-courses & coffee £22.50 + 10% service charge
Food served: 8.00-16.30 Mon-Fri. 9.30-16.30 Sat. 19.00-23.00 Fri (last sitting 21.30). 10.00-15.00 Sun. Pottery and Gallery open 9.30-16.30 Mon-Sat.
Closed: 25, 26 Dec. Easter 2 days & 12 July (possibly for one week).
Cuisine: Modern Irish.
Other Points: Non-smoking. Children welcome. Craft shop. Pottery and Gallery. Car Park. Sue Farmers Cookbook now available - £20. Winner - Special Award 2006.
Directions: From Belfast take the Bangor Road, turn off at Palace Barracks. Restaurant is opposite the police station.

for online reservations

Ireland North

Kircubbin Co Down

Paul Arthurs
Town centre restaurant with rooms

66 Main Street, Kircubbin,
Co Down BT22 2SP
Tel. +44(0)28 4273 8192
Email. info@paularthurs.com
www.paularthurs.com

Local man Paul Arthurs' contemporary dining room has recently seen the addition of five ensuite rooms next to the restaurant. This may prove to be a huge boon to those who prefer to linger until well after bedtime over the refreshingly no-fuss menu. Arthurs crams plenty of his abundant local produce into his spot-on dishes, including plump Strangford Lough prawns, Portaferry mussels, Finnebrogue venison and Kircubbin Bay crab claws and smoked salmon. Beef comes direct from Paul's father's farm, as does the game. Dinner might start with lobster bisque, followed by grilled Barbarie duck fillet "teriyaki" style, hot chocolate pudding with homemade vanilla ice cream. Arthurs is to be applauded for offering regular vegan dishes - tempura of seasonal vegetables with sweet soy & ginger, alongside the vegetarian choices, which include buttery asparagus, fresh penne, lemon and fine herbs, which are taken

Rooms: 5 ensuite. Double from £70. Single from £50. Family from £70 + £10 per child.
Prices: Sunday lunch main course from £14. Dinner main course from £14. House wine from £12.
Food Served: 12.00-14.30 Sun. 17.00-21.00 Tue-Thur. 17.00-21.30 Fri-Sat.
Closed: Mondays. January.
Cuisine: Modern Irish.
Other Points: No-smoking area. Children welcome.
Directions: From Newtownards follow the A20 for 14 miles to Kircubbin, restaurant situated on the left hand side in the middle of the main street.

from Paul's own herb garden. The well-selected wine list offers eight by the glass - a great way to broaden your wine-drinking horizons. 2007 will see the addition of a new herb garden and orchard.

Symbols

- ◇ Accommodation
- ✕ Restaurant
- ● Café
- ▯ Pub/Bar
- ☼ Daytime opening only
- ♪ Deli
- ♀ Wine
- ➤ Bakery
- ● Gourmet/Farm Shop
- ⇒ Leisure Centre/Spa
- CS Craft Shop
- VC Visitor Centre
- FP Food Producer

Good Food Ireland Awards

- ★ 2002 Award Winner
- ★ 2003 Award Winner
- ★ 2004 Award Winner
- ★ 2005 Award Winner
- ★ 2006 Award Winner

Ireland North

www.goodfoodireland.ie

Castle Ward & Strangford Lough Wildlife Centre — *Place to Visit*

Strangford, Downpatrick, Co Down,
BT30 7LS
Tel. +44 (0)28 4488 1204
Fax. +44 (0)28 4488 1729
Email. castleward@nationaltrust.org.uk

Castle Ward was built, inside and out, in two distinct architectural styles, Classical and Gothic. It gives a full flavour of how a house and estate worked with its upstairs downstairs tales, its Victorian laundry and the water-driven cornmill. Inside the beautiful 750 acre walled estate you will find an exotic sunken garden, paths that wind their way through woodland and suddenly open onto the quiet shores of the Lough. Look out for the Artists in Residence programme working in a traditional cottage with studio. Children will adore the paradise of fun at the adventure play area.

Other Points

Historic house, Industrial heritage, Farm, Garden, Park, Countryside, Coast, Nature Reserve, Adventure Playground, Shop, Refreshments, Guided tours, Suitable for picnics, Country walk, Available for functions, Programme of events,

Access for visitors with disability, Facilities for families, Learning, Dogs welcome on leads in grounds/garden only.

Admission Charged

Hours

Grounds
Oct - Apr: 10.00 - 16.00 daily
Ma - Sept: 10.00 - 20.00 daily
House & Wildlife Centre
17 Mar 1.00 - 18.00
01 Apr - 25 Jun 1.00 - 18.00 w/ends & BH/PH
Easter 14 Apr - 23 Apr: 1.00 - 18.00 daily
1 Jul - 31 Aug: 1.00 - 18.00 daily
2 Sept - 30 Sept: 1.00 - 18.00 w/ends
Last tour 1hr before closing
Tea room & shop open as per House and close at 5.30pm

Directions

On A25, 7ml from Downpatrick and 1.5ml from Strangford.
Drive time: Belfast 45 mins, Dublin 2.5 hrs

Mount Stewart House & Gardens — *Place to Visit*

Portaferry Road, Newtownards,
Co Down, BT22 2AD
Tel. +44 (0)28 4278 8387
Fax. +44 (0)28 4278 8569
Email. mountstewart@nationaltrust.org.uk

Home of the Londonderry family, the house and its contents reflect the remarkable history of the family. The house tour includes world famous paintings and stories about the prominent guests and the people who have worked there over the centuries. From the manicured formal terraces to the grandeur of the lake and the views from the Temple of the Winds, Mount Stewart's breathtaking gardens over-flow with the vibrant colour of the rare plants that thrive in the mild climate of the Ards Peninsula.

Other Points

Historic house, Gardens, Shop, Restaurant, Guided tours, Suitable for picnics, Lakeside walks, Available for functions, Programme of events, Access for visitors with disability, Facilities for families, Learning, Dogs welcome on leads in grounds/garden only.

Admission Charged

Hours

For opening times please contact property
Lakeside Gardens: Open all year daily 10.00 - sunset
Formal Gardens : 11- 26 Mar: w/ends & BH/PH only. Apr - Oct: daily
House: 11 Mar - 30 Apr: w/ends & BH/PH
Easter 14 - 23 Apr: daily. May: daily (except Tues). Jun - Aug: daily. Sept: daily (except Tues). Oct: w/ends. Nov - Feb: closed.
Last admission to House & Formal Gardens 1 hour before closing
Temple of the Winds: 2 Apr - 24 Sept
Sun & BH/PH only

Directions

Bus: Ulsterbus no 10 between Belfast & Portaferry, bus stop at garden gates.
Car: On A20, 5ml from Newtownards on the Portaferry Road. Drive time: 25 mins from Belfast.

for online reservations   **Ireland North**

St Patrick Centre   *Place to Visit*

Downpatrick, Co Down
Tel. +44 (0)28 4461 9000
Fax. +44 (0)28 4461 9111
Email. director@saintpatrickcentre.com
www.saintpatrickcentre.com

The St Patrick Centre is situated beside the Patron Saint's Grave in Downpatrick, medieval capital of County Down. This award winning building, within the shadow of the Mourne Mountains houses Ireland's newest visitor attraction. Bold graphics, sculptures and interactive videos allow visitors to explore the fascinating story of Patrick and how his legacy helped develop the Irish Golden Age which brought the light of Christianity to Dark Age Europe. Finally, take a flight through Ireland to all of the sites associated with Patrick in our 180 degree cinema. The St Patrick Centre is an essential destination for those who believe that Ireland really is the land of Saints and Scholars.

Other points
Guided Tours, Craft Shop, Restaurant, Art Gallery, Tourist Information Centre, Gardens, Euro Notes Accepted.

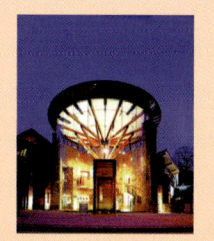

Hours
Oct to Mar: Mon-Sat 10.00 - 17.00
St Patrick's Day: 9.30 - 19.00
Apr, May & Sep: Mon-Sat 9.30 - 17.30.
Sunday 13.00 - 17.30
Jun to Aug: Mon-Sat 9.30 - 18.00
Sunday 10.00 - 18.00

Admission Charged

Directions
From Dublin: M1 Dublin to Newry and take A25 through Castlewellan and Clough. First left turn in Downpatrick at St Patrick's Square.
From Belfast: Take A24 to Carryduff and A7 at the roundabout through Saintfield and Crossgar. Turn Right at Roundabout in Downpatrick and follow signs.

Ulster Folk and Transport Museum   *Place to Visit*

Cultra, Holywood, Co Down,
BT18 0EU
Tel. +44 (0)28 9042 8428
Fax. +44 (0)28 9042 8728
Email. louise.willis@magni.org.uk
www.uftm.org.uk

The Ulster Folk and Transport Museum, Irish Museum of the Year, illustrates the way of life and the traditions of the people of the north of Ireland. At the open air Folk Museum 60 acres are devoted to illustrating the way of life of people in the early 1900s. The Transport Museum boasts the most comprehensive transport collection in Ireland. The Museum has a full programme of major events from Vehicle Days in the spring to Halloween and Christmas events in the winter. For the full programme of Events and Exhibitions please contact the Museum +44(0)2890428428 or visit the web site www.uftm.org.uk .

Other Points
Tea Rooms, Shop, Tours by arrangement, Disabled Access, Family Facilities, Educational Programmes, Picnic Area, Parking, Guide Dogs welcome, Dogs welcome on a lead, Baby Changing Facilities, Corporate Hire.

Hours
Mon - Sat 10.00 - Closing.
Sun 11.00 - Closing. (Times vary from 16.00pm to 18.00pm according to the season).

Directions
The Museum is situated on the main Belfast to Bangor Road, just ten minutes outside Belfast with excellent access by road, rail and bus and close to Belfast City Airport. Nearest rail station to the Museum is Cultra Halt. Buses stop outside the Museum entrance.

Ireland North

www.goodfoodireland.ie

Belleek Pottery

Place to Visit

Belleek, Co Fermanagh, BT3 3FY
Tel. +44 (0)28 6865 9300
Fax. +44 (0)28 6865 8625
Email. visitorcentre@belleek.ie
www.belleek.ie

Step into the world of Belleek Pottery and you enter one of Northern Ireland's oldest and most fascinating attractions.
This is an especially exciting time as Irelands oldest pottery celebrates its 150th anniversary. Established in 1857, Belleek Pottery holds a very special place in the cultural and commercial heritage of Co Fermanagh. Situated in the picturesque village of Belleek on the banks of the river erne, this imposing building is home to the world famous Belleek Fine Parian China and Belleek Visitor Centre, where facilities include guided tours, museum, audio visual theatre, showroom and restaurant.

Other Points
Guided Pottery Tours, Museum, Audio Visual Theatre, Showroom & Restaurant.

Hours
Apr - Jun: Mon - Fri 9.00 - 18.00,
Sat 10.00 - 18.00, Sun 14.00 - 18.00
Jul - Aug: Mon - Fri 9.00 - 18.00, 
Sat 10.00 - 18.00, Sun 11.00 - 18.00
Sep: Mon - Fri 9.00 - 18.00,
Sat 10.00 - 18.00, Sun 14.00 - 18.00
Oct: Mon - Fri 9.00 - 17.30,
Sat 10.00 - 17.30, Sun 14.00 - 18.00
Nov - Mar: Mon - Fri 9.00 - 17.30,
Sat & Sun Closed
Tours run Mon – Fri 9.30 – 12.15 and after lunch from 13.45 – 16.00 our last tour on Friday leaves at 15.00

Directions
Take the M1 to Dungannon. Continue on the A4 for approximately 9 miles to the Ballygawley roundabout. Follow the A4 through Augher, Clogher and Fivemiletown until you reach Enniskillen. In Enniskillen follow the signs for Belleek (A46). By car - 2 hours.

Castle Coole

Place to Visit

Enniskillen, Co Fermanagh, BT74 6JY
Tel. +44 (0)28 6632 2690
Fax. +44 (0)28 6632 5665
Email.
castlecoole@nationaltrust.org.uk

Situated in a stunning landscaped parkland on the edge of Enniskillen this majestic 18th century house built by James Wyatt was created to impress. We highly recommend the house tour to soak up the opulent Regency interior with its rich decoration, furnishings and furniture, including the ornate state bedroom prepared for George IV in 1821. You can also walk through the servants' tunnel and see the stableyard and coaches. Castle Coole is one of the finest neo-classical houses in Ireland.

Other Points
Historic house, Park, Shop, Refreshments, Guided tours, Suitable for picnics, Country walk, Available for functions, Programme of events, Access for visitors with disability, Facilities for families, Learning, Dogs welcome on leads in grounds/garden only.

Admission Charged

Hours
Grounds
30 Oct - 31 Mar: 10.00 - 16.00 daily
1 Apr - 29 Oct: 10.00 - 20.00 daily
House
17-19 Mar: 1.00 - 18.00
1 Apr - 31 May: 1.00 - 18.00 w/ends & BH/PH
Easter, 14 Apr - 23 Apr: 1.00 - 18.00 daily
1 - 30 June: 1.00 - 18.00 daily (except Thur)
1 Jul - 31 Aug: 12.00 - 18.00 daily
1 - 30 Sept: 1.00 - 18.00 w/ends
Last tour 1 hr before closing
Tea room & shop open as per House and close at 5.30pm

Directions
On A4, 1.5 ml from Enniskillen, on main Enniskillen to Belfast road. Drive time: Enniskillen 5 mins, Belfast 1.5 hrs, Dublin 2.5 hrs.

for online reservations

Ireland North

Dungannon Co Tyrone

Grange Lodge
Period country house & cookery school

7 Grange Road, Dungannon,
Co Tyrone BT71 7EJ
Tel. +44(0)28 8778 4212
Email. stay@grangelodgecountryhouse.com
www. grangelodgecountryhouse.com

Twenty years on, the Browns, Norah and Ralph to those of you not familiar with Grange Lodge, have a relaxed but confident way about them, which helps to put the weary traveller at their ease on arrival. The beautiful, stone Georgian house, which originates back to 1698 has been revamped (but not too much!) over the years, and is situated on three and a half acres of well established gardens with the most magnificent, almost regal pines and horse chestnuts. This in turn is surrounded by another seventeen acres of parklands, so you are never far from nature! The bedrooms are individually decorated, country cottage in style, with en suite bath or shower room. When it comes to dining, the elaborately decorated, formal dining room, which hosts various photos and trophies that Norah has won for her food is the place to be. Focusing on local produce is important to Norah, and she sources the speciality beef, lamb, pork and chicken from the farm shops and markets in the Dungannon area. Apart from the evening meal, the Bushmills Porridge that Norah cooks with organic oats and salt and water on the Aga the night before, and boasts a healthy shot

Rooms: 5 ensuite. Double from £78. Single from £55.
Prices: Set dinner from £26. House wine from £10.
Food Served: Sit down 7.30-20.00 for residents (must be booked in advance).
Closed: 20 Dec - 1 Feb.
Cuisine: Traditional Irish with a modern flavour with emphasis on using fresh local produce.
Other Points: Bedrooms non-smoking. Garden. Children welcome over 12 years old. Car park. Snooker table. Private dining for small groups by prior arrangement. Cookery school.
Winner - B&B of the Year 2006.
Directions: One mile from M1 Junction 15 on A29 Armagh Road. Turn left at Grange Lodge sign, almost immediately right, then white walled entrance on right.

of Bushmills will put a smile on your face! Combine that with free range eggs, dry cured bacon, home made bread, the local apple juice (another speciality of the house!) and you are set up for the day.

Grange Lodge

225

Ireland North

Ulster American Folk Park

Place to Visit

2 Mellon Road, Castletown, Omagh,
Co Tyrone, BT78 5QY
Tel. +44 (0)28 8224 3292
Fax. +44 (0)28 8224 2241
Email. uafp.info@.org.uk

An outdoor museum of emigration which tells the story of millions of people who emigrated from these shores throughout the 18th and 19th centuries. The Old World and New World layout of the Park illustrates the various aspects of emigrant life on both sides of the Atlantic. Traditional thatched buildings, American log houses and a full-scale replica emigrant ship and the dockside gallery help to bring a bygone era back to life. Costumed demonstrators go about their everyday tasks including spinning, open-hearth cookery, printing and textiles. The museum also includes an indoor Emigrants Exhibition and includes a Centre for Migration Studies/library. A full programme of special events is organised throughout the year.

Other Points
Guided Tours available, Residential Centre, Gift Shop, Restaurant, Coffee Shop, Bureau de Change, Free Car and Coach Parking, Cycle Shelter, Wheelchair Accessible

Hours
Oct - Mar: Mon - Fri 10.30 - 15.30
Museum closes at 17.00
Closed weekends and public holidays.
Apr- Sep: Mon - Sat 10.30 - 16.30
Museum closes at 18.00
Sun and public holidays 11.00 - 17.00
Museum closes 18.30

Directions
3 miles north of Omagh on A5 Road to Strabane. M1 to A5 from Belfast. N2 from Dublin on main North West Passage route.

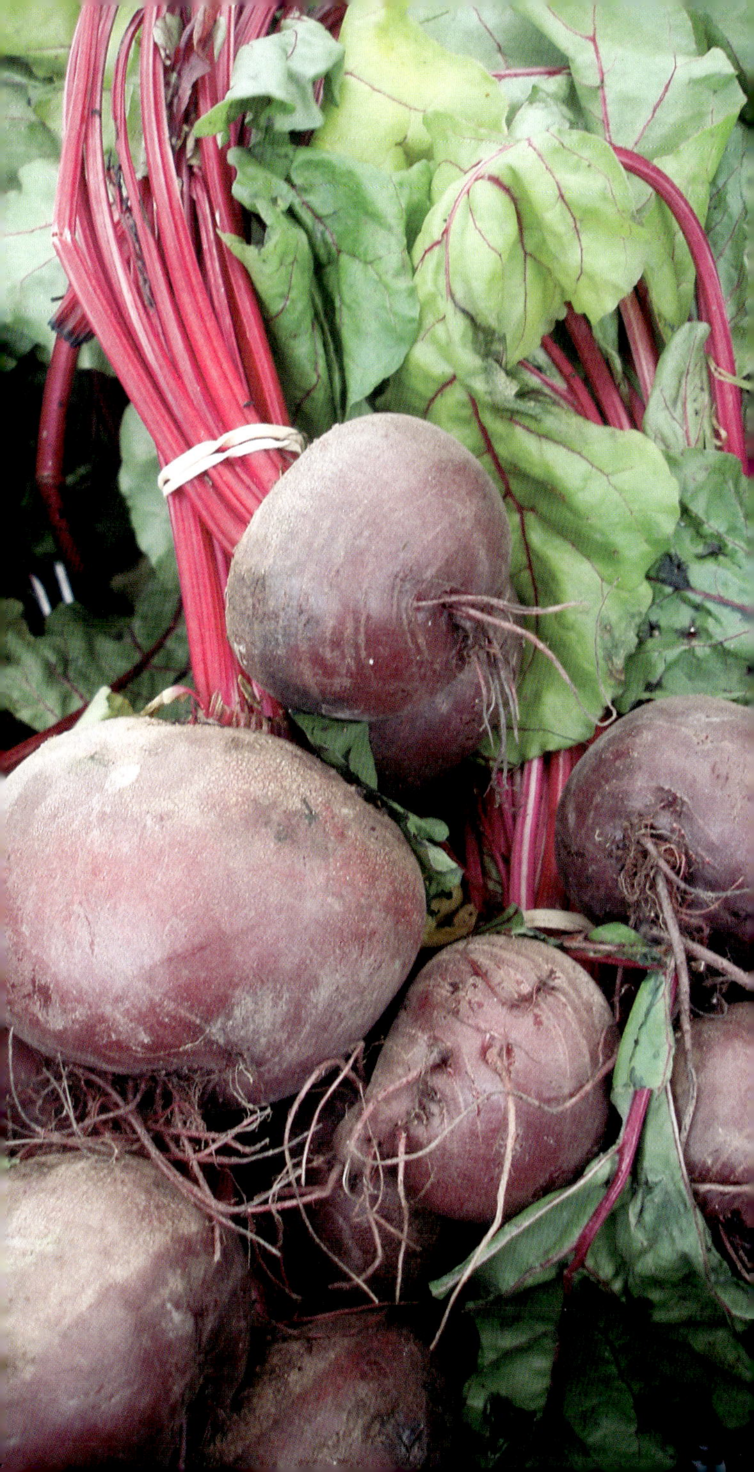

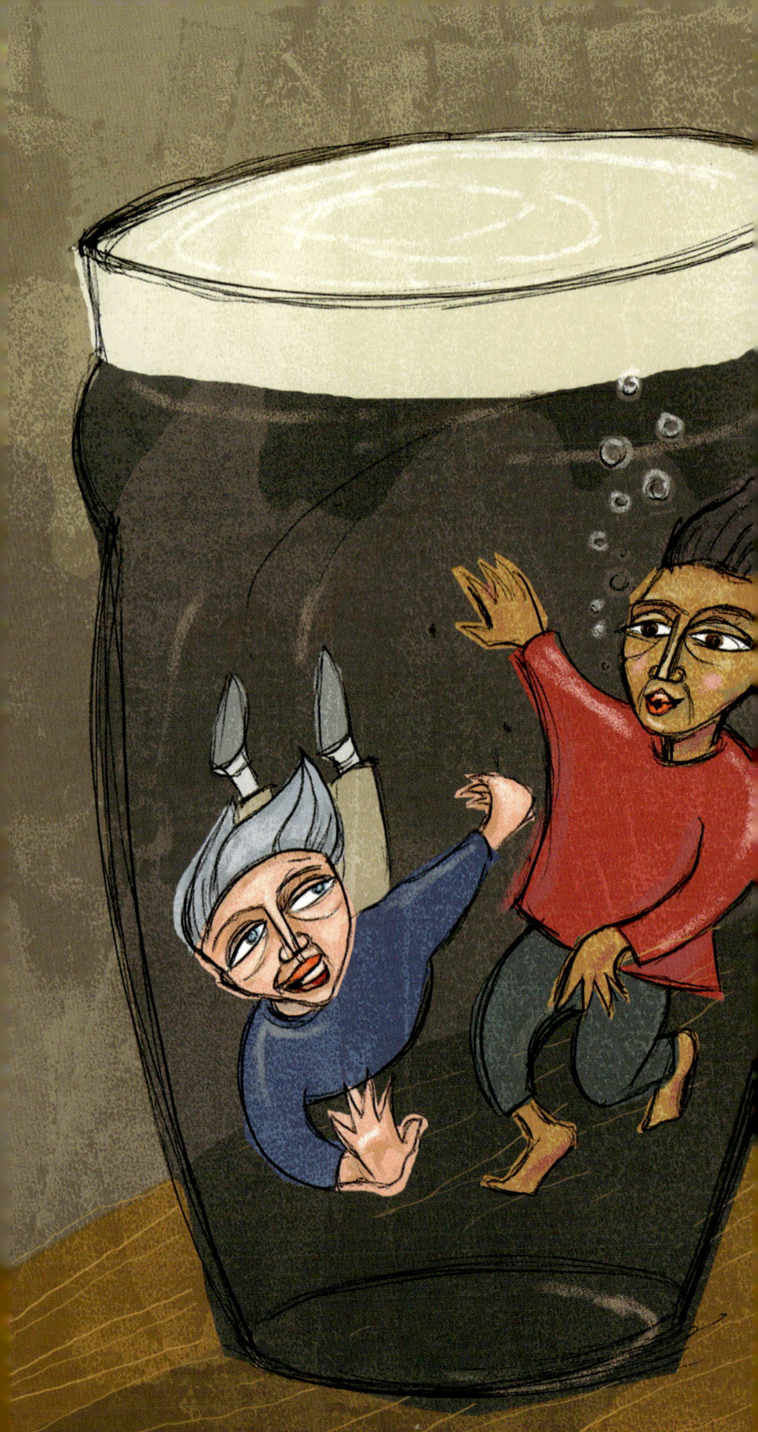

Underneath the
BLACK STUFF

Porter is Ireland's drink. Has been for years. It's a long and fascinating story. John Wilson dives into a pint.

John Wilson is a consultant specialising in wine and is author of the annual and much-respected The Wine Guide. He writes a weekly wine column in the Sunday Tribune and is a regular contributor to Wine Ireland and Food and Wine Magazine.

The Workman's Friend

When things go wrong and will not come right,
Though you do the best you can,
When life looks black as the hour of night -
A pint of plain is your only man.

When money's tight and is hard to get
And your horse has also ran,
When all you have is a heap of debt -
A pint of plain is your only man.

When health is bad and your heart feels strange,
And your face is pale and wan,
When doctors say that you need a change,
A pint of plain is your only man.

When food is scarce and your larder bare
And no rashers grease your pan,
When hunger grows as your meals are rare -
A pint of plain is your only man.

In time of trouble and lousy strife,
You have still got a darlint plan,
You still can turn to a brighter life -
A pint of plain is your only man.

Flann O'Brien (Brian O'Nolan)

It is the national drink, a symbol of Ireland throughout the world. Strange then, that it was invented across the water, by the old enemy England. The first records of porter appear in London around the 1730's, although this may initially have been a mixture of several different kinds of beer. Named after the porters of London, men who carried goods along the city streets, it rapidly became very popular. This popularity did not go unnoticed by one young Arthur Guinness (see below) a brewer over the sea in Dublin, who soon became market-leader, a position the firm has never lost. He was joined by other Irish brewers, and soon it became the national drink.

Irish stout is a different animal, with a distinctive, slightly bitter burnt flavour. This is because the Irish version uses malted barley, whereas other brews are made with lighter brown malts. Stout originally meant any kind of strong beer; these days it is reserved for stronger porters alone.

In the past, a publican was responsible for keeping his beers in good condition, and true stout drinkers knew which pubs served the best pint. Nowadays modern technology has taken much of the guesswork out of buying a pint, but it is still considered important to buy your pint in a busy pub, where the stout has not been lying on the feed-pipes for too long. In recent years, stout has been losing market share to lighter lagers as well as spirit-based drinks in the spiritual home of every true Irishman, the pub. It is easier for 'new' drinkers to swallow something with very little discernable flavour, served well-chilled, or with the sweetness of a cocktail. Old-timers accuse the breweries of 'dumbing down' stout, steadily lessening the flavour and character of their favourite drink. Certainly modern-day stout is a very different drink to its predecessor, which was much more powerful in both alcohol and flavour. But stout still remains close to the heart of the Irishman. Newer innovations, such as canned draught, with its ingenious widget, have helped the burgeoning off-sales. With one exception, it is only recently that drinkers are beginning to realize that stout is a great partner for many foods, including the national dish, Irish Stew. That exception is of course oysters; the two have been drunk together since the 1800s, when oysters were plentiful, and the food of the poor. Today many a pint is sunk in the great Oyster festival in Galway every September.

In the late 19th century, stout gained a reputation as a healthy drink, perfect for building up the sick and nursing mothers. Guinness used this to the full in their famous 'Guinness is good for you' advertising slogan. Until very recently, it was prescribed by doctors in the various maternity hospitals of Dublin!

The Irish Beweries

There are three major brewers of stout in Ireland. All are now owned by multinational companies. In recent years, a small number of micro-breweries have sprung up, all of which produce a stout.

MURPHYS

The brewing company of James P. Murphy was founded in 1856 by the sons of Jeremiah James Murphy. The wealthy family of traders and merchants had played an important role in the commercial life of the city for over a century prior to that, and had established a distillery in Midleton in 1825.

The company was successful from the start, quickly reaching a capacity of 100,000 barrels of stout and ale, and began exporting to the U.K. The family connection survived until 1980, with the death of John Fitzjames Murphy. John Fitzjames, known to many in Cork as 'the colonel' was formerly a Lieutenant Colonel in the British army. He joined the company in 1946 on his father's death, and served in various capacities for the next thirty-four years. The brewery is now owned by Heineken.

Tribal loyalties run deep in Ireland, and Corkmen always consider themselves superior to Dubliners. No true Corkman will ever be seen drinking Guinness. It's either Beamish or Murphy's. Murphy's is less bitter than Guinness, smooth with a slightly bitter dry finish, and hints of smoke. You can buy bottled, or bottled draught Murphys, but it is best appreciated in draught form, in one of our recommended Good Food Ireland establishments in Cork.

BEAMISH & CRAWFORD

Beamish & Crawford was founded in 1792 by William and William. They bought a long-establish brewery in the oldest part of Cork city, and within 15 years had grown to 100,000 barrels, making it the largest in Ireland at that time, and the third largest on these islands. The company went public in the early twentieth century, and is now owned by Scottish and Newcastle Breweries. Beamish is rich, nutty and lightly fruity, creamy and less dry than Guinness.

GUINNESS

This world-famous firm was founded in 1759 by Arthur Guinness, a brewer from Kildare. He took out a 9,000 year lease on a four acre site at St. James's Gate by the river Liffey in Dublin. Obviously an astute businessman, he also managed to acquire the water rights too, although this led to a bitter dispute with Dublin City Council that simmered on until 1784. Although he brewed various kinds of beer, Arthur chased the rapidly growing market for porter in London with great success. By his death in 1803, he had built up a thriving business, with its headquarters in Saint James's Gate, where Guinness is still brewed today. Guinness has traditionally been the most intensely-flavoured of stouts, with notes of caramel and coffee, and a dry, bitter finish. ∎

Artisan & Al Fresco

There is no excuse for plastic sandwiches. Ireland has come of age and scattered around the country are Good Food Ireland members brimming with the best. Pick up a picnic and head for the hills, writes Clodagh McKenna

Clodagh McKenna is a chef presenter on the UK Food Network and is the editor of the 'Slow Food Ireland Guide to Producers'. She runs farmers' markets at Farmleigh and has a commercial kitchen in West Cork where she produces her own line of products.

If you were driving round Ireland twenty years ago your picnic would probably have been a glorified packed lunch. You may have fantasised about the gourmet picnic feasts so famously depicted in impressionist paintings but you'd have made do with a hard boiled egg, a couple of pan bread sandwiches wrapped in clingfilm and a penguin biscuit for afters.

Those days are long gone. The superb local fare being produced in all regions; our rich heritage of artisan producers combined with the Irish food revolution of recent years have spawned an abundance of specialist food shops and delis. Today our picnic hampers can be packed with a feast of delicious, fresh, locally produced fare whatever region you are touring in or visiting. Try some of the artisan breads with an award winning native cheese and home made pickle; Brothers Kevin and Seamus Sheridan's cheese shops in Dublin and Galway stock over thirty native cheeses such as Gubbeen, Durrus and Ardrahan. The Farmshop at Aillwee Cave, Co Clare, produce and sell their own award winning Burren Gold cheese alongside local cheeses like St Tola goat's cheese and Cratloe sheep's cheese. Most of the outlets that sell cheese also sell a wide range of pickles and jams.

A staple of any self respecting picnic is good fresh bread; The Yellow Door, Portadown, Co Armagh have an in house bakery and also stock delicious sausages from Moyallon foods, a great addition to any picnic. Ditty's Home Bakery, Magherafelt, focus on traditional handmade breads from Northern Ireland, griddle baked soda and a diverse range of "wee buns". They will even put a hamper together for you!

Smoked meats and fish work well on picnics. The Burren Smokehouse, Lisdoonvarna, sell their own smoked organic salmon as do the Connemara Smokehouse, Co Galway who use traditional smoking methods - no artificial flavours, colours or preservatives. Both smokehouses will make up hampers on request.

Shopping for a picnic really can be as much fun as consuming it. I love a buzzy early morning market; the great selection of produce; picking what looks good on the day; taking tips from the stall holders. St George's Market - Belfast City, Co. Antrim was voted one of the UK's best markets in the Observer's Waitrose Food Awards 2004. Over 248 market stalls selling everything from apples to antiques to shark meat. I always make a bee line for Farmgate Café in the Old English Market in Cork. All their food is sourced locally from producers and growers in the area and they have a fantastic selection of freshly made sandwiches and mouth watering cakes.

If you are driving through Tipperary you have to stop in at Mary and Peter Ward's Country Choice shop in Nenagh, home cooked hams, perfectly kept farmhouse cheeses, their own fresh bread and a fantastic range of wines - picnic paradise! On the road from Dublin to Limerick stop off in Portlaoise at Jim Tynan's, Kitchen and Foodhall. Don't miss it! Jim makes all his breads and scones on the premises and there is lots of choice in cold deli meats, patés and terrines. The homemade cakes are sumptuous. For those of you heading North West, Kate's Kitchen in Sligo town is well worth a stop. Kate Pettit's shop is a treasure throve for the best of regional and local food and is perfect to get good food to go.

One of my favourite smells is walking into food halls and inhaling that mixture of coffee, chacuterie and cheese. Andersons Food Hall, Dublin offer a wide selection of Irish and continental cheeses, charcuterie, gourmet sandwiches, soups, patés, homemade breads and cakes. Cavistons Food Emporium, Dun Laoghaire have an impressive range of fresh seafood along with European salamis, farmhouse cheeses, organic vegetables and speciality breads, salads and pre-cooked meals. Dunne & Crescenzi, Dublin stock a wide selection of artisan ingredients including olive oils, pastas and preserved fruits.

If you have a sweet tooth there is a mouth watering selection of chocolates and patisserie to round off your picnic. Murphy's Ice Cream, Dingle and Killarney offer gourmet ice creams, chocolates and desserts in a wide variety of flavours. You can watch Benoit Lorge Chocolates being made from the shop floor - what better way to tempt the public! The gourmet chocolate shop's handmade Irish cream truffle milk and Irish whisky bitter truffle have won seven awards. Try them, you'll see why.

Of course a glass of fine wine is a wonderful accompaniment to a gourmet picnic but if you're steering clear why not try a wonderful cool apple juice? Ballycross Apple Farm in Wexford have a delicious range of apple and blackcurrant juices

What better way to pass a leisurely afternoon than picnicking on delicious Irish fare with good friends, looking out on wonderful scenery. I think any Impressionist painter would be proud to paint it. ■

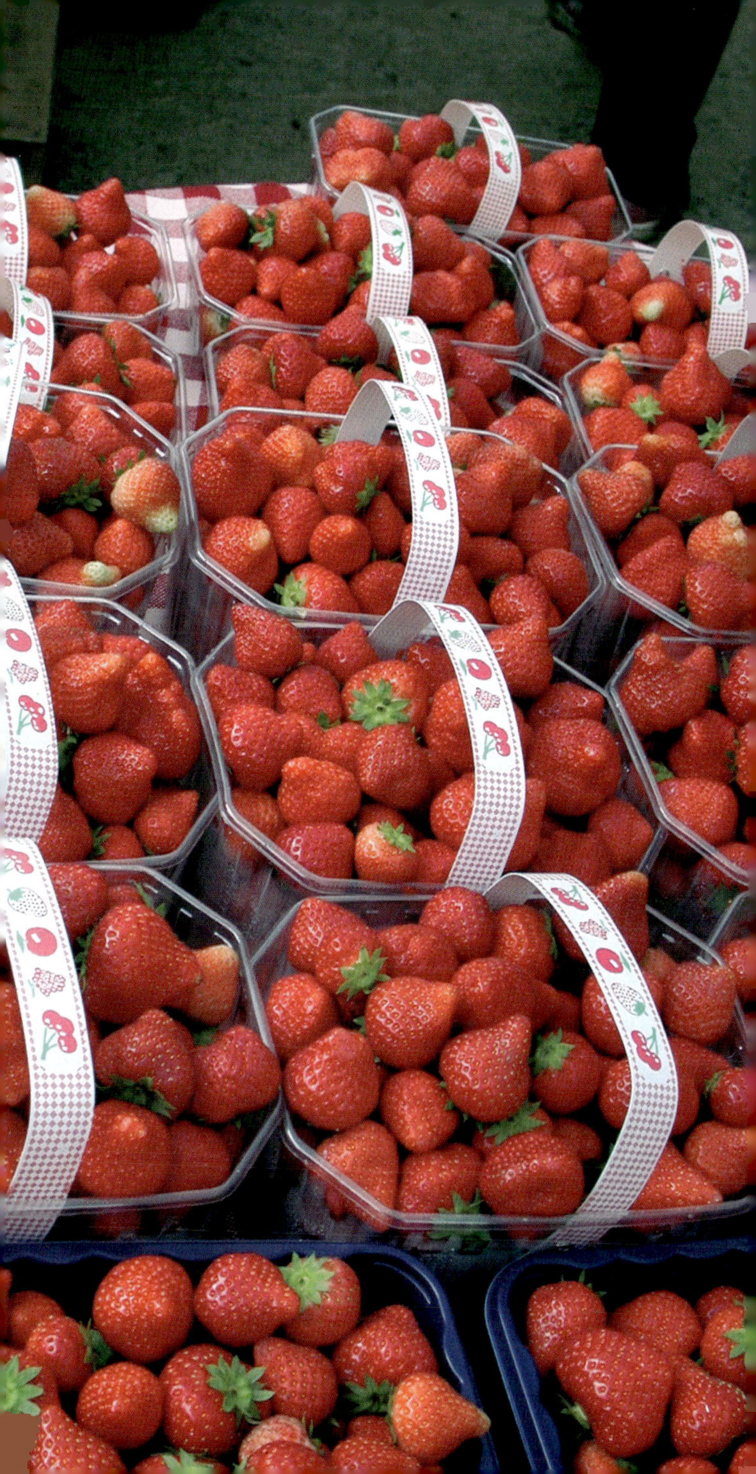

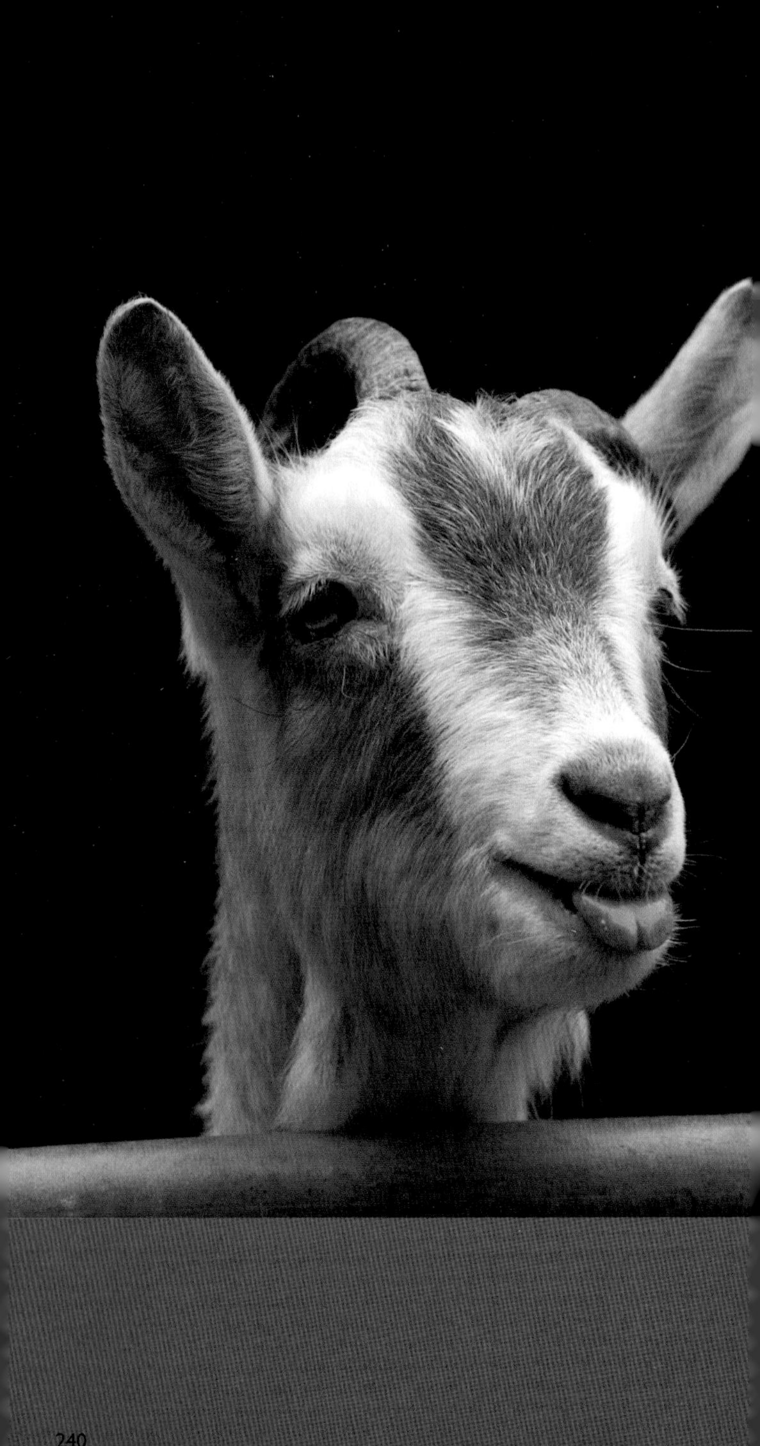

… Food Producers

My carrots have mud on them, my potatoes too. I expected rocket but got watercress instead. The lady beside me was cross because there were no tomatoes. But it's April I pointed out, what did she expect.

Being a food producer is not easy. Weather intervenes, slugs eat the crops, the sun shines too much or not at all. Getting up early is not to everyone's taste and the hours are undoubtedly long. Making cheese requires dedication, but so too does smoking fish, making jam, or ice-cream for that matter.

We like to think of ourselves as a food island and in a very real sense this is true. Up and down the country there are people producing food with individuality, love, care and attention. It is a passion that flies in the face of much of the modern world and we are all the richer for it.

The people are the heros in the following pages. Their souls reside to be enjoyed by those of us who buy their products. But what we taste is them and their understanding of the resource they have to hand. Of the seasons, of the land. Go on, be different, you'll be amazed.

Arbutus Breads

Rathdene, Montenotte, Cork
Tel. +353(0)86 3805065
Email. arbutus@iol.ie

Artisan baker Declan Ryan is a former chef/restaurateur, producing a maximum of 900 finest quality, traditionally crafted real breads daily from his small bakery using a mixture of organic, French and traditional stone ground Irish flours. Breads are made to recipes unchanged since the introduction of yeast, breads made without any chemical additives or improvers whatsoever; breads allowed to prove naturally and slowly (up to 20 hours in the case of pure sour-dough loaves). The range includes wholemeal,

Contact: Declan Ryan.

white and rye sour-dough, white and wholemeal and spelt yeast breads, baguettes, and other interesting breads using additional ingredients like walnuts, red wine, tomatoes and herbs. And of course traditional West Cork soda cake, made with the addition of Macroom oatmeal.

Ballycross Apple Farm

Bridgetown, Co Wexford
Tel. +353(0)53 9135160
Email. cve@indigo.ie

There is no doubting the main focus at Ballycross - apples don't get much more of a star billing than they do here. The orchards are a delight, but so too are the farm buildings with their well manicured courtyard, farm shop and café. The Irish climate is particularly well suited to growing apples and Ballycross does it all with considerable style. The apples here eat well and make the most fantastic juice - a good balance of sweetness with acidity and a depth of flavour not always found in other juices. You may choose to settle in for a glass of well chilled juice and a light lunch or to take a bottle or two home. A case is to be

Contact: Chris Von Englebrechtan.
Opening Hours: 2pm-6pm Sat&Sun.
Closed: Mid Feb-mid Aug.
Directions: Coming from Wexford in to Bridgetown go straight, through the railway crossing and take the next right. Ballycross Apple Farm is the 2nd turn on the right.

recommended, a bottle never quite seems to be enough.

Bellvelly Smokehouse

Cobh, Co Cork
Tel. +353(0)21 4811089
Email. mail@frankhederman.com
www.frankhederman.com

Belvelly Smokehouse's customer list reads like a star-studded cast; Rick Stein, Ballymaloe, L'Ecrivain and Avoca. Critical acclaim has strectched as far as the New York Times and the list of products means you can enjoy not just smoked salmon, but mussels, eel and mackerel. Frank Hederman has been smoking for years and his individuality shines through. The salmon, whether wild or organic, has a silky smoothness that marries perfectly with the smokey tones. Cutting the richness of this king of the sea requires a peculiar finesse and Belvelly samon delivers it every time.

Contact: Frank Hederman.

The baked smoked salmon is also a delight, either to be eaten as a starter of as a main course. The smoking is very gentle and along with some plainly boiled potatoes and some hollandaise it makes for a welcome change. Or try the smoked mussles in vinaigrette. These can be eaten on their own, made into a salad or used to dress pasta. Perfect simplicity

243

Boozeberries Ltd

Ballyconnell Lodge, Tullow,
Co Carlow
Tel. +353(0)59 9156312
Email. info@boozeberries.com
www.boozeberries.com

'Cottage Garden Herbs' has branched out with a fruity libation that has many glorious uses. Michelle Power has come up with her own version of what Italy, Spain and many other countries have enjoyed for generations. 'Boozeberries' delivers exactly what its name suggests. Wonderful whole berries infused in alcohol, with no added colours or flavourings - giving you a berry liqueur. Winner of Gold and Bronze

Contact: Michelle Power.

in 2006 Great Taste Awards, these rich and vibrant liqueurs are fantastic drizzled over ice cream, mixed with champagne or just simply as an after dinner shot.

Born Free Organic Chickens

Ballymabin, Dunmore East, Co Waterford
Tel. +353(0)51 383565
Email. paul_crotty@eircom.net

Producing good chickens doesn't require much. A bit of time, love care and attention. Which is exactly what Born Free is all about. Buy one of their chickens and it will be between 70 and 90 days old. That is more than twice the age of a conventionally farmed chicken. Not only this but it will have spent its time outdoors, scratching around on green fields living in sheds that are constantly moved. For a chicken that is a pretty good offering. So much so that

Contact: Paul Crotty.

these birds are certified (by IOFGA) as organic tablebirds. Just the thing to ensure the perfect roast. Born Free are Hubbard chickens, a breed that delivers a bird with superior flavour. Something deep and rounded and deliciously satisfying. The way chicken used to be.

Cocoa Bean Artisan Chocolates

Unit 3b, Limerick Food Kitchens,
Crossagalla Industrial Estate
Ballysimon Road, Limerick
Tel. +353(0)61 446615
info@cocoabeanchocolates.com
www.cocoabeanchocolates.com

Forget the green tea. Just sit back and relax with one of the beautifully packaged and deliciously mouth watering chocolates from 'The Cocoa Bean Artisan Chocolate Company' and let the 'loving feeling' begin! They say that 'chocolate triggers love', but we now know that it has some noteworthy health benefits. Chocolate is higher in antioxidants than green tea or tomatoes and certainly appeals to more of

Contact: Sarah Hehir & Emily Stanford.

the senses! This highly successful Limerick based operation was initially inspired by the interest and passion of two sisters Sarah Hehir and Emily Stanford. 'The Cocoa Bean Artisan Chocolate Company' offers a sumptuous variety of chocolate products from sleek and stylish 'wafer thin chocolate squares' to chunky 'fruit and nut clusters' full of eastern fruits.

Connemara Smokehouse

Bunowen Pier, Aillebrack,
Ballyconneely, Co Galway
Tel. +353(0)95 23739
Email. info@smokehouse.ie
www.smokehouse.ie

The setting is one of the most beautiful areas in Ireland, the ingredients some of the purest; fish, salt, smoke, herbs, sugar, honey and Irish whiskey. The Connemara Smokehouse is the oldest in the region and for over 25 years the family have been perfecting this ancient craft. What you get are well balanced foods, the smoking always playing a supporting role; enhancing rather than dominating so the sweetness of the salmon, for example, comes through gently. Not content to work with salmon only however, you can also buy smoked mackerel, tuna, cod and kippers. While the company

Contact: Graham & Saoirse Roberts.
Opening Hours: 9.00-17.00 Mon-Fri. Closed 13.00-14.00
Closed: Sat. & Sun. Seasonal & bank holidays.
Directions: About 5 miles south of Clifden on the L102.

Ditty's Home Bakery & Coffee Shop

3 Rainey Street, Magherafelt,
Co Derry BT45 5AA
Tel. +44(0)28 7963 3944
Email. dittybky@aol.com
www.dittysbakery.com

With their emphasis on the handmade breads locally traditional to Northern Ireland, which range from wheaten and soda breads to griddle-baked fluffy soda farls (served toasted and topped with homemade jam) and earthy potato farls (crisp-fried in butter), it's no wonder Robert and Helen Ditty's local bakery is a popular spot for breakfast. They do also offer the likes of fresh fruit and berries with natural yoghurt to those customers who can resist the farls and fries. Lunch includes homemade soups, burgers and tartlets, alongside more substantial fare such as minute steak with red onion marmalade and fresh green salad. Their baking is in demand farther afield too; Ditty's oatcakes can be bought in prestigious delis throughout Ireland and the UK, and bespoke hampers and cakes for anniversaries and special occasions can be ordered directly from the bakery.

Contact: Robert & Helen Ditty.
Prices: Main course from £5.
Food served: 8.00-17.30 Mon-Sat.
Closed: Sundays. 25, 26 Dec. 1 Jan. Easter Mon & Tue. First Mon in May. 12,13 July.
Cuisine: Traditional Irish.
Other Points: Non-smoking. Children welcome.
Directions: From Belfast: M22/M2 (by pass Toomebridge), follow A6 until you reach Derry/Magherafelt/Castledawson roundabout, take left to Magherafelt, go to centre of town, taking a right at top of hill in Rainey Street. The shop is located on corner roundabout.

G's Gourmet Jams

Abbeyleix, Co Laois
Tel. +353(0)57 8731058

Making award-winning jam requires a lot of attention to detail. Top quality fruit, just the right amount of sugar and a cooking process that allows for the flavours to develop. G's Gourmet Jams tick all the right boxes, allowing the fruit to shine through. This is a traditional way of doing things. It's about as close to homemade as you can get and the jams speak for themselves. Helen Gee's approach is to keep things simple. Uncomplicated. Getting the best ingredients and doing as little to them as possible. That

Contact: Helen Gee.

way the fruit plays the main role, which is just how it should be. Established in 1999, the awards have continued to flow over the years. Choose from the likes of raspberry or gooseberry jams, three-fruit marmalade and a range of chutneys which include red pepper and autumn varieties.

Gallweys Chocolates

Abbeylands Business Park, Ferrybank
Co Waterford
Tel. +353(0)51 830860
Email. gallweyschocolates@eircom.net
www.gallweys.com

Two great tastes in one. For those partial to a drop of Irish whiskey here's something extremely special. Handmade chocolates filled with pure old Irish whiskey. The Gallwey family recipe has been passed down for generations and is available for sale at quality food purveyors throughout Ireland and the UK. Gallweys 'Irish Coffee Truffles' have creamy white chocolate and a dark coffee, pure cream and an old Irish whiskey centre. Not to be missed especially

Contact : Ciara Power.

for the Christmas season or for that corporate gift is their 'Exclusive Collection Box', which is a collection of their award-winning handmade truffles, as well as a dozen 'Royal Pralines'. Delicious.

Inagh Farmhouse Cheese Ltd

Inagh, Co Clare
Tel. +353(0)65 6836633
Email. info@st-tola.ie
www.st-tola.ie

St Tola Goat Cheese has been made near the village of Inagh, just south of the Burren, for 20 years. In 1999, Siobhan Ní Ghairbhith took over and the farm has continued to produce organic cheeses. The company philosophy of producing organic and healthy goat cheese in an ethically, environmentally and sustainable manner is an achievement recognised by the number of awards the cheese have won. Some 120 milking goats are milked twice daily, the milk enhanced by the rich organic grass on the 65-acre farm. The cheeses are handcrafted daily, without the use of additives or preservatives. Low in salt and fat, they are suitable for vegetarians and those who have allergies such as asthma or eczema. The range includes the original St Tola log, St Tola Crottin, St Tola Hard Cheese and St Tola Feta. The farm is certified organic with I.O.F.G.A. (the Irish Organic Farmers and Growers Association).

Contact: Siobhan Ní Ghairbheith.

La Maison des Gourmets Bakery

15 Castle Market, Dublin 2
Tel. +353(0)1 6727258

Tucked away on a pedestrians-only street in the heart of the city's smartest shopping area, this charming boulangerie and salon de The specialises in authentic French bread, viennoiserie and patisserie products, offering a true taste of France in Dublin. For breakfast indulge in the Petit Dejeuner Francais, a selection of mini viennoiseries to accompany your favourite coffee or freshly squeezed juices, to be enjoyed there or to go. Light lunch dishes, served in a chic, understated space at the top of a winding staircase might include French onion soup and tartine of Bayonne ham and artichoke or smoked salmon with chive cream accompanied by a glass of wine. After a busy day drop in for a delicious afternoon tea that includes a selection of hand made delights which are all made in full view. The shop also does a brisk trade in custom-made, ultra-rich special-occasion cakes.

Contact: Olivier Qunet.
Prices: Main course from €10-€12. Wine from €22.
Food served: 8.00-19.00 Mon-Sat. Lunch only served 12.00-15.00.
Closed: Sundays and bank holidays. 1 week after Christmas.
Cuisine: French.
Other Points: Children welcome. French language lessons at breakfast.
Directions: Between Georges St. Arcade and Powerscourt Shopping Centre or between Dury St. and South William St.

Lorge Chocolatier

Bonane, Kenmare, Co Kerry
Tel. +353(0)87 9917172
Email. chocolatecrust@eircom.net

What used to be a post office in Kenmare has now become Lorge Chocolatier. You can sample, see chocolates being made, enrol on a course and make them yourself or, best of all, buy some to take home. Previously pastry chef at the nearby Sheen Falls, Benoit Lorge has a passion for chocolate and what started out as a way to raise money for charity has since been turned into a business. He supplies shops and top hotels with his creations but is happiest when selling from his own shop direct to the public. He runs popular courses including one specially geared to children. Awards keep coming his way, including two golds from the Great Taste Awards. This is a must-stop for anyone interested in the fascinating complexities of this ancient food.

Contact: Benoit Lorge.
Opening Hours: 10.00-18.00.
Closed: Jan.
Directions: Between Kenmare and Glengariff on the N71 before the church in the village of Bonane.

Mossfield Organic Farm

Clareen, Birr, Co Offaly
Tel. +353(0)57 9131002
Email. mossfieldorganicfarm@eircom.net

Creating a new cheese is no easy matter and is not a business renowned for its speed. Yet in a very short time Ralph Haslam has developed an organic gouda-style cheese which keeps winning awards. The cheese is complex, with long, lingering flavours that come with herbaceous notes. The milk is organic which gives the cheese a well-balanced richness. With time this develops into an even more powerful force but always with a balancing and charming sweetness. You can buy the cheese direct from the farm or from a number of speciality shops throughout Ireland. Choose from young or mature and there are a number of flavoured cheeses including cumin and basil and garlic. The added flavours are well chosen and complementary, particularly the cumin.

Contact: Ralph Haslam.

Moyallon Foods

76 Crowhill Road, Craigavon,
Co Armagh BT66 7AT
Tel. +44(0)28 3834 9100
Email. mail@moyallonfoods.com
www.moyallonfoods.com

Fancy a bacon sandwich as it used to be? All sweetness and meatiness, the sort of succulence that had you leaping out of bed on a Sunday morning just to make one with a large pot of coffee? Moyallon bacon hits just this spot. A family-owned business with over 12 years experience, their aim is to supply a 'carefully sourced range of delicious and unique speciality food products, supporting farmers, gamekeepers and producers from Ireland and abroad'. Avoiding unnecessary artificial additives, preservatives and colourings, and sourcing produce locally where possible, why not head to the 'Yellow Door Deli' in Portadown or Belfast or even their stall at St. George's Speciality Food and Garden Market in Belfast every Saturday and try out their hand-made sausages. Perhaps 'Lamb, mint and rosemary' catches your eye? Or for a more Mediterranean feel 'Pork with sundried tomato and basil'. These knowledgeable and skilful food enthusiasts deliver top quality.

Contact: Jilly Dougan.

Murphy's Ice Cream

Strand Street, Dingle, Co Kerry
Tel. +353(0)66 9152644
Email. sean@murphysicecream.ie
www.murphysicecream.ie
www.icecreamireland.com

You might be forgiven for thinking Murphy's in Dingle is a pub. It almost looks like one and the name certainly sounds right. Inside however it is not creamy pints of Guinness you will find but creamy tubs of ice-cream made by brothers Sean and Kieran Murphy. Kerry cream to be precise which is what many claim lies at the heart of Murphy's deliciousness. Others think it is the flavours; top-quality Valrhona chocolate, top flight vanilla, home made caramel. Suffice to say you can sit back in the comfort of this relaxed café and enjoy a scoop or several. You can also enjoy coffee, or one of the freshly made cakes. This is dessert heaven, there is very little reason to want to go home. Unless that is you buy something to take home which is always an option.

Contact: Sean & Kieran Murphy.
Opening Hours: Daily. 11.00-22.00 summer. 11.00-18.00 winter.
Closed: Dec to Feb.
Directions: In the centre of town, close to the marina and Post Office.

Murphy's Ice Cream

37 Main Street, Killarney, Co Kerry
Tel. +353(0)66 9152644
Email. sean@murphysicecream.ie
www.murphysicecream.ie
www.icecreamireland.com

Right in the heart of Killarney on Main Street Murphy's beautifully blends the art of shop and café. You can buy to go, or buy to stay. It might be a coffee. It could be one of the freshly baked cakes but for most it is the ice-cream which attracts. There is a passion inherent in Murphy's ice-cream. And its not just the great flavours. You may pick from pure chocolate, rum and raisin or great, rather than just, vanilla but it is also Kerry milk and cream. Why not sit and enjoy a scoop or three. Wash them down with a coffee or maybe wait a while. The ice-cream tends to linger. The flavours are long in this part of the world. Should you wish to takes some home that is unlikely to be a problem. That is if you can wait that long.

Contact: Sean & Kieran Murphy.
Opening Hours: Daily. 11.00-22.00 summer. 11.00-18.00 winter.
Closed: Jan.
Directions: In the centre of town.

Cocoa Bean Artisan Chocolates

The Burren Smokehouse

Lisdoonvarna, Co Clare
Tel. +353(0)65 7074432
Email. info@burrensmokehouse.ie
www.burrensmokehouse.ie

With over 30,000 visitors a year, this traditional stone smokehouse with its visitor's centre and gourmet shop have become something of a landmark in the heart of the Burren country. The shop itself sells everything from music, books and maps to crafts and kitchen utensils, but it is the food that takes centre stage, much of it local: Clare jams and Burren honeys, Cocoa Bean chocolates and award-winning cheeses such as the locally made St Tola's Goat Cheese and Burren Gold. They also smoke the local Kilshanny cheese, but Birgitta and Peter Curtin are most famed for their award-winning smoked fish: their cold smoked Irish salmon recently won them yet another Gold in the Great Taste Awards 2005. They also smoke their own trout, and mackerel. A great place to stock up for gourmet gifts or treats for yourselves: make up your own selection from the various smoked fish available or pick up one of the cane picnic baskets brimming with specially selected goodies.

Contact: Birgitta Curtin.
Opening hours: 9.00-17.00 & 9.00-18.00 Jun & Aug and weekends. 10.00-16.00 Jan to Mar.
Closed: Good Friday. 25, 26 Dec.
Other Points: Video presentation on smoking of fish. Craft shop. Children welcome. Car park.
Directions: Eight kilometres from the Cliffs of Moher. Five hundred metres from the square in Lisdoonvarna on the Doolin side of the town. Two hundred metres from The Roadside Tavern.

The Farmshop at Aillwee Cave

Ballyvaughan, Co Clare
Tel. +353(0)65 7077036
Email. barbara@aillweecave.ie
www.aillweecave.ie

Visitors to the two-million-year-old cave at Aillwee, in the spectacular limestone landscape of the Burren, should make time for the splendid farm shop alongside. Ben Johnson, cheesemaker and apiarist, is responsible for the production of award-winning Burren Gold, a Gouda-type cheese which you can watch being made before tasting. If inspiration strikes, you can sign up to one of Ben's cheesemaking courses. A wide range of other local cheeses - Poulcoin goat's cheese, Cratloe sheep's cheese - as well as pickles, homemade jams, pestos, oil and spiced vinegars fill the shelves. Ben dons his beekeeping hat to produce honeycombs and wildflower honey. The shop also stocks up to 20 varieties of homemade fudge, ranging from triple chocolate to maraschino cherry. There's a potato bar, with attractive stone seating and outsize images of local wildflowers, as well as a tea room for freshly made soups, sandwiches, quiches and ginger bread, and a kiosk selling hot dogs and muffins in peak season only.

Contact: Ben Johnson.
Hours: Open daily. 10.00-18.30 April-September. 10.00-17.00 October-March.
Other Points: Car Park. Children welcome. Cheese making.
Directions: Located 5km south of Ballyvaughan on the R480.

The Heatherlea Bakery

90-96 Main Street, Bangor,
Co Down BT20 4AG
Tel. +44(0)28 9145 3157

Situated right in the heart of Bangor, this traditional cafÉ and bakery is run by Paul and Patricia Getty. There has been a bakery on the site since 1937 but the building today is bright, modern and airy. Although the food might be described as good, plain and traditional, there's an excellent choice offered throughout the day. Get a hearty breakfast early in the morning - the traditional Ulster fry is joined on the menu by a breakfast bap or bacon roll or, unusually, rich fruit loaf toasted with banana. Morning or afternoon shoppers and visitors drop in for a flavoured latte or cappuccino to accompany one - or two - of the delicious pastries. Scones, doughnuts, fresh cream pastries and pancakes are fresh from the bakery. The dessert range has regulars such as apple sponge, rhubarb tart, lemon meringue, butter sponge and pavlova. The children's' menu has home made soup and Irish stew. Lunch specials include deep-layered lasagne, chicken and ham pie and mango chicken.

Prices: Lunch main course from £4
Food Served: 8.30-16.30 Mon-Sat.
Closed: Sundays. 25,26 Dec. 1 Jan. Easter Mon & Tues. May Day. 12, 13 July.
Cuisine: Traditional/modern Irish.
Other Points: Children welcome. Parking nearby.
Directions: Follow A2 to Bangor from Belfast. Drive to Main Street. The Heatherlea is situated between the two town churches on left hand side facing the sea.

The Stoneoven

Kingshill, Arklow, Co Wicklow
Tel. +353(0)402 39418
Email. stoneoven@eircom.net
www.stoneoven.com

Germany's loss was Ireland's gain when Egon and Liane Friedrich arrived in Arklow some 20 years ago. They founded the Stoneoven, a small bakery that hand-crafts wonderful breads. Their ambition was to craft excellent quality, healthy, delicious bread specialities from selected nutritious ingredients, with a preference for organic raw materials. And they have more than succeeded. The aroma of baking bread wafts along the streets of Arklow as the doors to the small shop opens and closes. There are seven spelt breads, two ryes, a gluten free, and four European classics, as well as some delicious sweet and diabetic treats. At Christmas time they produce Christollen, the German speciality and savouries based on rye, spelt and almond. Part of the secret of Stoneoven's success is long, slow cooking, locking in moisture and giving slow nutrient release.

Contact: Egon and Liane Friedrich.

252

Cookery Schools

Learning to cook is like so many things a combination of knowledge and confidence but it is confidence particularly that many lack. In the old days much of this was picked up 'at mother's apron strings'. How old-fashioned that sounds.

Today we experience nothing of the sort and to fill that void the cookery school has emerged. When much of our life seems so fast and furious it is comforting, reassuring to spend time over food. The following pages feature the best schools in the country where you can spend as little as few hours or in some cases many months.

The more advanced, like Ballymaloe have integrated their courses right back to the farm. In some instances you can meet the hen that produced the egg you are holding. In others you are given an opportunity to go and literally fish for your supper.

What they all share is a belief in putting food where it rightly belongs, at the centre of our lives. Obtaining the skill requires time, but there are gifted cooks and teachers up and down the country running classes expertly tuned to providing just that. Go on, grab a wooden spoon. You deserve it.

Ballymaloe House
Period country house, restaurant & cookery school

Shanagarry, Midleton, Co Cork
Tel. +353(0)21 4652531
Email. res@ballymaloe.ie
www.ballymaloe.ie

With a history dating back to 1450 when a Norman Castle was built on lands at Ballymaloe, this is one of Ireland's best-known guesthouses. The buildings in use today are built into and around the castle. In 1967, rooms were ready for guests and these continue to provide comfort and olde-world charm. New rooms have been built over the years, offering guests all the luxuries associated with this charming guesthouse. Eating in Ballymaloe is always a treat, whether it's breakfast, lunch or dinner. With the highest quality ingredients in the capable hands of head chef Jason Fahy, cooking is inspired. Lunch may be warm salad of Gubbeen cheese and bacon or escalope of beef. After an aperitif in the drawing room, a five-course dinner may begin with Ballycotton fish soup or locally smoked fish tart, followed by roast Kassler or guinea fowl. With Irish Farmhouse cheeses and homemade biscuits and a dessert from the trolley, you may just manage coffee and petit fours. Ballymaloe is unusual in that it still lays down stocks of fine vintage wines. The list has some 200 carefully selected wines.

Rooms: 33 ensuite. High season rates - double from €260. Single from €160. Family from €410.
Prices: Lunch (4 course) from €35. Dinner (5 course) from €70. House wine from €25.
Food served: Lunch 13.00 daily. Dinner 19.00-21.00 daily.
Closed: Christmas and 2 weeks in Jan.
Cuisine: Traditional Irish.
Other Points: Cookery School. Afternoon tea and light lunches residents only. Bedrooms non-smoking. Children welcome. Garden. Car park. Heated outdoor pool (summer only). Tennis. Five-hole golf course. Croquet. Children's outdoor play area. Annual Wine Weekend Courses in March and April. Craft shop. Winner - Newcomer of the Year 2006
Directions: From Cork airport, turn left towards the city. At the Kinsale roundabout follow road markings and signs for N25 East. At the roundabout at the end of the tunnel take the third exit heading for Rosslare. Bypass Midleton at the roundabout, take the third exit and watch for signs for Cloyne and Ballycotton. Ballymaloe is 2 miles beyond Cloyne on the Ballycotton road.

Ballymaloe Cookery School
Cookery School

Shanagarry, Midleton, Co Cork
Tel. +353(0)21 4646785/4646727
Email. enquiries@cookingisfun.ie
www.cookingisfun.ie

You could be forgiven for thinking the Ballymaloe Cookery School is somebody's house. The building is a delight, the garden a sea of green and everywhere happy smiling faces. Students range in age from the young to the not so young, from those taking time out to those embarking on careers. You don't just learn how to cook at Ballymaloe. It starts with the ingredients; eggs from the farm, fish from nearby Ballycotton, herbs and vegetables from the strictly organic garden, fruit from the trees that boarder the outside seating areas. The kitchens themselves are homely and welcoming with large generous demonstration areas and lots of natural light. And seemingly everywhere is the dominating, infectious enthusiasm of Darina Allen, the guiding force behind what has become a world-wide name for quality and integrity.

Darina Allen

Ghan House
Coastal country house, restaurant & cookery school

Carlingford, Co Louth
Tel. +353(0)42 937 3682
Email. ghanhouse@eircom.net
www.ghanhouse.com

Paul Carroll's attractive Georgian country house and cookery school stands in walled grounds in a lovely village close to Carlingford Lough The small lake to the front catches the reflection of the long, white, two-storey building and breathtaking views of Slieve Foy encircle the house. Inside, a large hallway with old timber floors and an open fireplace create an atmosphere of warmth and comfort which permeates the house. The twelve ensuite bedrooms, all with mountain views, are furnished with family antiques and filled with fresh flowers and old-fashioned attention to detail. The restaurant offers intimate dining in classic surroundings, with home-baked bread and dishes such as ceviche of tuna loin with spicy lime dressing, or roasted local red legged partridge setting the elegant tone. Vegetables and herbs come from the garden and fresh local produce is used where possible including Cooley lamb, Carlingford mussels and oysters.

Rooms: 12 ensuite. Double from €180. Single from €75.
Prices: Dinner main course from €27,50. House Wine from €18.50.
Food Served: Fri, Sat, Sun (booking recommended) and at any other time by prior arrangement.
Closed: 24-26, 31 Dec. 1-6 Jan.
Cuisine: Modern Irish.
Other Points: Garden. Dogs welcome in stable. Children welcome. Cookery school. Private dining.
Directions: 1 hour from Dublin & Belfast Airports, 15 minutes from N1, signposted to Medieval Carlingford. Ghan House is a tree length away from Carlingford.

The cookery school attracts high calibre guest chefs such as Ursula Ferrigno and Paula McIntyre, and the impressive programme of events includes fishing trips on Carlingford Lough, whiskey tasting and eight-course gourmet nights.

Grange Lodge
Period country house & cookery school

7 Grange Road, Dungannon,
Co Tyrone BT71 7EJ
Tel. +44(0)28 8778 4212
Email.
stay@grangelodgecountryhouse.com
www. grangelodgecountryhouse.com

Twenty years on, the Browns, Norah and Ralph to those of you not familiar with Grange Lodge, have a relaxed but confident way about them, which helps to put the weary traveller at their ease on arrival. The beautiful, stone Georgian house, which originates back to 1698 is situated on three and a half acres of well established gardens with the most magnificent, almost regal pines and horse chestnuts. This in turn is surrounded by another seventeen acres of parklands, so you are never far from nature! The bedrooms are individually decorated, country cottage in style, with en suite bath or shower room. When it comes to dining, the elaborately decorated, formal dining room, which hosts various photos and trophies that Norah has won for her food is the place to be. At Norah's Cookery School you can learn how entertaining is made easy with the specially arranged morning and afternoon programmes held in Norah's kitchen, reflecting the best use of seasonal produce. This is important to Norah, and she sources the speciality beef, lamb, pork and chicken from the farm shops and markets in the Dungannon area. Apart from the evening meal, the Bushmills Porridge that Norah cooks with organic oats and salt and water on the Aga the night be-

Rooms: 5 ensuite. Double from £78. Single from £55.
Prices: Set dinner from £26. House wine from £10.
Food Served: Sit down 7.30-20.00 for residents (must be booked in advance).
Closed: 20 Dec - 1 Feb.
Cuisine: Traditional Irish with a modern flavour with emphasis on using fresh local produce.
Other Points: Bedrooms non-smoking. Garden. Children welcome over 12 years old. Car park. Snooker table. Private dining for small groups by prior arrangement. Cookery school.
Winner - B&B of the Year 2006.
Directions: One mile from M1 Junction 15 on A29 Armagh Road. Turn left at Grange Lodge sign, almost immediately right, then white walled entrance on right.

---

fore, and boasts a healthy shot of Bushmills will put a smile on your face! Combine that with free range eggs, dry cured bacon, home made bread, the local apple juice (another speciality of the house!) and you are set up for the day.

Powersfield House
Country house bed & breakfast & cookery school

Ballinamuck, Co Waterford
Tel. +353 (0)58 45594
Email. powersfieldhouse@cablesurf.com
www.powersfield.com

With its gracious, Georgian-style lines, lovely mature gardens, on-site cookery school - offering lots of invaluable tips, and location just outside Dungarvan in one of the prettiest and most golfer-friendly areas of West Waterford, Eunice Power's delightful house boasts many of the comforts of a much grander establishment. Its warm, inviting lounge is antiques-furnished and decorated in restful beige and gold, while each of the 6 light-filled bedrooms are individually designed using tasteful colours with fresh floral arrangements. Smart bathrooms feature fluffy towels, spacious showers (some have baths), and a tempting basket of toiletry "goodies." Don't miss Eunice's delectable breakfasts and dinners, which might include Greek yoghurt with granola, bananas and Cappagh Runny Honey; local Helvic smoked salmon with scrambled eggs; mussels and monkfish in a Thai broth with wild rice; and hot chocolate pudding with vanilla ice cream. Powersfield House offers a great escape at excellent value. Eunice also runs a wide variety of cookery courses throughout the year.

Rooms: 6 ensuite, Double from €110. Single from €60. Family from €120.
Prices: Set dinner from €28-€38.
Food served: Dinner by arrangement for residents.
Closed: Christmas to mid Jan.
Cuisine: Contemporary Irish food, focusing on local organically grown ingredients.
Other Points: Non-smoking bedrooms. Garden. Children welcome. Car park. Cookery school.
Directions: Take the main Killarney road R672 from Dungarvan, second turn left, first house on the right.

Eunice Power

260

ORGANIC CENTRE

Farmers Markets

Farmers' markets have made an enormous impact on the culinary landscape of Ireland. And not just for shoppers. Artisan producers are able, with very little cost, to set up their stalls to see if what they have produced will sell.

For many they are a return to the old ways of doing things. Local people buying and selling local produce. There is also the chance to talk to the person who has produced what you are buying, to undertand the complexities of what is involved in its making.

Some markets are bigger than others, some more regular. But throughout Ireland there is a recognition that this is the way things should be, at least some of the time.

Ireland East & Dublin

Dublin

City Centre — Temple Bar Food Market
Meeting House Square, Temple Bar
Saturday morning and now Wednesday, 11am - 3pm

Wolfe Tone Park Gourmet Food Market
Jervis Street
Friday, 11am - 3pm

Pearse Street Market /Food Co-Op
St. Andrews Centre, 114-116 Pearse St., Dublin 2
Saturday, 9.30am - 3pm

Dalkey — Dalkey Market
Town Hall, Main Street, Dalkey
Friday, 10am - 4pm

Donnybrook — Donnybrook Village Market
St Mary's Church, Anglesa Road, Ballsbridge, Dublin 4
Thursday, 11am - 7pm

Dublin Docklands — Docklands Market
The IFSC on Excise Walk
Thursday, 10am - 3pm

Dun Laoghaire — Dun Laoghaire Shopping Centre
Shopping Centre
Thursday, 10am - 5pm

Dun Laoghaire Peoples' Park Market
Peoples' Park
Sunday, 11am - 4pm

Dun Laoghaire Harbour Market
Dun Laoghaire Harbour offices/Yacht club
Saturday, 10am - 4pm

Dundrum — Dundrum Market
Airfield Trust Grounds
Saturday, 10am - 4pm

Howth — Howth Market
Sunday

Leopardstown — Leopardstown Racecourse Market
Leopardstown Racecourse
Friday, 11am - 6pm

Malahide — Malahide Market
St Sylvesters GAA
Saturday, 10am - 4pm

Monkstown — Monkstown Village Market
Monkstown Parish Church, Monkstown, Co Dublin
Saturday, 10am - 4pm

Ranelagh — Ranelagh Market
Multi Denominational School
Sunday, 10am - 4pm

Rathfanham — Marley Park Market
Marley Park, Craft Courtyard Rathfanham
Saturday, 10am - 4pm

Rush   **Fingal Food Fayre**
                    Fingal Arts Centre
                    Last Sunday of every month

Kildare

Athy   **Athy Farmers Market and Craft Fair**
                    Heritage Square
                    Sunday, 10am - 3pm

Kildare   **Kildare Folly Market**
                    3rd Sunday of every Month, 11am - 6pm

Naas   **Naas Market**
                    Storehouse Restaurant, Friary Lane
                    Saturday 10am - 3pm

Newbridge   **Newbridge Farmers Market**
                    Courtyard Shoppping Centre (by Lidl)
                    Friday, 9am - 2pm

Laois

Portlaoise   **Portlaoise Farmers' Market**
                    Shaws Centrepoint Car Park
                    Friday, 9am - 3pm

Longford

Longford   **Longford Farmers' Market**
                    Temperance Hall, Longford Town
                    Saturday, 9.30am - 1pm

Louth

Castle Bellingham   **Castle Bellingham Market**
                    Castle Bellingham
                    1st Sunday of every month 11am - 6pm

Meath

Enfield   **Enfield Country Market**
                    Friday

Kells   **Kells Farmers Market**
                    Saturday, 10am - 2pm

Kells   **Kells Country Market**
                    Friday

Oldcastle   **Oldcastle Country Market**
                    Friday

Trim   **Trim Farmers' Market**
                    Loman Street, Trim
                    Last Saturday of every month, 10am

Offaly North

Clara
Clara Market
7am until evening usually 5 or 6pm

Tullamore
Tullamore County Fair
Millennium Square, Main Street
Saturday, 9am - 4pm

Westmeath

Athlone
Fernhill Farmers' Market
Fernhill Garden Centre
Last Sunday of every month

Athlone Town
Athlone Farmers' Market
Market Square
Saturday, 10am - 3pm

Mullingar
Mullingar Market
Harbour Place Car Park
Every Sunday

Wicklow

Arklow
Arklow Market
Masonic Hall
Saturday, 10.30am - 12am

Avoca
Avoca Market
Parish Hall
Sundays in July and August, 2.30pm - 5.30pm

Blessington
Blessington Market
Saturdays, 2.30am - 4.30pm

Bray
Bray Market
Killarney Road near the Boghall Road
Saturday, 10am - 3pm

Glendalough
Glendalough Market
Laragh
2nd Sunday of Every Month, 11am - 4pm

Kilcoole
Kilcoole Market
Saturday, 10.30 - 11.30am

Macreddin village
Brooklodge Market
Brooklodge
1st & 3rd Sunday of every month

Powerscourt
Waterfall Market
Farmyard, almost next to Powerscourt Waterfall
2nd & 4th Sunday of every month

Roundwood
Roundwood Market
Parish Hall
Sunday, 3 - 5pm

Ireland South

Carlow

Carlow Town — **Potato Market**
Saturday, 9am - 2pm

Cork

Ballincollig — **Ballincollig Farmers' Market**
Village Shopping Centre on the Main Street
Wednesday, 10am - 2.30pm

Ballydehob — **Ballydehob Market**
Ballydehob Community Hall
Friday, 10.30am - noon

Bandon — **Bandon Market**
Car park of Mace Supermarket
Thursday

Bantry — **Bantry Market**
The Square
Friday, 9am - 1pm

Castletownbere — **Castletownbere Market**
1st Thursday of every month

Clonakilty — **Clonakilty Market**
McCurtain Hill
Thursday and Saturday, 10am - 2pm

Cobh — **Cobh Market**
Sea Front
Friday, 10am - 1pm

Cork City — **English Market**
Entrances on Princes St., Patrick St.
and the Grand Parade
Open every day

Coal Quay Market
Cornmarket Street
Saturday, 9am - 4.30pm

Douglas — **Douglas Market**
Douglas Community Park
Saturday

Dunmanway — **Dunmanway Market**
Market Square
Saturday, 10am - 1pm

Fermoy — **Fermoy Market**
Saturday

Inchigeelagh — **Inchigeelagh Market**
Creedons Hotel
Last Saturday of every month

Kanturk — **Duhallow Farmers' Market**
Rear of Super Valu Kanturk
Thursday and Saturday, 10.30am - 2.00pm

Killavullen — **Blackwater Valley Farmers' Markets**
Nano Nagle Centre (Signposted from N22, Mallow-Fermoy)
Saturday Fortnightly

Kinsale	**Kinsale Market** Short Quay, in front of Jim Edwards restaurant Tuesday, 9.30am - 1.30pm
Macroom	**Macroom Market** The Square Tuesday, 9am - 4pm
Mahon Point	**Mahon Point Market** Mahon Point Shopping Centre Thursday, 10am - 2pm
Mallow	**Blackwater Valley Farmers' Market** Nano Nagle Centre, Kilavullen Fortnightly, Saturday, 10.30am - 1pm
Midleton	**Midleton Farmers' Market** Hospital Road Saturday, 10am - 2pm
Mitchelstown	**Mitchelstown Farmers' Market** The Town Square Saturday
Schull	**Schull Market** Car Park near the Pier Sunday, 11am - 3pm
Skibbereen	**Skibbereen Market** Old Market Square (opposite AIB Bank) Saturday, 9am - 1.30pm
Youghal	**The Clock Gate Farmers' Market** Beside the Clock Gate, Youghal Friday, 11am - 3pm

Kerry

Caherdaniel	**Caherdaniel Market** Friday, 10am - 12am (June-September and Christmas)
Cahirciveen	**Cahirciveen Market** Cahirciveen Community Centre Thursday, 11am - 2pm June - Sept.
Dingle	**Dingle Market** Opposite the harbour Friday, 10am - 4pm
Kenmare	**Kenmare Market** An Cro, Bridge Street. Wednesday-Sunday, 10am - 6pm & 7 days during July and August
Killarney	**Killarney Country Market** Parish Hall, Anne's Rd. Friday, 11.30 - 1.30
Killorglin	**Killorglin Market** CYMS Hall Friday, 11am - 1pm
Listowel	**Listowel Food Fair** Thursday, 10am - 1pm

Milltown	**Milltown Organic Market** The Old Church Saturday, 10am - 2pm
	Milltown Organic Market Organic Centre Tuesday-Thursday, 2pm - 5pm
Sneem	**Sneem Market** Tuesday, 11am - 2pm (June -September and Christmas)
Tralee	**Tralee Market** Friday, 9am - 5pm

Kilkenny

Kilkenny City	**Gowran Park Market** 2nd Sunday of every Month

Tipperary South

Cahir	**Cahir Market** Beside Craft Granary, Craft Yard Carpark Saturday, 9am - 1pm
Carrick-on-Suir	**Carrick-on-Suir Market** Heritage Centre, Main Street Friday, 10am - 2pm
Clonmel	**Clonmel Market** St Peter & Paul's Primary School, Kickham St., beside Oakville Shopping Centre Saturday, 10am -2pm

Waterford

Dungarvan	**Dungarvan Farmers' Market** Gratton Square Thursday, 10am - 1.30pm
Dunhill	**Dunhill Market** Parish Hall Last Sunday of every month, 11.30am - 2pm
Waterford City	**Jenkins Lane Market** Saturday, 10am - 4pm
	The Quay's Market 46 The Quay Every Day

Wexford

Campile	**Dunbrody Farmers' Market** Dunbrody Abbey Centre, New Ross Sunday, 12am - 3.30pm
Enniscorthy	**Enniscorthy Market** Saturday, 9am-2pm
New Ross	**Conduit Lane Market** Saturday, 9am - 2pm
Wexford	**Wexford Town Market** Mallin St. Car Park Friday, 9am - 2pm

Ireland West

Clare

Ballyvaughan	**Ballyvaughan Market** The Old Schoolhouse Saturday, 10am - 2pm
Ennis	**Ennis Farmers' Market** Upper Market Street Car Park Friday, 8am - 2pm
Killaloe	**Killaloe Farmers' Market** Between The Waters Sunday, 11am - 3pm
Kilrush	**Kilrush Farmers' Market** The Market Square Thursday, 9am - 2pm
Shannon	**Skycourt Farmers' Market** Skycourt Shopping Centre Friday, 11am - 6pm

Donegal

Donegal Town	**Donegal Town Market** Diamond Saturdays Monthly
Letterkenny	**Letterkenny Market** Mc Ginley's Car Park, Pearse Road 1st & 3rd Saturday of every month 9am - 3pm

Galway

Ballinasloe	**Ballinasloe Market** Croffey Centre, Main Street Friday, 10am - 3pm
Galway City	**Galway Market** Beside St Nicholas' Church Saturday, 8.30am - 4pm

Leitrim

Carrick-on-Shannon	**Carrick-on-Shannon Farmers' Market** Market Yard Centre Thursday, 10am - 2pm
Manorhamilton	**Manorhamilton Farmers' Market** Friday

Limerick

Abbeyfeale	**Abbeyfeale Market** Parish Hall Friday, 9am - 1 pm
Limerick City	**Limerick Market** Milk Market Saturday, 8am - 2pm

Mayo

Westport	**Westport Market** Saturday

Roscommon

Boyle   **Boyle Market**
King House, Main Street, Boyle
Saturday, 10am - 2pm

Roscommon   **Roscommon Town Market**
Off Market Square
Friday, 10am - 3pm

Sligo

Sligo Town   **Sligo Farmers' Market**
Sligo IT car park
Saturday, 9am - 1pm

Tipperary North

Thurles   **Thurles Farmers' Market**
The Greyhound Track, Thurles
Saturday, 9.30am - 1.00pm

Ireland North

Antrim

Belfast   **St Georges Market**
12-20 East Bridge Street
Friday, 6.00 - 13.00. Saturday, 9.00 - 15.00

Lisburn   **Lisburn Market**
Saturday

Templepatrick   **Templepatrick Market**
4th Sunday of every month, 11am - 6pm

Armagh

Portadown   **Portadown Market**
Last Saturday of every month

Tyrone

Dungannon   **Dungannon Market**
Tesco's carpark
1st Saturday of every month, 8.30am - 1pm

Spicy Wok Oil
250ml
Herb & Garlic Oil
250ml
Herb & Garlic Oil
250ml
Red Hot Chilli Oil
250ml

Food Shops

Dotted about the country there are shops selling real food. They tend to be quite small, are run by their owners and are filled with bottles and jars you are unlikely to find elsewhere, certainly not a supermarket.

Along with jars there will be cheese, usually several kinds, maybe some ham and smoked salmon. Olive oil is likely, as is a good vinegar. These are the kind of places where putting a picnic together is simple, where you can shop for a whole meal and come out with something fantastic.

The choice is likely to be limited to a few of each thing, maybe two or three olive oils, a few different jams. But they will all be very different as each is likely to have real character. The sort that reflects where they have come from, who has made them.

This is all something to be celebrated and enjoyed, variety coupled with excellence.

Micro Breweries

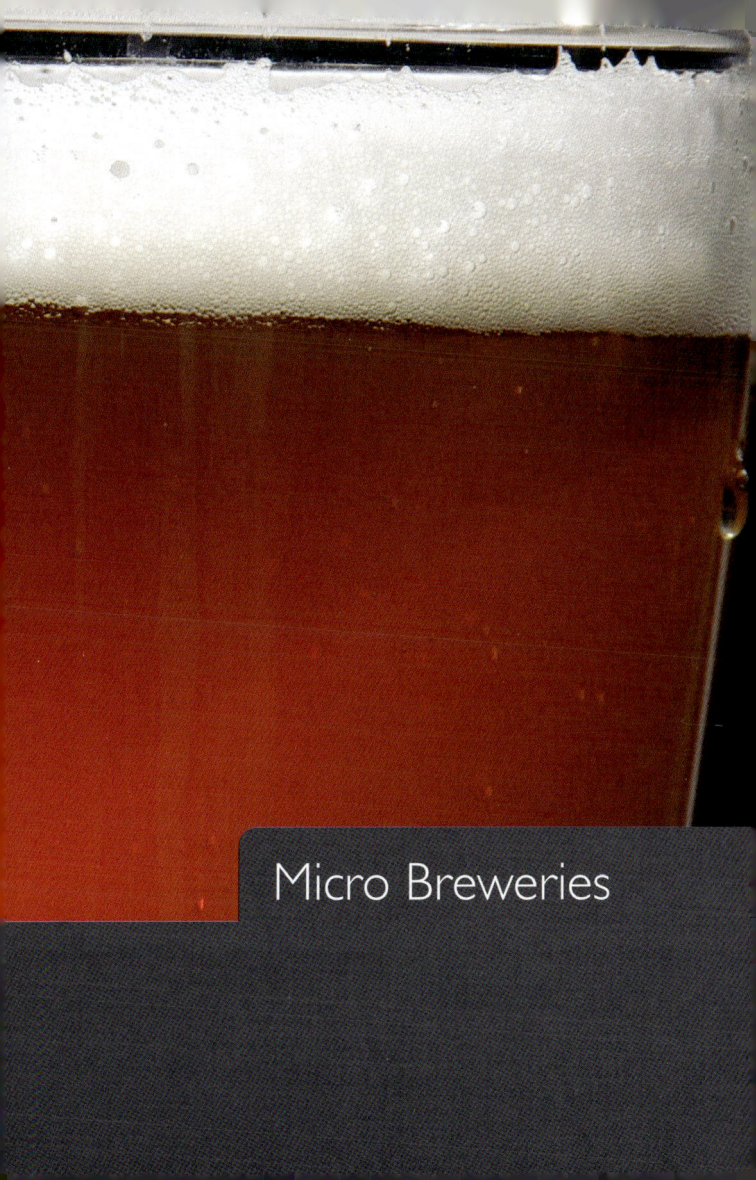

Making Macro out of Micro

The revolution started about twenty years ago. A small section of beer drinkers in the UK and the USA began to question the way their favourite tipple was being made. They felt that over the years, the larger breweries had steadily reduced the flavour of their beers, until they were now distinctly watery. The breweries logic was simple; if a beer doesn't taste of anything, how can you dislike it? It would naturally appeal to the mass market. You can also drink a lot more of it, particularly if it is served very cold. Beer-drinkers had slowly succumbed to cheaper, blander brews, backed up by intensive advertising campaigns.

In each country, disgruntled beer-lovers began to demand beers that offered something different. Some looked to the European continent, to countries such as Germany, Belgium and Czechoslovakia, where excellent beers were still the order of the day, and in the case of Germany were governed by strict regulations. In the UK, many looked back to the once-vibrant brewing industry that had thrived in every town the length of the country. What they were looking for was real beer; beers that tasted of something, complex, satisfying beers with attitude.

The answer came in the form of the micro-brewery. Small, artisan breweries sprang up, making small quantities of individual hand-made beers. They eschewed the long list of foaming agents, stabilizers and other additives used by the large breweries. Instead they stuck to the basic five ingredients; water, yeast, hops, malt and water.

The difference is simple; flavour. Micro-breweries will never be able to compete with the larger companies on marketing and advertising spend. Their beers are never going to have mass appeal. Instead, they offer beer with a difference; beer filled with hoppy, malty flavours, beer with complexity; beer that makes you think, and beer that you can actively enjoy.

A warning - most of the mass-produced beers are 'session' beers, designed to be drunk in quantity, as quickly as possible. Artisan brews can be something of a shock to the uninitiated. It can take a while to get used to all that flavour. It is highly unlikely that you will be able to knock back fifteen pints on a night out. Most have a far higher alcohol content anyway. Think of them like wine, to be sipped and enjoyed slowly over an extended period. Oliver Hughes of the Porterhouse micro-brewery recommends reading the newspaper with a pint of his Wrassler stout!

In Ireland we have been a bit slower to join the revolution. It may be down to an innate conservatism, or the fact that a few giant breweries enjoyed a virtual duopoly of business in our pubs. But in recent years, we have joined in wholeheartedly. Any decent off-licence will have a good range of foreign beers from all over the world. Instead of buying a six-pack or crate of the one beer, customers now buy a mixed case, and experiment in the comfort of their own homes.

In Good Food Ireland we now recommend a number of microbreweries. It has not been easy for them fighting the might of the larger breweries. Bottling lines are very expensive to buy, so often the only opportunity to taste an Irish beer with real flavour is to visit the micro-brewery. ∎

Porterhouse North
Cross Guns, Bridge, Glasnevin, Dublin 9
Tel. +353(0)1 8309884
Email.
info@porterhousebrewco.com
www.porterhousebrewco.com

The Porterhouse
16-18 Parliament Street,
Temple Bar, Dublin 2
Tel. +353(0)1 6798847
Email.
info@porterhousebrewco.com
www.porterhousebrewco.com

Porterhouse Central
45-47 Nassau Street, Dublin 2
Tel. +353(0)1 6774180
Email.
info@porterhousebrewco.com
www.porterhousebrewco.com

Porterhouse Bray
Strand Road, Bray, Co Wicklow
Tel. +353(0)1 2860668
Email.
info@porterhousebrewco.com
www.porterhousebrewco.com

The Porterhouse Brew Pubs in Dublin were the brainchild of Oliver Hughes and his cousin Liam LaPlant. Hughes had become fascinated by brew pubs when studying law in the U.K. At the same time, Liam was working in London pubs. Back in 1989, they set up the original Porterhouse in Bray, Co. Wicklow. It is still there. The idea then as now was to make serious beer and have a bit of fun too. There are four pubs in Dublin offering a range of Porterhouse beers alongside an eclectic range of foreign beers. A taste of the three Porterhouse stouts - the Oyster Stout, Plain Porter and Wrassler is an essential part of any visit to Dublin. Ask nicely and you may even receive a bottle of the amazing Celebration Stout, brewed to commemorate years in Dublin's bustling Temple Bar. I can promise you it bears no resemblance to whatever beer you are drinking now.

Franciscan Well Brew Pub

North Mall, Cork
Tel. +353(0)21 4210130 Brewery
Tel. +353(0)21 4393434 Pub
Email. shane_long@hotmail.com
www.franciscanwellbrewery.com

Founded in 1998 on Cork's North Mall, across the street from the river, the Franciscan Well Brewery is built on the site of an old Franciscan Monastery dating back to 1219. It was believed that water from the well had miraculous and curative properties, though you'll have to try the brewery's own lager, ale, stout and wheat beer yourself to see if they could claim similar benefits. All the beers brewed here are free from chemical additives and preservatives. Enjoy them from the taps of the large serving vessels behind the bar. Try the creamy Shandon stout, the fruity Blarney Blonde ale or the robust Rebel Red ale with a distinct caramel flavour. Several European beers are also available. There's a barbecue every Thursday and Friday from May to September, and regular traditional live music, as well as beer festivals twice yearly: at Easter and the October bank holiday weekend, inspired by the German Oktoberfest. What would the monks have made of it all? Find out more on a special brewery tour.

282

One for the Road

Stops Along the Way

Rosslare to Cork
Dublin to Wexford to Rosslare
Belfast to Derry
Belfast to Sligo
Dublin to Sligo
Galway to Sligo
Dublin to Limerick to Tralee
Dublin to Belfast
Dublin to Cork to Killarney
Limerick to Galway
Dublin to Waterford
Waterford to Limerick
Westport to Sligo to Donegal

Listings in BLUE denote
places to visit

Rosslare to Cork

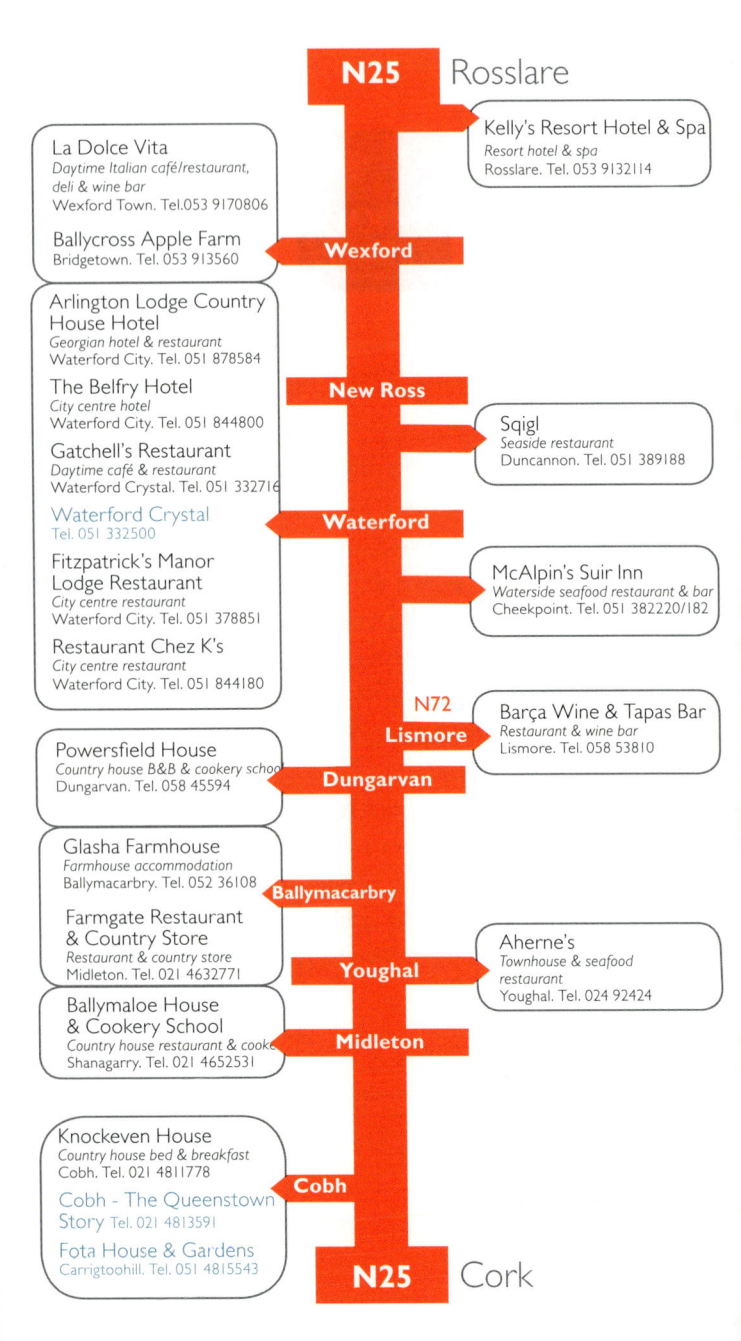

N25 — Rosslare

Kelly's Resort Hotel & Spa
Resort hotel & spa
Rosslare. Tel. 053 9132114

La Dolce Vita
Daytime Italian café/restaurant, deli & wine bar
Wexford Town. Tel.053 9170806

Ballycross Apple Farm
Bridgetown. Tel. 053 913560

Wexford

Arlington Lodge Country House Hotel
Georgian hotel & restaurant
Waterford City. Tel. 051 878584

The Belfry Hotel
City centre hotel
Waterford City. Tel. 051 844800

Gatchell's Restaurant
Daytime café & restaurant
Waterford Crystal. Tel. 051 332716

New Ross

Sqigl
Seaside restaurant
Duncannon. Tel. 051 389188

Waterford Crystal
Tel. 051 332500

Waterford

Fitzpatrick's Manor Lodge Restaurant
City centre restaurant
Waterford City. Tel. 051 378851

Restaurant Chez K's
City centre restaurant
Waterford City. Tel. 051 844180

McAlpin's Suir Inn
Waterside seafood restaurant & bar
Cheekpoint. Tel. 051 382220/182

N72 Lismore

Barça Wine & Tapas Bar
Restaurant & wine bar
Lismore. Tel. 058 53810

Powersfield House
Country house B&B & cookery school
Dungarvan. Tel. 058 45594

Dungarvan

Glasha Farmhouse
Farmhouse accommodation
Ballymacarbry. Tel. 052 36108

Ballymacarbry

Farmgate Restaurant & Country Store
Restaurant & country store
Midleton. Tel. 021 4632771

Youghal

Aherne's
Townhouse & seafood restaurant
Youghal. Tel. 024 92424

Ballymaloe House & Cookery School
Country house restaurant & cookery
Shanagarry. Tel. 021 4652531

Midleton

Knockeven House
Country house bed & breakfast
Cobh. Tel. 021 4811778

Cobh - The Queenstown Story Tel. 021 4813591

Fota House & Gardens
Carrigtoohill. Tel. 051 4815543

Cobh

N25 — Cork

286

Dublin to Wexford to Rosslare

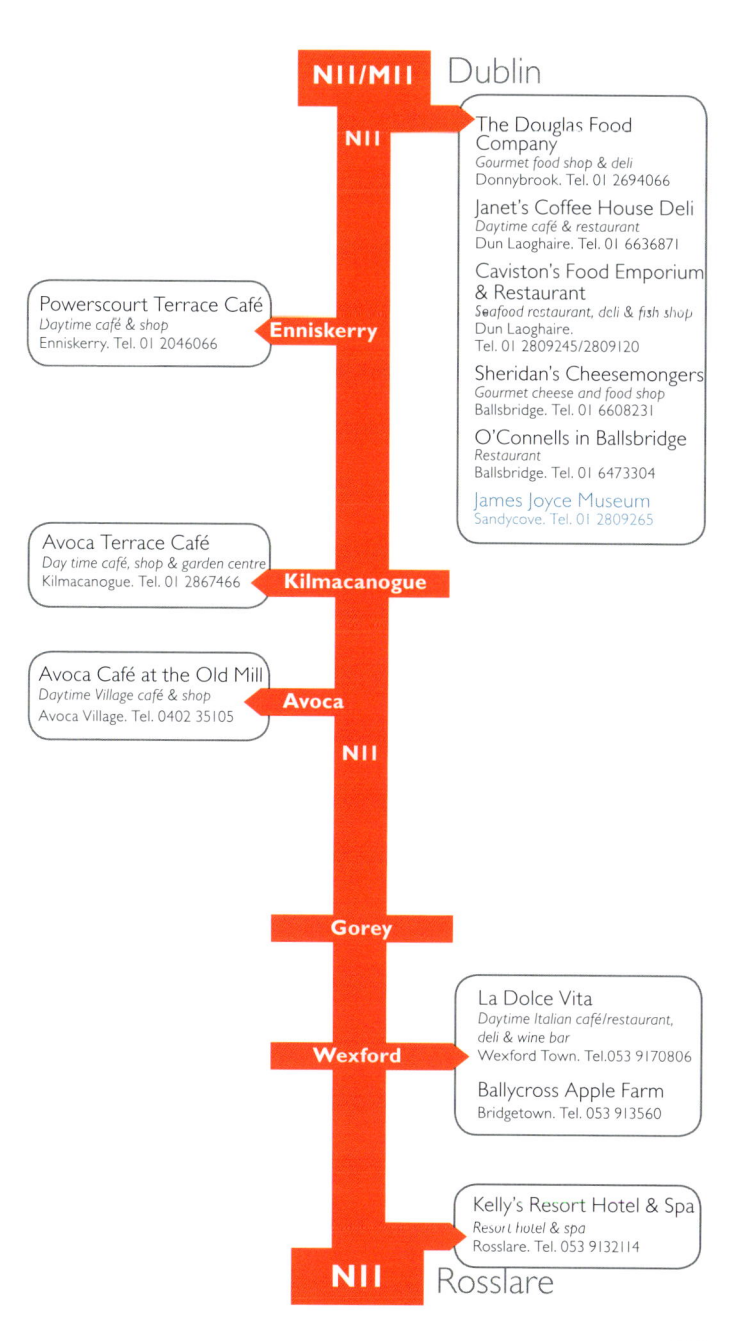

N11/M11 — Dublin

N11

- The Douglas Food Company
  Gourmet food shop & deli
  Donnybrook. Tel. 01 2694066

- Janet's Coffee House Deli
  Daytime café & restaurant
  Dun Laoghaire. Tel. 01 6636871

- Caviston's Food Emporium & Restaurant
  Seafood restaurant, deli & fish shop
  Dun Laoghaire.
  Tel. 01 2809245/2809120

- Sheridan's Cheesemongers
  Gourmet cheese and food shop
  Ballsbridge. Tel. 01 6608231

- O'Connells in Ballsbridge
  Restaurant
  Ballsbridge. Tel. 01 6473304

- James Joyce Museum
  Sandycove. Tel. 01 2809265

Enniskerry

- Powerscourt Terrace Café
  Daytime café & shop
  Enniskerry. Tel. 01 2046066

Kilmacanogue

- Avoca Terrace Café
  Day time café, shop & garden centre
  Kilmacanogue. Tel. 01 2867466

Avoca

- Avoca Café at the Old Mill
  Daytime Village café & shop
  Avoca Village. Tel. 0402 35105

N11

Gorey

Wexford

- La Dolce Vita
  Daytime Italian café/restaurant, deli & wine bar
  Wexford Town. Tel. 053 9170806

- Ballycross Apple Farm
  Bridgetown. Tel. 053 913560

- Kelly's Resort Hotel & Spa
  Resort hotel & spa
  Rosslare. Tel. 053 9132114

N11 — Rosslare

Belfast to Derry

From the North dial 028. From the Republic dial 048

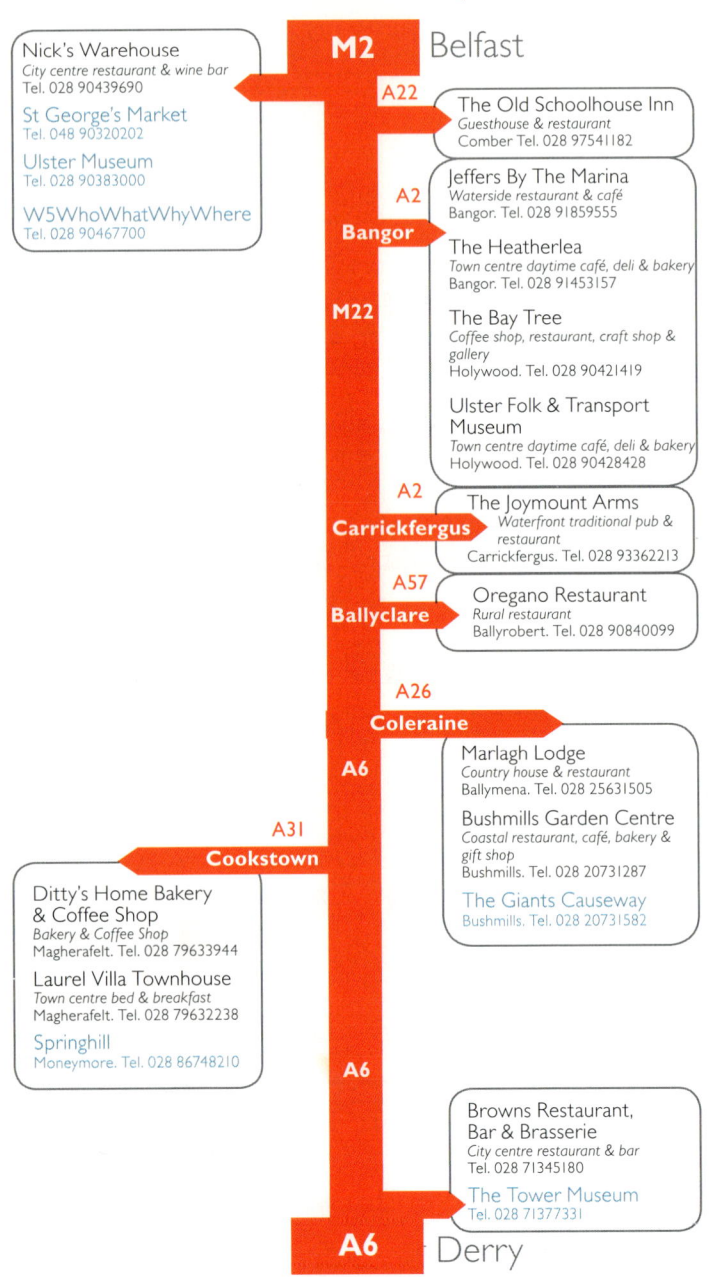

M2 — Belfast

Nick's Warehouse
City centre restaurant & wine bar
Tel. 028 90439690

St George's Market
Tel. 048 90320202

Ulster Museum
Tel. 028 90383000

W5WhoWhatWhyWhere
Tel. 028 90467700

A22

The Old Schoolhouse Inn
Guesthouse & restaurant
Comber Tel. 028 97541182

A2

Jeffers By The Marina
Waterside restaurant & café
Bangor. Tel. 028 91859555

Bangor

The Heatherlea
Town centre daytime café, deli & bakery
Bangor. Tel. 028 91453157

M22

The Bay Tree
Coffee shop, restaurant, craft shop & gallery
Holywood. Tel. 028 90421419

Ulster Folk & Transport Museum
Town centre daytime café, deli & bakery
Holywood. Tel. 028 90428428

A2

Carrickfergus

The Joymount Arms
Waterfront traditional pub & restaurant
Carrickfergus. Tel. 028 93362213

A57

Ballyclare

Oregano Restaurant
Rural restaurant
Ballyrobert. Tel. 028 90840099

A26

Coleraine

A6

Marlagh Lodge
Country house & restaurant
Ballymena. Tel. 028 25631505

Bushmills Garden Centre
Coastal restaurant, café, bakery & gift shop
Bushmills. Tel. 028 20731287

The Giants Causeway
Bushmills. Tel. 028 20731582

A31

Cookstown

Ditty's Home Bakery & Coffee Shop
Bakery & Coffee Shop
Magherafelt. Tel. 028 79633944

Laurel Villa Townhouse
Town centre bed & breakfast
Magherafelt. Tel. 028 79632238

Springhill
Moneymore. Tel. 028 86748210

A6

Browns Restaurant, Bar & Brasserie
City centre restaurant & bar
Tel. 028 71345180

The Tower Museum
Tel. 028 71377331

A6 — Derry

288

Belfast to Sligo
From the North dial 028. From the Republic dial 048

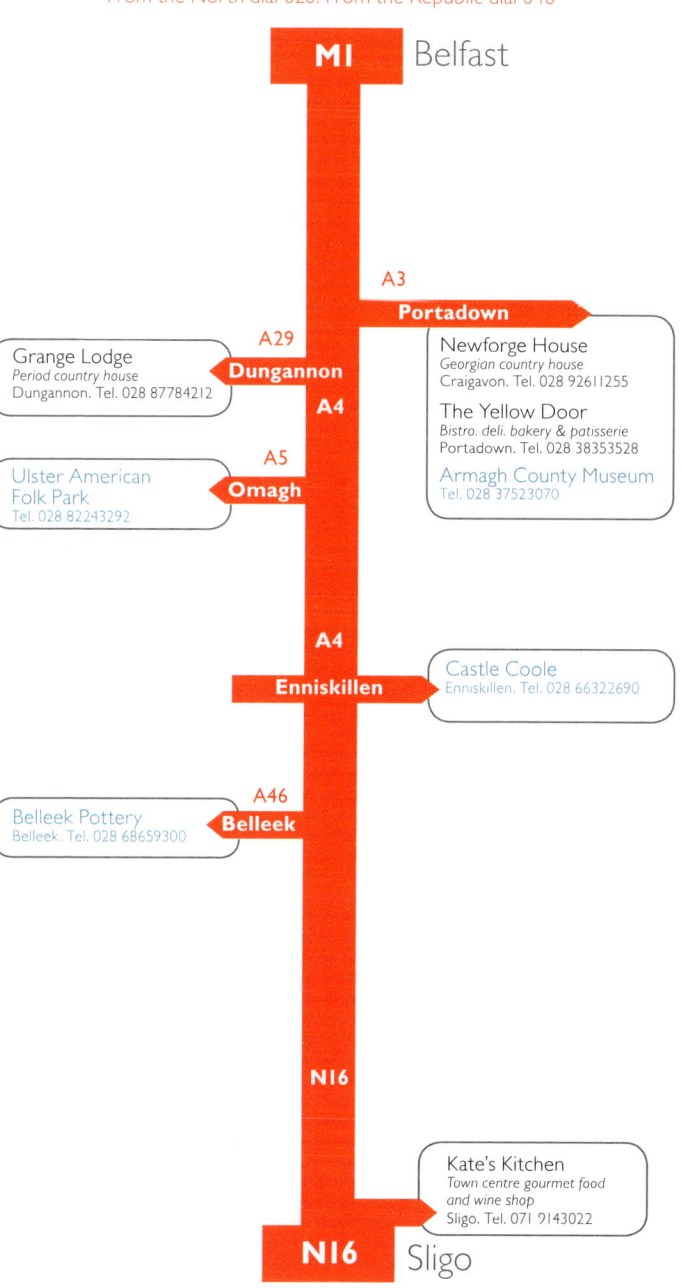

M1 — Belfast

A3 — **Portadown**

A29 — **Dungannon**

Grange Lodge
Period country house
Dungannon. Tel. 028 87784212

Newforge House
Georgian country house
Craigavon. Tel. 028 92611255

The Yellow Door
Bistro, deli, bakery & patisserie
Portadown. Tel. 028 38353528

Armagh County Museum
Tel. 028 37523070

A4

A5 — **Omagh**

Ulster American Folk Park
Tel. 028 82243292

A4

Enniskillen

Castle Coole
Enniskillen. Tel. 028 66322690

A46 — **Belleek**

Belleek Pottery
Belleek. Tel. 028 68659300

N16

Kate's Kitchen
Town centre gourmet food and wine shop
Sligo. Tel. 071 9143022

N16 — Sligo

Dublin to Sligo

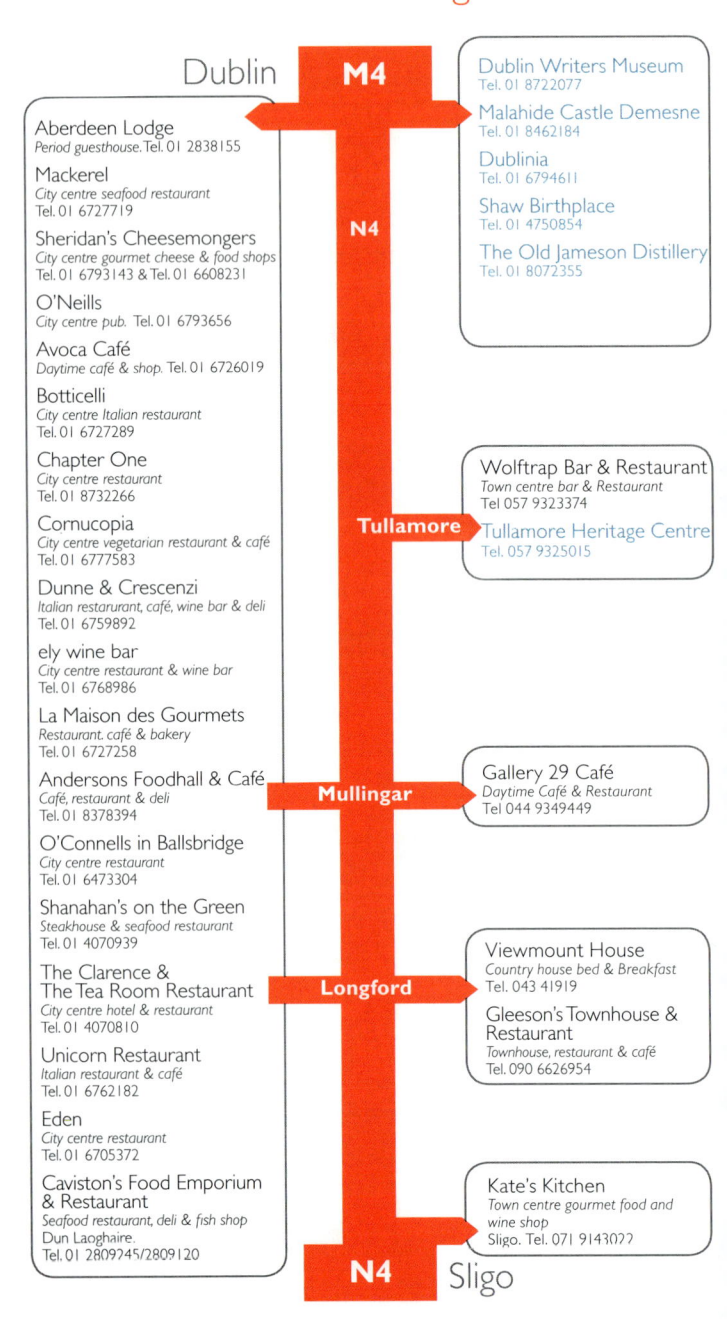

Dublin

M4 → **N4**

Dublin

- **Aberdeen Lodge**
  Period guesthouse. Tel. 01 2838155
- **Mackerel**
  City centre seafood restaurant
  Tel. 01 6727719
- **Sheridan's Cheesemongers**
  City centre gourmet cheese & food shops
  Tel. 01 6793143 & Tel. 01 6608231
- **O'Neills**
  City centre pub. Tel. 01 6793656
- **Avoca Café**
  Daytime café & shop. Tel. 01 6726019
- **Botticelli**
  City centre Italian restaurant
  Tel. 01 6727289
- **Chapter One**
  City centre restaurant
  Tel. 01 8732266
- **Cornucopia**
  City centre vegetarian restaurant & café
  Tel. 01 6777583
- **Dunne & Crescenzi**
  Italian restaurant, café, wine bar & deli
  Tel. 01 6759892
- **ely wine bar**
  City centre restaurant & wine bar
  Tel. 01 6768986
- **La Maison des Gourmets**
  Restaurant, café & bakery
  Tel. 01 6727258
- **Andersons Foodhall & Café**
  Café, restaurant & deli
  Tel. 01 8378394
- **O'Connells in Ballsbridge**
  City centre restaurant
  Tel. 01 6473304
- **Shanahan's on the Green**
  Steakhouse & seafood restaurant
  Tel. 01 4070939
- **The Clarence & The Tea Room Restaurant**
  City centre hotel & restaurant
  Tel. 01 4070810
- **Unicorn Restaurant**
  Italian restaurant & café
  Tel. 01 6762182
- **Eden**
  City centre restaurant
  Tel. 01 6705372
- **Caviston's Food Emporium & Restaurant**
  Seafood restaurant, deli & fish shop
  Dun Laoghaire.
  Tel. 01 2809245/2809120

Dublin (attractions)

- **Dublin Writers Museum**
  Tel. 01 8722077
- **Malahide Castle Demesne**
  Tel. 01 8462184
- **Dublinia**
  Tel. 01 6794611
- **Shaw Birthplace**
  Tel. 01 4750854
- **The Old Jameson Distillery**
  Tel. 01 8072355

Tullamore

- **Wolftrap Bar & Restaurant**
  Town centre bar & Restaurant
  Tel 057 9323374
- **Tullamore Heritage Centre**
  Tel. 057 9325015

Mullingar

- **Gallery 29 Café**
  Daytime Café & Restaurant
  Tel 044 9349449

Longford

- **Viewmount House**
  Country house bed & Breakfast
  Tel. 043 41919
- **Gleeson's Townhouse & Restaurant**
  Townhouse, restaurant & café
  Tel. 090 6626954

Sligo

- **Kate's Kitchen**
  Town centre gourmet food and wine shop
  Sligo. Tel. 071 9143022

N4 → Sligo

Galway to Sligo

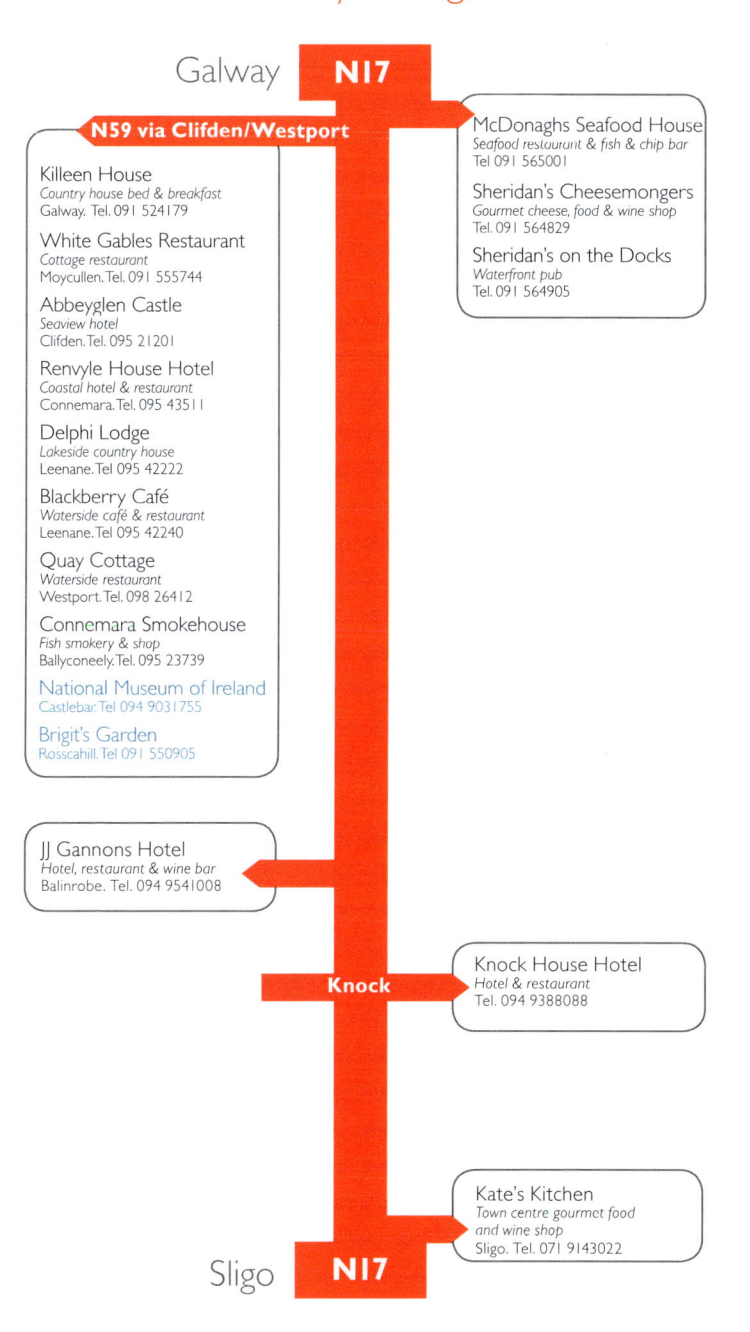

Galway — **N17**

N59 via Clifden/Westport

Killeen House
Country house bed & breakfast
Galway. Tel. 091 524179

White Gables Restaurant
Cottage restaurant
Moycullen. Tel. 091 555744

Abbeyglen Castle
Seaview hotel
Clifden. Tel. 095 21201

Renvyle House Hotel
Coastal hotel & restaurant
Connemara. Tel. 095 43511

Delphi Lodge
Lakeside country house
Leenane. Tel 095 42222

Blackberry Café
Waterside café & restaurant
Leenane. Tel 095 42240

Quay Cottage
Waterside restaurant
Westport. Tel. 098 26412

Connemara Smokehouse
Fish smokery & shop
Ballyconeely. Tel. 095 23739

National Museum of Ireland
Castlebar. Tel 094 9031755

Brigit's Garden
Rosscahill. Tel 091 550905

McDonaghs Seafood House
Seafood restaurant & fish & chip bar
Tel 091 565001

Sheridan's Cheesemongers
Gourmet cheese, food & wine shop
Tel. 091 564829

Sheridan's on the Docks
Waterfront pub
Tel. 091 564905

JJ Gannons Hotel
Hotel, restaurant & wine bar
Balinrobe. Tel. 094 9541008

Knock

Knock House Hotel
Hotel & restaurant
Tel. 094 9388088

Kate's Kitchen
Town centre gourmet food and wine shop
Sligo. Tel. 071 9143022

Sligo — **N17**

Dublin to Limerick to Tralee

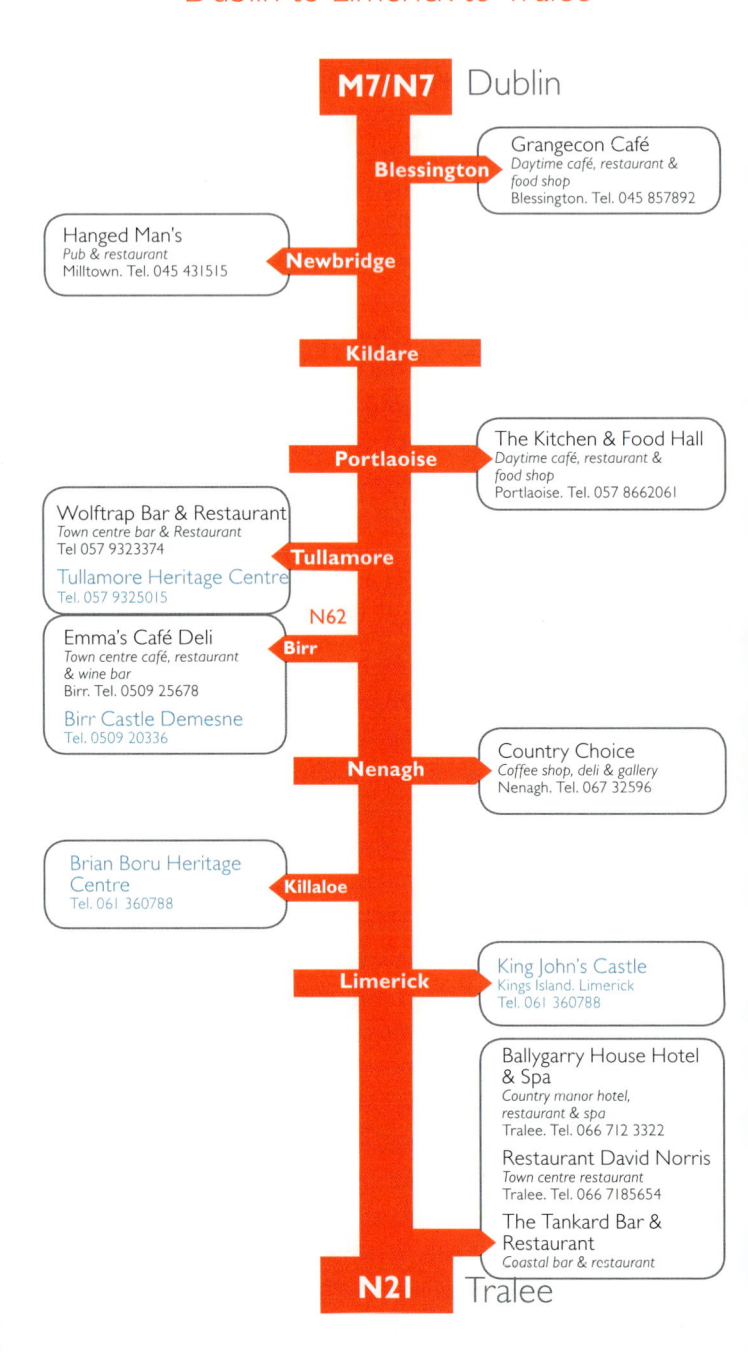

M7/N7 Dublin

Blessington
- Grangecon Café
  Daytime café, restaurant & food shop
  Blessington. Tel. 045 857892

Newbridge
- Hanged Man's
  Pub & restaurant
  Milltown. Tel. 045 431515

Kildare

Portlaoise
- The Kitchen & Food Hall
  Daytime café, restaurant & food shop
  Portlaoise. Tel. 057 8662061

Tullamore
- Wolftrap Bar & Restaurant
  Town centre bar & Restaurant
  Tel 057 9323374
- Tullamore Heritage Centre
  Tel. 057 9325015

N62

Birr
- Emma's Café Deli
  Town centre café, restaurant & wine bar
  Birr. Tel. 0509 25678
- Birr Castle Demesne
  Tel. 0509 20336

Nenagh
- Country Choice
  Coffee shop, deli & gallery
  Nenagh. Tel. 067 32596

Killaloe
- Brian Boru Heritage Centre
  Tel. 061 360788

Limerick
- King John's Castle
  Kings Island. Limerick
  Tel. 061 360788

- Ballygarry House Hotel & Spa
  Country manor hotel, restaurant & spa
  Tralee. Tel. 066 712 3322
- Restaurant David Norris
  Town centre restaurant
  Tralee. Tel. 066 7185654
- The Tankard Bar & Restaurant
  Coastal bar & restaurant

N21 Tralee

292

Dublin to Belfast

From the North dial 028. From the Republic dial 048

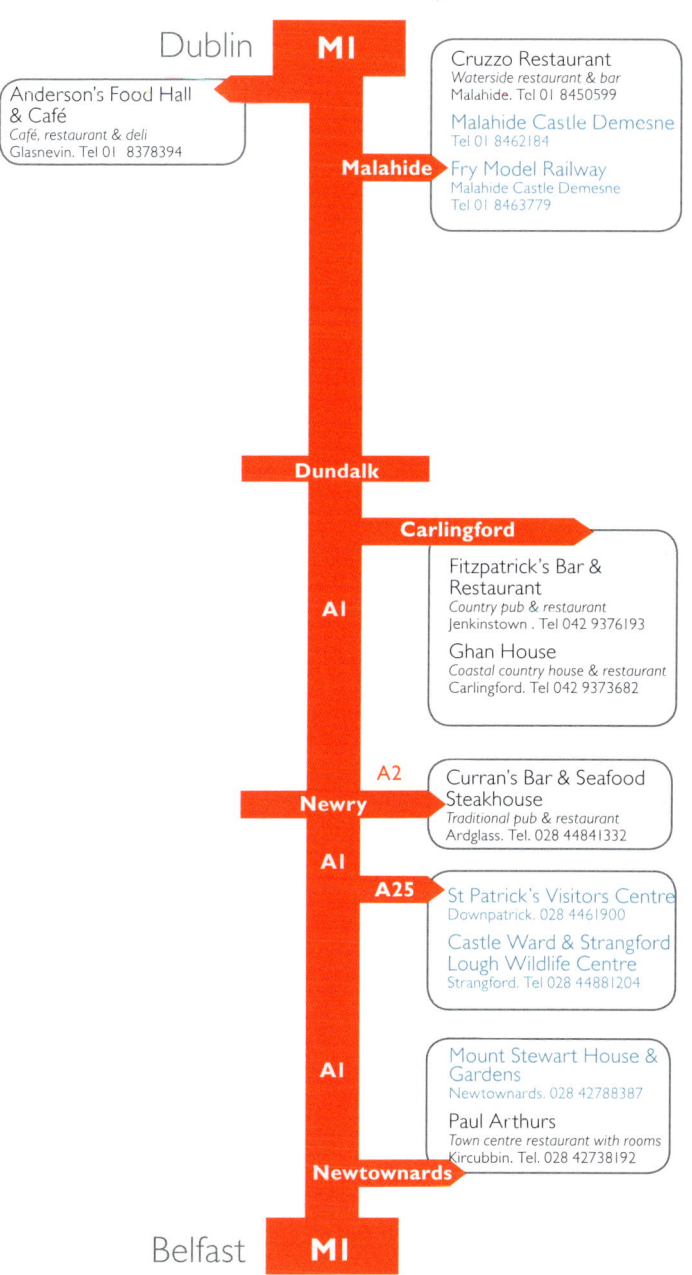

Dublin — M1

Anderson's Food Hall & Café
Café, restaurant & deli
Glasnevin. Tel 01 8378394

Malahide

Cruzzo Restaurant
Waterside restaurant & bar
Malahide. Tel 01 8450599

Malahide Castle Demesne
Tel 01 8462184

Fry Model Railway
Malahide Castle Demesne
Tel 01 8463779

Dundalk

Carlingford

A1

Fitzpatrick's Bar & Restaurant
Country pub & restaurant
Jenkinstown. Tel 042 9376193

Ghan House
Coastal country house & restaurant
Carlingford. Tel 042 9373682

A2
Newry

Curran's Bar & Seafood Steakhouse
Traditional pub & restaurant
Ardglass. Tel. 028 44841332

A1

A25

St Patrick's Visitors Centre
Downpatrick. 028 4461900

Castle Ward & Strangford Lough Wildlife Centre
Strangford. Tel 028 44881204

A1

Mount Stewart House & Gardens
Newtownards. 028 42788387

Paul Arthurs
Town centre restaurant with rooms
Kircubbin. Tel. 028 42738192

Newtownards

Belfast — M1

293

Dublin to Cork to Killarney

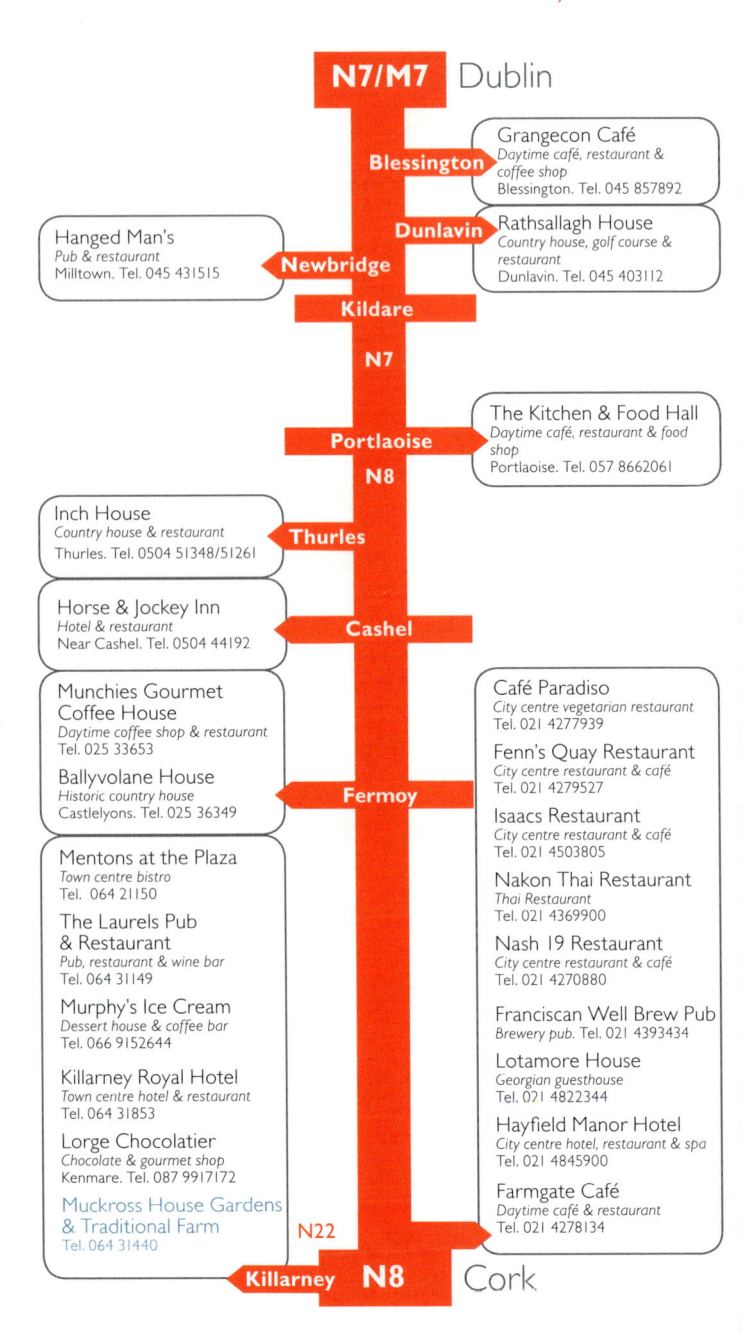

N7/M7 Dublin

Blessington
- Grangecon Café
  Daytime café, restaurant & coffee shop
  Blessington. Tel. 045 857892

Dunlavin
- Rathsallagh House
  Country house, golf course & restaurant
  Dunlavin. Tel. 045 403112

Newbridge
- Hanged Man's
  Pub & restaurant
  Milltown. Tel. 045 431515

Kildare

N7

Portlaoise
- The Kitchen & Food Hall
  Daytime café, restaurant & food shop
  Portlaoise. Tel. 057 8662061

N8

Thurles
- Inch House
  Country house & restaurant
  Thurles. Tel. 0504 51348/51261

Cashel
- Horse & Jockey Inn
  Hotel & restaurant
  Near Cashel. Tel. 0504 44192

Fermoy
- Munchies Gourmet Coffee House
  Daytime coffee shop & restaurant
  Tel. 025 33653
- Ballyvolane House
  Historic country house
  Castlelyons. Tel. 025 36349

- Mentons at the Plaza
  Town centre bistro
  Tel. 064 21150
- The Laurels Pub & Restaurant
  Pub, restaurant & wine bar
  Tel. 064 31149
- Murphy's Ice Cream
  Dessert house & coffee bar
  Tel. 066 9152644
- Killarney Royal Hotel
  Town centre hotel & restaurant
  Tel. 064 31853
- Lorge Chocolatier
  Chocolate & gourmet shop
  Kenmare. Tel. 087 9917172
- Muckross House Gardens & Traditional Farm
  Tel. 064 31440

Cork
- Café Paradiso
  City centre vegetarian restaurant
  Tel. 021 4277939
- Fenn's Quay Restaurant
  City centre restaurant & café
  Tel. 021 4279527
- Isaacs Restaurant
  City centre restaurant & café
  Tel. 021 4503805
- Nakon Thai Restaurant
  Thai Restaurant
  Tel. 021 4369900
- Nash 19 Restaurant
  City centre restaurant & café
  Tel. 021 4270880
- Franciscan Well Brew Pub
  Brewery pub. Tel. 021 4393434
- Lotamore House
  Georgian guesthouse
  Tel. 021 4822344
- Hayfield Manor Hotel
  City centre hotel, restaurant & spa
  Tel. 021 4845900
- Farmgate Café
  Daytime café & restaurant
  Tel. 021 4278134

N22

Killarney **N8**

Limerick to Galway

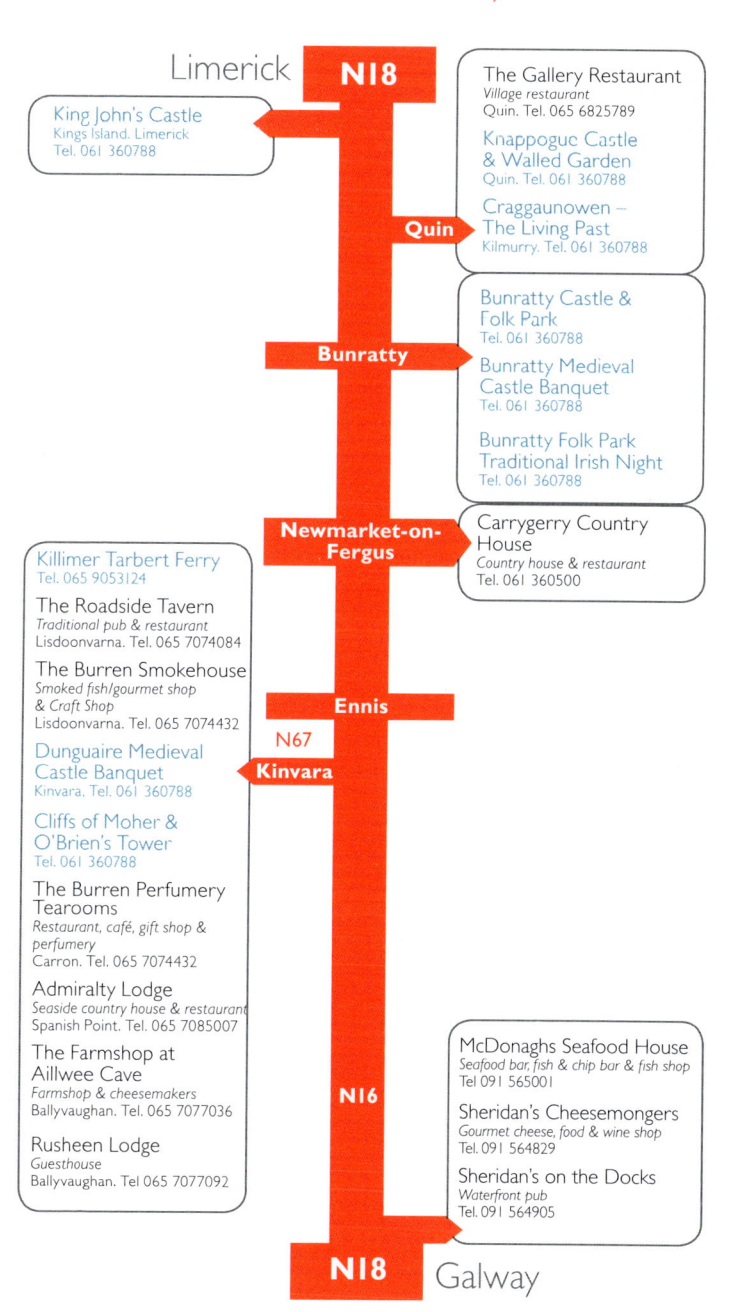

Limerick — **N18**

King John's Castle
Kings Island, Limerick
Tel. 061 360788

The Gallery Restaurant
Village restaurant
Quin. Tel. 065 6825789

Knappogue Castle & Walled Garden
Quin. Tel. 061 360788

Craggaunowen – The Living Past
Kilmurry. Tel. 061 360788

Quin

Bunratty

Bunratty Castle & Folk Park
Tel. 061 360788

Bunratty Medieval Castle Banquet
Tel. 061 360788

Bunratty Folk Park Traditional Irish Night
Tel. 061 360788

Newmarket-on-Fergus

Carrygerry Country House
Country house & restaurant
Tel. 061 360500

Killimer Tarbert Ferry
Tel. 065 9053124

The Roadside Tavern
Traditional pub & restaurant
Lisdoonvarna. Tel. 065 7074084

The Burren Smokehouse
Smoked fish/gourmet shop & Craft Shop
Lisdoonvarna. Tel. 065 7074432

Ennis

N67

Kinvara

Dunguaire Medieval Castle Banquet
Kinvara. Tel. 061 360788

Cliffs of Moher & O'Brien's Tower
Tel. 061 360788

The Burren Perfumery Tearooms
Restaurant, café, gift shop & perfumery
Carron. Tel. 065 7074432

Admiralty Lodge
Seaside country house & restaurant
Spanish Point. Tel. 065 7085007

The Farmshop at Aillwee Cave
Farmshop & cheesemakers
Ballyvaughan. Tel. 065 7077036

Rusheen Lodge
Guesthouse
Ballyvaughan. Tel 065 7077092

N16

McDonaghs Seafood House
Seafood bar, fish & chip bar & fish shop
Tel 091 565001

Sheridan's Cheesemongers
Gourmet cheese, food & wine shop
Tel. 091 564829

Sheridan's on the Docks
Waterfront pub
Tel. 091 564905

N18 — **Galway**

Dublin to Waterford

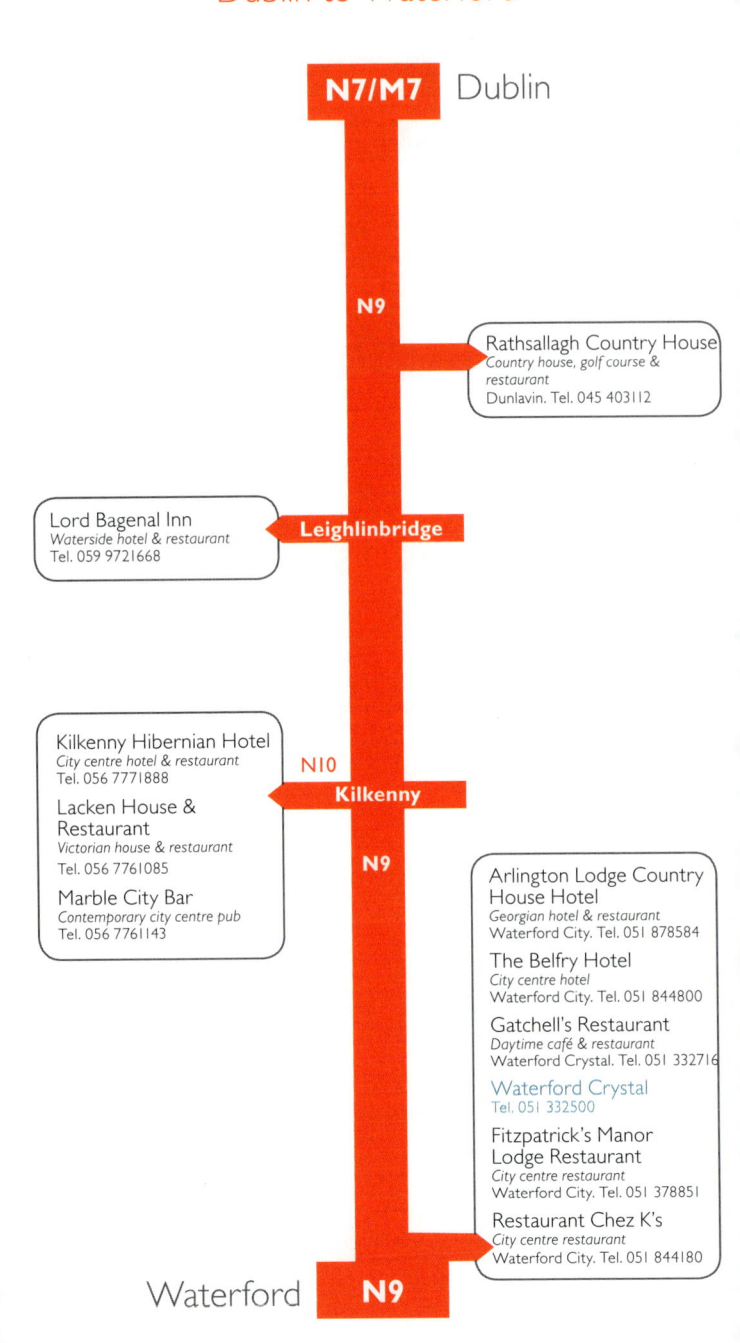

N7/M7 Dublin

N9

Rathsallagh Country House
Country house, golf course & restaurant
Dunlavin. Tel. 045 403112

Lord Bagenal Inn
Waterside hotel & restaurant
Tel. 059 9721668

Leighlinbridge

Kilkenny Hibernian Hotel
City centre hotel & restaurant
Tel. 056 7771888

Lacken House & Restaurant
Victorian house & restaurant
Tel. 056 7761085

Marble City Bar
Contemporary city centre pub
Tel. 056 7761143

N10

Kilkenny

N9

Arlington Lodge Country House Hotel
Georgian hotel & restaurant
Waterford City. Tel. 051 878584

The Belfry Hotel
City centre hotel
Waterford City. Tel. 051 844800

Gatchell's Restaurant
Daytime café & restaurant
Waterford Crystal. Tel. 051 332716

Waterford Crystal
Tel. 051 332500

Fitzpatrick's Manor Lodge Restaurant
City centre restaurant
Waterford City. Tel. 051 378851

Restaurant Chez K's
City centre restaurant
Waterford City. Tel. 051 844180

Waterford **N9**

Waterford to Limerick

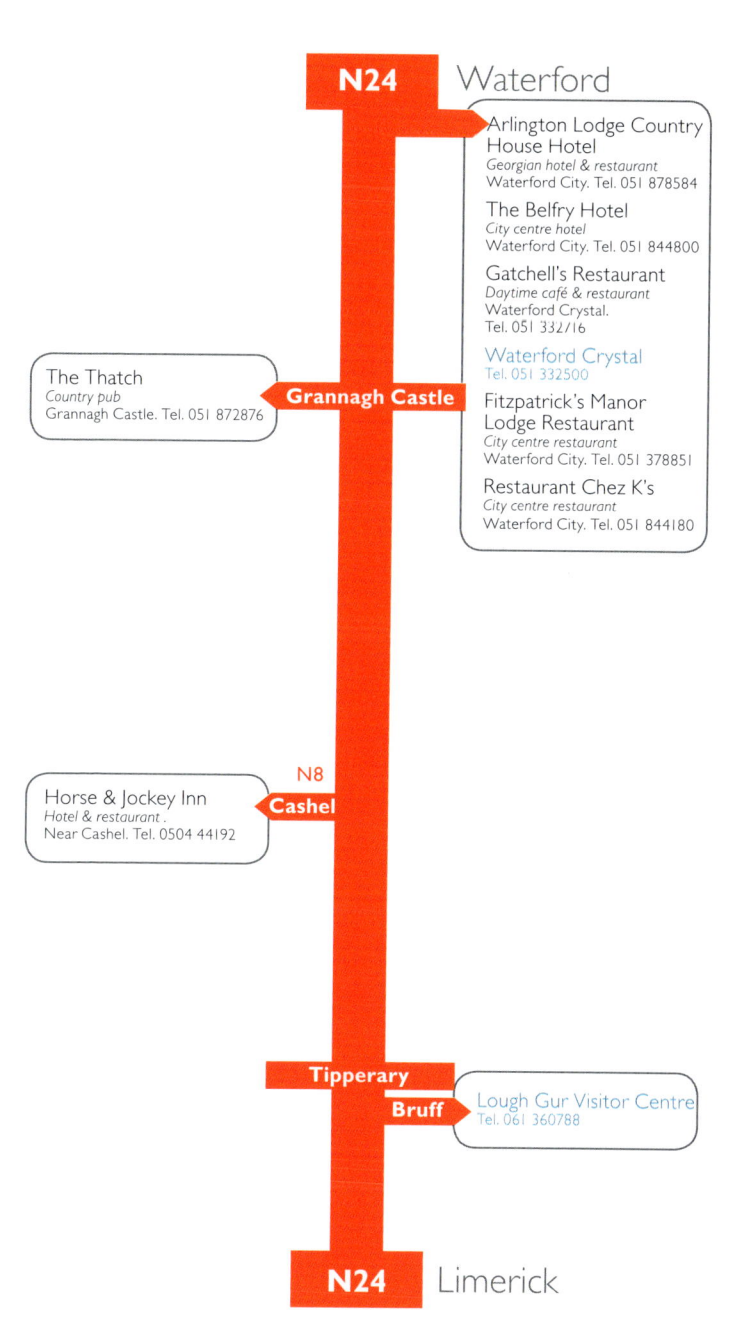

N24

Waterford

Arlington Lodge Country House Hotel
Georgian hotel & restaurant
Waterford City. Tel. 051 878584

The Belfry Hotel
City centre hotel
Waterford City. Tel. 051 844800

Gatchell's Restaurant
Daytime café & restaurant
Waterford Crystal.
Tel. 051 332716

Waterford Crystal
Tel. 051 332500

Fitzpatrick's Manor Lodge Restaurant
City centre restaurant
Waterford City. Tel. 051 378851

Restaurant Chez K's
City centre restaurant
Waterford City. Tel. 051 844180

Grannagh Castle

The Thatch
Country pub
Grannagh Castle. Tel. 051 872876

N8
Cashel

Horse & Jockey Inn
Hotel & restaurant
Near Cashel. Tel. 0504 44192

Tipperary

Bruff

Lough Gur Visitor Centre
Tel. 061 360788

N24 Limerick

297

Westport to Sligo to Donegal

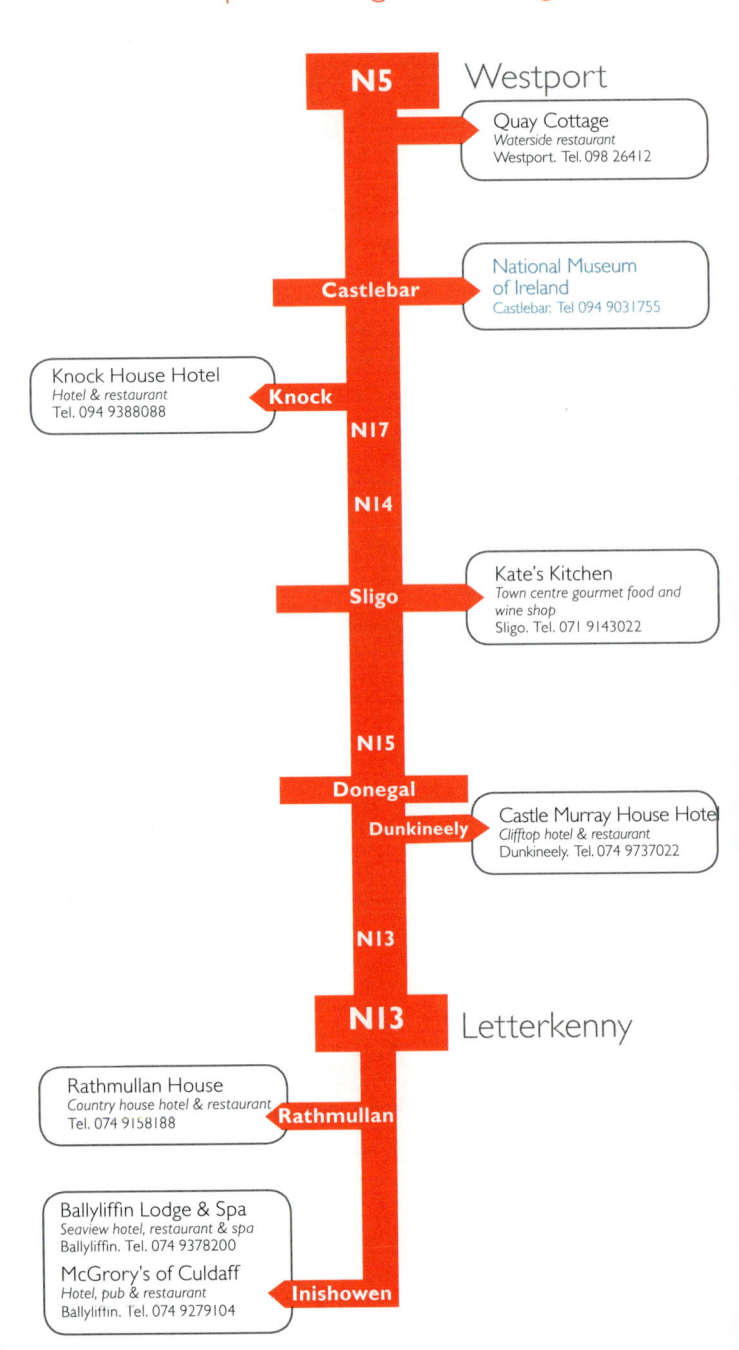

N5 — Westport

> Quay Cottage
> *Waterside restaurant*
> Westport. Tel. 098 26412

Castlebar

> National Museum of Ireland
> Castlebar. Tel 094 9031755

Knock House Hotel
Hotel & restaurant
Tel. 094 9388088

Knock

N17

N14

Sligo

> Kate's Kitchen
> *Town centre gourmet food and wine shop*
> Sligo. Tel. 071 9143022

N15

Donegal

Dunkineely

> Castle Murray House Hotel
> *Clifftop hotel & restaurant*
> Dunkineely. Tel. 074 9737022

N13

N13 — Letterkenny

Rathmullan House
Country house hotel & restaurant
Tel. 074 9158188

Rathmullan

Ballyliffin Lodge & Spa
Seaview hotel, restaurant & spa
Ballyliffin. Tel. 074 9378200

McGrory's of Culdaff
Hotel, pub & restaurant
Ballyliffin. Tel. 074 9279104

Inishowen

Index of Establishments A-Z

Name	Location	County	Page
Abbeyglen Castle	Clifden	Co Galway	173
Aberdeen Lodge	Ballsbridge	Dublin 4	68
Admiralty Lodge	Spanish Point	Co Clare	159
Aherne's	Youghal	Co Cork	115
An Sugan	Clonakilty	Co Cork	99
Anderson's Food Hall & Café	Glasnevin	Dublin 9	70
Arlington Lodge Country House Hotel		Waterford City	136
Avoca Café	Dublin City	Dublin 2	59
Avoca Café	Molls Gap	Co Kerry	124
Avoca Café at The Old Mill	Avoca	Co Wicklow	81
Avoca Terrace Café	Kilmacanogue	Co Wicklow	83
Ballycross Apple Farm	Bridgetown	Co Wexford	141
Ballygarry House Hotel & Spa	Tralee	Co Kerry	125
Ballyliffin Lodge & Spa	Ballyliffin	Co Donegal	168
Ballymaloe House & Cookery School	Shanagarry	Co Cork	114
Ballyvolane House	Fermoy	Co Cork	109
Barça Wine & Tapas Bar	Lismore	Co Waterford	135
Bay Tree (The)	Holywood	Co Down	220
Belfry Hotel (The)		Waterford City	139
Blackberry Café	Leenane	Co Galway	176
Blue Haven Hotel	Kinsale	Co Cork	112
Botticelli	Temple Bar	Dublin 2	59
Brown's Restaurant, Bar & Brasserie		Derry City	215
Burren Perfumery Tea Rooms (The)	Carron	Co Clare	156
Burren Smokehouse (The)	Lisdoonvarna	Co Clare	156
Bushmills Garden Centre	Bushmills	Co Antrim	206
Café Paradiso		Cork City	101
Carbery Cottage Guest Lodge	Durrus	Co Cork	108
Carrygerry Country House	Newmarket-on-Fergus	Co Clare	158
Castle Murray House Hotel	Dunkineely	Co Donegal	169
Cavistons Food Emporium & Restaurant	Dun Laoghaire	Co Dublin	71
Chapter One	Dublin City	Dublin 1	58
Clarence & Tea Room Restaurant (The)	Dublin City	Dublin 2	67
Connemara Smokehouse	Ballyconeely	Co Galway	173
Cornucopia	Dublin City	Dublin 2	60
Country Choice	Nenagh	Co Tipperary	193
Cruzzo Restaurant	Malahide	Co Dublin	72
Currans Bar & Seafood Steakhouse	Ardglass	Co Down	219
Delphi Lodge	Leenane	Co Galway	177
Ditty's Home Bakery & Coffee Shop	Magherafelt	Co Derry	215
Douglas Food Company (The)	Donnybrook	Dublin 4	70

Name	Location	County/City	Page
Dunne & Crescenzi	Dublin City	Dublin 2	60
Eden	Dublin City	Dublin 2	61
ely wine bar	Dublin City	Dublin 2	62
Emma's Café Deli	Birr	Co Offaly	187
Farmgate Café		Cork City	102
Farmgate Restaurant & Country Store	Midleton	Co Cork	113
Farmshop at Aillwee Cave (The)	Ballyvaughan	Co Clare	154
Fenn's Quay Restaurant		Cork City	103
Fisherman's Cottage	Inishere	Aran Islands	172
Fitzpatrick's Bar & Restaurant	Jenkinstown	Co Louth	78
Fitzpatricks Manor Lodge Restaurant		Waterford City	137
Franciscan Well Brew Pub		Cork City	103
Gallery 29 Café	Mullingar	Co Westmeath	81
Gallery Restaurant (The)	Quin	Co Clare	159
Gatchell's Restaurant at Waterford Crystal		Waterford City	137
Ghan House	Carlingford	Co Louth	77
Glasha Farmhouse	Ballymacarbry	Co Waterford	133
Gleesons	Clonakility	Co Cork	99
Gleeson's Townhouse & Restaurant		Roscommon Town	192
Glin Castle	Glin	Co Limerick	181
Gorman's Clifftop House and Restaurant	Dingle Peninsula	Co Kerry	120
Grange Lodge	Dungannon	Co Tyrone	225
Grangecon Café	Blessington	Co Wicklow	82
Hanged Man's	Newbridge	Co Kildare	75
Hayfield Manor Hotel		Cork City	104
Heatherlea (The)	Bangor	Co Down	218
Heron's Cove (The)	Goleen	Co Cork	110
Horse & Jockey Inn	Horse & Jockey	Co Tipperary	132
Inch House	Thurles	Co Tipperary	132
Íragh Tí Connor	Ballybunion	Co Kerry	118
Isaacs Restaurant		Cork City	105
Janet's Coffee House Deli	Dun Laoghaire	Co Dublin	72
Jeffers by the Marina	Bangor	Co Down	218
JJ Gannons	Ballinrobe	Co Mayo	184
Joymount Arms (The)	Carrickfergus	Co Antrim	207
Kate's Kitchen		Sligo Town	193
Kelly's Resort Hotel & Spa	Rosslare	Co Wexford	142
Kilkenny Hibernian Hotel		Kilkenny City	130
Killarney Royal Hotel	Killarney	Co Kerry	123
Killeen House	Bushy Park	Co Galway	178
Kitchen & Food Hall (The)	Portlaoise	Co Laois	76
Knock House Hotel	Knock	Co Mayo	185
Knockeven House	Cobh	Co Cork	101

La Dolce Vita		Wexford Town	143
La Maison des Gourmets	Dublin City	Dublin 2	62
Lacken House & Restaurant		Kilkenny City	131
Laurel Villa Townhouse	Magherafelt	Co Derry	216
Laurels Pub & Restaurant (The)	Killarney	Co Kerry	124
Lime Tree Restaurant (The)	Kenmare	Co Kerry	121
Lord Bagenal Inn	Leighlinbridge	Co Carlow	96
Lorge Chocolatier	Kemare	Co Kerry	121
Lotamore House	Tivoli	Cork City	105
Mackerel	Dublin City	Dublin 2	64
Marble City Bar		Kilkenny City	130
Marlagh Lodge	Ballymena	Co Antrim	205
McAlpin's Suir Inn	Cheekpoint	Co Waterford	133
McDonagh's Seafood House		Galway City	175
McGrory's of Culdaff	Inishowen Peninsula	Co Donegal	170
Mentons at the Plaza	Killarney	Co Kerry	123
Munchies Gourmet Coffee House	Fermoy	Co Cork	108
Murphy's Ice Cream	Dingle	Co Kerry	120
Murphy's Ice Cream	Killarney	Co Kerry	125
Nakon Thai Restaurant	Douglas	Co Cork	106
Nash 19 Restaurant		Cork City	106
Newforge House	Craigavon	Co Armagh	211
Nick's Warehouse		Belfast City	206
O'Connells in Ballsbridge	Ballsbridge	Dublin 4	69
O'Connor's Seafood Restaurant	Bantry	Co Cork	98
Old Bank House	Kinsale	Co Cork	113
Old Schoolhouse Inn (The)	Comber	Co Down	219
O'Neills	Dublin City	Dublin 2	64
Oregano Restaurant	Ballyclare	Co Antrim	204
Paul Arthurs	Kircubbin	Co Down	221
Powerscourt Terrace Café	Enniskerry	Co Wicklow	83
Powersfield House	Dungarvan	Co Waterford	134
QC's Seafood Bar & Restaurant	Cahirciveen	Co Kerry	119
Quay Cottage	Wesport	Co Mayo	185
Rathmullan House	Rathmullan	Co Donegal	171
Rathsallagh Country House	Dunlavin	Co Wicklow	82
Renvyle House Hotel	Renvyle	Co Galway	174
Restaurant Chez K's		Waterford City	138
Restaurant David Norris	Tralee	Co Kerry	126
Roadside Tavern (The)	Lisdoonvarna	Co Clare	157
Rusheen Lodge	Ballyvaughan	Co Clare	154
Shanahans On The Green	Dublin City	Dublin 2	65
Sheridans Cheesemongers		Galway City	175
Sheridans Cheesemongers	Dublin City	Dublin 2	65
Sheridans Cheesemongers	Ballsbridge	Dublin 4	69
Sheridans on the Docks		Galway City	176

Sqigl Restaurant	Duncannon	Co Wexford	141
Tankard Bar & Restaurant (The)	Fenit	Co Kerry	126
Thatch (The)	Grannagh Castle	Via Waterford	134
Tigh Ned (The)	Inishere	Aran Islands	172
Unicorn Restaurant (The)	Dublin City	Dublin 2	68
Viewmouunt House (The)	Longford	Co Longford	76
White Gables Restaurant (The)	Moycullen	Co Galway	178
Wolftrap Bar & Restaurant (The)	Tullamore	Co Offaly	79
Yellow Door (The)	Portadown	Co Armagh	212

Good Food Ireland Guide 2007
Did you enjoy your visit?

We would like to hear how the properties in the guide matched up to your expectations. Good Food Ireland has inspectors who visit each property in an effort to ensure that the experience we describe is accurate. Please let us know how you enjoyed your visit as your efforts will assist us in monitoring standards. If any property exceeded your expectations you may like to recommend them for an award. Quality, Value, Individual Hospitality and Good Food are the key principles of the Good Food Ireland ethos and we do hope our members live up to your expectations and ours.

We look forward to hearing from you.

Property Name ....

PLEASE PRINT IN BLOCK CAPITALS

Address ....

....

....

I had ❏ lunch ❏ dinner ❏ stayed there on (date) ....

Details ....

....

....

....

Reports received up to the end of May 2007 will be used in the research of the 2008 edition

Would you recommend this establishment for an award? ❏

Why?..

....

....

....

❏ I am not in any way connected to the proprietors.

Name ....

Address ....

....

....

As a result of your sending Good Food Ireland this form, we may send you information on Good Food Ireland in the future. If you would prefer not to receive such information. please tick this box ❏

Please send completed form to
GUEST COMMENTS
Good Food Ireland
Ballykelly House, Drinagh, Wexford, Ireland
Tel. +353 (0)53 9158693. Fax. +353 (0)53 9158688
Email. info@goodfoodireland.ie

Good Food Ireland Guide 2007
Did you enjoy your visit?

We would like to hear how the properties in the guide matched up to your expectations. Good Food Ireland has inspectors who visit each property in an effort to ensure that the experience we describe is accurate. Please let us know how you enjoyed your visit as your efforts will assist us in monitoring standards. If any property exceeded your expectations you may like to recommend them for an award. Quality, Value, Individual Hospitality and Good Food are the key principles of the Good Food Ireland ethos and we do hope our members live up to your expectations and ours.

We look forward to hearing from you.

Property Name

PLEASE PRINT IN BLOCK CAPITALS

Address

I had ❑ lunch ❑ dinner ❑ stayed there on (date)

Details

Reports received up to the end of May 2007 will be used in the research of the 2008 edition

Would you recommend this establishment for an award? ❑

Why?

❑ I am not in any way connected to the proprietors.

Name

Address

As a result of your sending Good Food Ireland this form, we may send you information on Good Food Ireland in the future. If you would prefer not to receive such information. please tick this box ❑

Please send completed form to
GUEST COMMENTS
Good Food Ireland
Ballykelly House, Drinagh, Wexford, Ireland
Tel. +353 (0)53 9158693. Fax. +353 (0)53 9158688
Email. info@goodfoodireland.ie

Good Food Ireland Guide 2007
Did you enjoy your visit?

We would like to hear how the properties in the guide matched up to your expectations. Good Food Ireland has inspectors who visit each property in an effort to ensure that the experience we describe is accurate. Please let us know how you enjoyed your visit as your efforts will assist us in monitoring standards. If any property exceeded your expectations you may like to recommend them for an award. Quality, Value, Individual Hospitality and Good Food are the key principles of the Good Food Ireland ethos and we do hope our members live up to your expectations and ours.

We look forward to hearing from you.

Property Name

PLEASE PRINT IN BLOCK CAPITALS

Address

I had ❏ lunch ❏ dinner ❏ stayed there on (date)

Details

Reports received up to the end of May 2007 will be used in the research of the 2008 edition

Would you recommend this establishment for an award? ❏

Why?

❏ I am not in any way connected to the proprietors.

Name

Address

As a result of your sending Good Food Ireland this form, we may send you information on Good Food Ireland in the future. If you would prefer not to receive such information. please tick this box ❏

Please send completed form to
GUEST COMMENTS
Good Food Ireland
Ballykelly House, Drinagh, Wexford, Ireland
Tel. +353 (0)53 9158693. Fax. +353 (0)53 9158688
Email. info@goodfoodireland.ie

Good Food Ireland Guide 2007
Did you enjoy your visit?

We would like to hear how the properties in the guide matched up to your expectations. Good Food Ireland has inspectors who visit each property in an effort to ensure that the experience we describe is accurate. Please let us know how you enjoyed your visit as your efforts will assist us in monitoring standards. If any property exceeded your expectations you may like to recommend them for an award. Quality, Value, Individual Hospitality and Good Food are the key principles of the Good Food Ireland ethos and we do hope our members live up to your expectations and ours.

We look forward to hearing from you.

Property Name
....

PLEASE PRINT IN BLOCK CAPITALS

Address
....

....

....

I had ❏ lunch ❏ dinner ❏ stayed there on (date)
....

Details
....

....

....

....

Reports received up to the end of May 2007 will be used in the research of the 2008 edition

Would you recommend this establishment for an award? ❏

Why?...

....

....

....

❏ I am not in any way connected to the proprietors.

Name
....

Address
....

....

....

As a result of your sending Good Food Ireland this form, we may send you information on Good Food Ireland in the future. If you would prefer not to receive such information. please tick this box ❏

Please send completed form to
GUEST COMMENTS
Good Food Ireland
Ballykelly House, Drinagh, Wexford, Ireland
Tel. +353 (0)53 9158693. Fax. +353 (0)53 9158688
Email. info@goodfoodireland.ie

GOOD FOOD IRELAND

the road to good food in Ireland

Good Food Ireland Guide 2007
Did you enjoy your visit?

We would like to hear how the properties in the guide matched up to your expectations. Good Food Ireland has inspectors who visit each property in an effort to ensure that the experience we describe is accurate. Please let us know how you enjoyed your visit as your efforts will assist us in monitoring standards. If any property exceeded your expectations you may like to recommend them for an award. Quality, Value, Individual Hospitality and Good Food are the key principles of the Good Food Ireland ethos and we do hope our members live up to your expectations and ours.

We look forward to hearing from you.

Property Name ....

PLEASE PRINT IN BLOCK CAPITALS

Address ....

....

....

I had ❏ lunch ❏ dinner ❏ stayed there on (date) ....

Details ....

....

....

....

Reports received up to the end of May 2007 will be used in the research of the 2008 edition

Would you recommend this establishment for an award? ❏

Why?..

....

....

....

❏ I am not in any way connected to the proprietors.

Name ....

Address ....

....

....

As a result of your sending Good Food Ireland this form, we may send you information on Good Food Ireland in the future. If you would prefer not to receive such information, please tick this box ❏

Please send completed form to
GUEST COMMENTS
Good Food Ireland
Ballykelly House, Drinagh, Wexford, Ireland
Tel. +353 (0)53 9158693. Fax. +353 (0)53 9158688
Email. info@goodfoodireland.ie

Good Food Ireland Guide 2007
Did you enjoy your visit?

We would like to hear how the properties in the guide matched up to your expectations. Good Food Ireland has inspectors who visit each property in an effort to ensure that the experience we describe is accurate. Please let us know how you enjoyed your visit as your efforts will assist us in monitoring standards. If any property exceeded your expectations you may like to recommend them for an award. Quality, Value, Individual Hospitality and Good Food are the key principles of the Good Food Ireland ethos and we do hope our members live up to your expectations and ours.

We look forward to hearing from you.

Property Name ....
PLEASE PRINT IN BLOCK CAPITALS

Address ....

....

....

I had ❏ lunch ❏ dinner ❏ stayed there on (date) ....

Details ....

....

....

....

Reports received up to the end of May 2007 will be used in the research of the 2008 edition

Would you recommend this establishment for an award? ❏

Why?..

....

....

....

❏ I am not in any way connected to the proprietors.

Name ....

Address ....

....

....

As a result of your sending Good Food Ireland this form, we may send you information on Good Food Ireland in the future. If you would prefer not to receive such information. please tick this box ❏

Please send completed form to
GUEST COMMENTS
Good Food Ireland
Ballykelly House, Drinagh, Wexford, Ireland
Tel. +353 (0)53 9158693. Fax. +353 (0)53 9158688
Email. info@goodfoodireland.ie